Football Economics and Policy

Also by Stefan Szymanski

WHY ENGLAND LOSE (*co-authored with Simon Kuper*)

PLAYBOOKS AND CHECKBOOKS: An Introduction to the Economics of Modern Sports

FANS OF THE WORLD, UNITE! A Capitalist Manifesto for Sports Consumers (*co-authored with Stephen F. Ross*)

NATIONAL PASTIME: How Americans Play Baseball and the Rest of the World Plays Soccer (*co-authored with Andrew Zimbalist*)

IL BUSINESS DEL CALCIO (*co-authored with Umberto Lago and Alessandro Baroncelli*)

WINNERS AND LOSERS: The Business Strategy of Football (*co-authored with Tim Kuypers*)

Football Economics and Policy

Stefan Szymanski

First published 2010 by
PALGRAVE MACMILLAN

Palgrave Macmillan in the UK is an imprint of Macmillan Publishers Limited,
registered in England, company number 785998, of Houndmills, Basingstoke,
Hampshire RG21 6XS.

Palgrave Macmillan in the US is a division of St Martin's Press LLC,
175 Fifth Avenue, New York, NY 10010.

Palgrave Macmillan is the global academic imprint of the above companies
and has companies and representatives throughout the world.

Palgrave® and Macmillan® are registered trademarks in the United States,
the United Kingdom, Europe and other countries.

ISBN-13: 978-0-230-23223-5 hardback

This book is printed on paper suitable for recycling and made from fully
managed and sustained forest sources. Logging, pulping and manufacturing
processes are expected to conform to the environmental regulations of the
country of origin.

A catalogue record for this book is available from the British Library.

A catalog record for this book is available from the Library of Congress.

10   9   8   7   6   5   4   3   2   1
19   18   17   16   15   14   13   12   11   10

Printed and bound in Great Britain by
CPI Antony Rowe, Chippenham and Eastbourne

Contents

List of Figures

List of Tables

Acknowledgements

I have been lucky enough to work with many outstanding co-authors over the years. I wish to thank those who agreed to have our joint papers republished here: Tunde Buraimo, David Forrest, Tom Hoehn, Umberto Lago, Rob Simmons and Ron Smith, as well as those I have worked with elsewhere: Kevin Alavy, Wladimir Andreff, Giles Atkinson, Luigi Buzzacchi, Filippo dell'Osso, Pedro Garcia del Barrio, Steve Hall, David Harbord, Takeo Hirata, Georgios Kavetsos, Stefan Késenne, Tim Kuypers, Stephanie Leach, Neil Longley, Susana Mourato, Susanne Parlasca, Ian Preston, Steve Ross, Tommaso Valletti and Andy Zimbalist. I have also been fortunate to work in sports economics at a time when the subject has been transformed from a minor curiosity into a genuine sub-field of economics with its own journals, associations and conferences. There are now hundreds of economists who have published papers on sports economics, most of whom I have met and learnt from, and to whom I owe many thanks for advice, support, and even, on occasion, correction.

I am grateful to Taiba Batool for initiating this project, to Gemma Papageorgiou for managing it Palgrave and to Cherline Daniel for her efficient project management.

Chapter 1 was originally published as "The English Football Industry: Profit Performance and Industrial Structure" (with Ron Smith) in *International Review of Applied Economics*, 1997, 11, 1, 135–153. http://www.informaworld.com. Reproduced with kind permission.

Chapter 2 was originally published as "The Market for Soccer Players in England after Bosman: Winners and Losers" in *Player Market Regulation in Professional Team Sports*, S. Késenne and C. Jeanrenaud (eds), Standaard Uitgeverij, Antwerp, 1999. Reproduced with kind permission.

Chapter 3 was originally published as "The Americanization of European Football" (with Tom Hoehn) in *Economic Policy*, 1999, 28, 205–233. Reproduced with kind permission.

Chapter 4 was originally published as "Hearts and Minds and Restrictive Practices Court Case" in *Football in the Digital Age*, S. Hamil, J. Michie, C. Oughton and S. Warby (eds), Mainstream, 2000, ISBN 1840183292.

Chapter 5 was originally published as "Broadcasting, Attendance and the Inefficiency of Cartels" (with David Forrest and Rob Simmons) in *Review of Industrial Organization*, 2004, 24, 243–265. With kind permission of Springer Science and Business Media.

Chapter 6 was originally published as "A Market Test for Discrimination in the English Professional Soccer Leagues" in *Journal of Political Economy*, 2000, 108, 3, 590–603. Reproduced with kind permission.

Chapter 7 was originally published as "The Financial Crisis in European Football: An Introduction" (with Umberto Lago and Rob Simmons) in *Journal of Sports Economics*, 2006, 7, 3–12. Reproduced with kind permission.

Chapter 8 was originally published as "English Football" (with Tunde Buraimo and Rob Simmons) in *Journal of Sports Economics*, 2006, 7, 29–46. Reproduced with kind permission.

Chapter 9 was originally published as "Income Inequality, Competitive Balance and the Attractiveness of Team Sports: Some Evidence and a Natural Experiment from English Soccer" in *Economic Journal*, 2001, 111, F69–F84. Reproduced with kind permission of Blackwell Publishers and the Royal Economic Society.

Chapter 10 was originally published as "The Champions League and the Coase Theorem" in *Scottish Journal of Political Economy*, 2007, 53, 355–373. Reproduced with kind permission of Blackwell Publishers and the Royal Economic Society.

Chapter 11 was originally published as "The Economic Impact of the World Cup" in *World Economics*, 2002, 3, 1, 169–177. Reproduced with permission from *World Economics* with permission. © Economic and Financial Publishing Ltd.

Introduction

In the last 20 years the economic dimensions of football have expanded dramatically. To take one simple example, the annual income of Liverpool football club in 2008 was greater than the annual income of all Premier League clubs in 1992 (the year it was founded); but Liverpool didn't even have the largest income in the Premier League in 2008 (Manchester United, Chelsea and Arsenal all made more). The year before the Premier League started, the combined income of the top division was in the region of £150 million; by 2008 this had increased to £1,930 million. This implies a compound annual growth rate of over 16%; even after allowing for the effects of inflation the annual growth rate of income has exceeded 13%, during a period when the UK economy grew by less than 3% per year in real terms. And while the Premier League has consistently topped the income growth tables, the national leagues of Italy, Germany, Spain and France have also seen incomes grow rapidly, as have the UEFA Champions League, the FIFA World Cup, the UEFA European Championship and a whole host of smaller domestic and international football competitions.

Looking at this phenomenon from the perspective of an economist, there are many questions that naturally come to mind. First, we can examine the causes of growth, the underlying changes in demand (and supply) that led to the influx of cash. Second, we can ask how the cash has been used, who has benefited (and who has lost out). These are essentially descriptive and analytical approaches, or 'positive' economics, meaning that we use theory and empirical research in order to understand how the football economy operates. However, the third type of question that an economist should be asking has to do with policy. Given the winners and losers from changes in football, can we say whether social welfare has increased as the football economy has grown? Is the organisation of football socially optimal, or are there reforms which would increase social welfare? In the end, economists should ask the same normative question that Lenin posed about pre-revolutionary Russia: What Is to Be Done? Moreover, economists should approach this task using the theory and data that they have accumulated in the positive analysis. In a sense, this is the purpose of economics and the economists. Just as in government economists are used to conducting a cost–benefit analysis of policy proposals,[1] so economists studying football should analyse the policies of the football authorities, actual or proposed, and evaluate them in terms of costs and benefits to the football public.

This has been my approach to writing about the economics of football over the last 20 years or so, and the chapters in this volume are intended to illustrate that approach. Over this period the number of published papers on football has expanded enormously. I recall an early rejection of a paper in which an anonymous referee took the paper to task for not referring to the existing literature, and proceeded to list fewer than ten papers, most of which were only tangentially related to the subject and some of which were already quite old. By 2006 the literature had grown to the point where Bill Gerrard was able to edit a two-volume collection of 54 papers on the economics of football, while only representing a small fraction of the total published research. Yet most of the new football research has focused on positive issues – estimating demand and production functions, trying to develop wage equations and so on – and only limited attention has been paid to policy issues. I find this disappointing. There is at present a continuing policy debate over the future of football, but much of that debate is emotional, confused and unstructured. Although this is only to be expected given the social significance of the sport, it is surely the case that economic analysis of policy issues can bring a structure to the debate which can help illuminate the true focus of the controversy and enable all sides to articulate their positions coherently and effectively. In my opinion, economists should try harder to enter the debate. Whether or not my papers have succeeded in clarifying policy issues, I hope that they might at least provoke some economists to advance their own policy analyses in order to broaden and deepen the existing debate.

In the rest of this chapter I will explain briefly the context of football economics research when I first started writing on it, then describe what I think is the contribution of each of the chapters in this volume, and finally I will analyse the current policy debates and the questions that I think are of significance.

1. How football changed in the 1990s

The first draft of my football industry paper co-authored with Ron Smith was written around 1992 (it took another five years to get the paper published, after a struggle which Ron declared to be one of the toughest in his distinguished publishing career). In that first draft we described English football as a typical rustbelt industry, characterised by underinvestment, poor quality products, falling demand and poor profitability. By the time the paper was published only the last of these descriptions remained true.

Much has been written on the causes of the transformation of English football.[2] There are five sets of indicators that help us to understand the transformation:

(i) Attendance at league football in England was in secular decline from 1949, falling from a total of 41 million across the four professional divisions to a low of 16.5 million in the 1985/86 season. Since then it has grown steadily to reach over 30 million in 2007/08. Premier League attendance increased from 7.8 million in 1988/89 to 13.5 million in 2007/08.

(ii) Ticket prices have also increased significantly since 1986/87, when the average ticket price for a top division game was around £2.50. Even before the Premier started in 1992/93, average ticket prices had already increased to around £10, and by 2007/08 they were over £30 on average. Allowing for inflation, £2.50 in 1986/87 was equivalent to around £5 in 2007/08, meaning that after accounting for inflation, ticket prices have risen about sixfold. Moreover, matchday income increased by even more, as clubs provided more services and better facilities (at higher prices) at the grounds.

(iii) The creation of the Premier League was motivated by the desire of the big clubs to take control of their broadcasting rights. Under the last contract, shared between the 92 Football League clubs, the League was paid £11 million by the terrestrial broadcaster ITV to show 18 live games per season. The initial contract with the satellite broadcaster Sky paid the 20 Premier League clubs around £60 million per season, and by 2009 the total value of broadcast rights sales nationally and internationally generated around £750 million per season.

(iv) Merchandising and sponsorship income has been transformed. Back in the mid - 1980s Manchester United generated about £250,000 per year from sponsorship by Sharp Electronics, £350,000 per year from its kit deal with Adidas, about £200,000 per year from selling advertising space inside the ground, plus a few hundred thousand from other business activities – just over £1 million per year in total. Most other clubs at this time would have generated much less. By 2007/08 the average Premier League club made about

£20 million per year from commercial activities (and Manchester United was estimated to make around £140 million).

(v) Throughout all the change football has remained resolutely unprofitable. In 1992 the top division clubs posted a combined pre-tax profit of £175,000 and half of the clubs reported a loss. In 2007 the Premier League clubs reported a combined pre-tax loss of £266 million, and only four teams reported a profit. Financial difficulties have been even greater in the lower divisions, and between 1992 and 2008 forty different clubs (in the three divisions below the Premier League) have entered insolvency proceedings (from which all the clubs have subsequently emerged).

Why did this happen? The story is not one that is specific to England and the Premier League, and the process of commercialisation was developing fastest in Italy during the 1980s. In Italy the key motivator was competition for TV rights. Until the early 1980s, in most of Europe TV broadcasting was dominated by state-run monopolies or near monopolies (RAI in Italy, the BBC in the UK, ARD and ZDF in Germany, TF1 in France). The advent of cable and satellite broadcasting technologies created competition from privately operated pay TV networks, hungry for content and which perceived football as one of the most powerful drivers of subscriptions. Increasing competition for the rights of Serie A, and the backing of powerful conglomerates (e.g. Fiat and Juventus), made it the richest league in Europe, capable of attracting the top stars. While football had always been chic in Italy, In England its image had been undermined by the scourge of hooliganism and a series of disasters, from the Heysel Stadium and the Bradford City fire in 1986 to Hillsborough in 1989. The latter finally provoked government intervention to improve stadium quality; at first this was largely subsidised by government, but as attendances grew in the 1990s clubs increasingly funded the expansion themselves. English clubs also looked increasingly to the marketing expertise of the major leagues in the USA to generate new revenue streams: football shirts became fashion items, and football culture dropped its working-class roots and became firmly established as the most popular entertainment of the middle classes, and by the 1990s that meant almost everyone in Britain.

The avalanche of money in the Premier League fell directly into the laps of the players, as the clubs competed for success. In the early 1990s many of England's best players were playing in Serie A; within a decade the trend had reversed and an increasing share of the world's top talent was gravitating to Premier League. Unlike the US major leagues, the clubs were unable to turn popularity into profit, largely because of the competitive structure of the leagues. In the US the leagues are closed, so that a team that comes bottom of the league can just wait until the following year and try again; in Europe the threat of relegation means that poor-performing teams are prone to spending heavily to avoid the drop, and this creates a financial pressure from beneath that drives every club to spend more than would be considered prudent. In the mid - 1990s there were around 20 clubs that issued shares to the market, which were enthusiastically bought in the expectation of profiting from the football boom. Within a few years almost all of these shares were worthless, as investors learned the power of competitive incentives within the promotion and relegation system. Nonetheless, the investors' loss was the fans' gain, as the quality of football on the pitch rose significantly.

Not that these developments pleased all the fans. Traditionalists felt that the soul of the game had been sold for commercial gain. Clubs had certainly become more businesslike, and many felt that business had no place in the national game. It was argued that higher ticket prices were driving out traditional fans. Despite the fact that clubs registered little by way of profit, many feared that businessmen were stripping clubs of their assets (most notably the ground, usually located close to the centre of town and extremely attractive in a housing boom). When the Labour Party came to power in 1997 it set up a football task force, intended to represent all the interests of the game, and many of the supporter groups called for increased regulation, by government if necessary, of commercial activities. Another set of concerns related to growing financial inequalities in football and the fear that these would ultimately destroy interest in the game. This 'uncertainty of outcome' hypothesis – the idea that without an adequate level of competitive balances fans will lose interest – has been a constant theme of critics (and many insiders) over the last two decades, despite the rise in attendances. Moreover, the constant reminders of financial instability, as lower-division clubs went in and out of bankruptcy, caused many to worry about the long-term security of the game (even if no club ever disappeared) and to call for tighter financial controls over the decisions of football club boards of directors. The influx of foreign players was also deemed problematic by many who thought that the reduction of opportunities for British-born players would undermine the performance of the England national team. And as the growing global popularity of English football attracted foreign investors – from Russia, the USA, Thailand and the United Arab Emirates – many people worried that the national game was moving beyond national control.

2. Papers

To study an industry you need to have data. In particular you want to know (a) what is produced and how it is valued and (b) how it is produced and what it costs. Armed with this information it should be possible to understand how competition works, and how the industry is structured. In most industries there is considerable heterogeneity in both outputs and inputs, making this kind of analysis problematic. For example, if we consider the clothing industry, what is the difference between the high-end fashionwear sold by a retailer such as Prada and the products sold in 'value retailers' such as Primark? How does one compare the market for specialist sportswear to the market for lingerie? The product space of the industry is broad, and many firms nominally in the same industry can scarcely be considered competitors. Comparing data on sales and costs across firms would in many cases be largely meaningless. For example, who would be considered more successful – a low-volume/high-margin specialist or a high-volume/low-margin mass market producer? Professional sports leagues are almost tailor-made for economic analysis, since in most cases a league forms a distinct market in its own right.[3]

In the late 1980s I worked for John Kay at London Business School's Centre for Business Strategy with a group of researchers interested in finding good ways to illustrate the use of economic concepts in business, and the idea that the English Football League might be a suitable case study came up. I then looked into the possibility of gathering data and discovered a remarkable peculiarity which has been the platform for much of the rest of my career. For various reasons, almost all professional English football clubs set themselves up as limited liability companies (between the 1880s and 1920s); under English law all limited liability companies have to file annual accounts with Companies House; these accounts are available for inspection by the public; and throughout their history English clubs have engaged in almost no activity other than playing professional football. Thus the microfiche reports from Companies House provided a complete financial picture of the operations of the league. In essence, teams buy players in the market, the performance of these players translates into success in the league competition, and success translates into revenues generated from players. The precise statistical measurement of these relationships for English league clubs between 1974 and 1989 was set out in the paper 'The English Football Industry: Profit, Performance and Industrial Structure'. For me, there are two key insights from the paper. The first is that success depends on share of total football resources deployed, rather than spending in the absolute and the second is that the correlation between spending and success implies that the market for players operates relatively efficiently.[4]

In 1997 I was invited by Stefan Késenne and Claude Jeanrenaud to a conference organised in Neuchatel, Switzerland, to discuss the implications of the Bosman judgement. Bosman was a Belgian player who had challenged the transfer system in Europe, and the European Court of Justice had declared it inconsistent with the freedom of movement guaranteed to all European citizens by the Treaty of Rome. It was hard to argue that Bosman himself was not entitled to redress (he wanted to move, his club was willing to sell him, a club had offered a reasonable fee to pay for him, and yet his club refused to agree to the transfer), but the football authorities declared that the consequences of the judgement would be widespread bankruptcy of clubs. This statement, of course, required some underlying view of how the player market worked, and the purpose of the conference was to bring together economists from Europe and the USA, where the problem of player market restraints had long been at issue, to try to establish some common frameworks. Afterwards Stefan and Claude edited a book of papers based upon the conference. My own contribution, 'The Market for Soccer Players in England after Bosman: Winners and Losers', was an attempt to place the judgement in the context of what I had learnt about the operation of the player market from the analysis of the accounting data. I argued that since the labour market operated competitively (and by this time I had already started to obtain some data from other European leagues suggesting that the wage–performance correlation was more or less as strong as that in England), the precise timing and rules of contracts would make little difference to the financial position of the clubs. The representatives of football clubs, not surprisingly, tended to dismiss this view, although with the benefit of hindsight it seems hard to argue, whatever the consequences of Bosman were in reality, that they involved widespread financial failure of football clubs.

Perhaps more interesting was the reaction of the American economists, who tended to argue from their experience that labour markets in professional sports did not work very efficiently. The opportunity to draw on the experience of the leading American economists, such as Roger Noll, Gerald Scully, Rodney Fort, Paul Staudohar, and the sports law expert Stephen F. Ross, who was to become a close collaborator, significantly broadened my horizons and forced me to develop an account of how the differences between the outcomes of league competition in the USA and in Europe could be accounted for by the different incentive structures and institutions adopted by the organisers of the leagues. My first real attempt to do this came in a paper co-authored with Tom Hoehn, the economic consultant and specialist in competition law. At the time there was much talk of the creation of a breakaway European superleague that might be modelled on the NFL or the NBA, and so we gave the paper the deliberately provocative title 'The Americanization of European Football'. The paper even described a model of a superleague that might preserve the best in European traditions while benefiting from more international competition. As financial inequalities in Europe have grown, there have been persistent demands to adopt measures such as salary caps, which are used to maintain balance in American leagues, and the paper showed how the nature of simultaneous competition in domestic leagues and international competitions such as the Champions League made the design of a salary cap impractical (although as Champions League revenues have increased, the concern that these are distorting domestic competitions has also increased). Perhaps the greatest strength of this chapter is in illustrating how the aim of preserving European football traditions frequently conflicts with measures that are called for to maintain more balance among the teams.

The other great footballing cause célèbre of the 1990s was the collective selling of broadcast rights. I became involved in this from around 1997 as the Office of Fair Trading in the UK challenged the selling arrangements of the FA Premier League in the Restrictive Practices Court (since superseded, following the Competition Act of 2000). As their 'football expert witness' I was asked to analyse collective selling and to comment on whether it brought benefits to football and whether its abolition would do harm. My own view was that collective selling did little to advance the alleged goal of increasing competitive balance, although this did not matter much since, contrary to received wisdom, the fans did not seem to care too much about competitive balance (recall that at this time Manchester United was becoming increasingly dominant on the field, while attendance at Premier League games was booming). The major harm caused by collective selling, in my view, was (and still is) the restriction on the number of live games broadcast, 66 at that date (138 now) out of 380 games played. Moreover, the logic of competition law in general is that agreements to restrain competition can be justified if they are indispensable for meeting some desirable goal (e.g. competitive balance, supposing for a moment that this really is desirable), but it is hard to see how collective selling is indispensable. As was argued in court, if mechanisms to share revenues are desirable, there are many ways the clubs could reach such agreements even if they were not allowed to sell broadcast rights collectively. In any case, the OFT lost their case, and I tried to set out the reasons for that defeat in the paper 'Hearts and Minds and the Restrictive Practices Court case'. The issue did not go away with that case, being taken up by the European Commission in 2003. A key argument raised by the Premier League in defence of collective selling was that it was necessary to restrict the number of games shown in order to protect attendances at the game itself. This is an empirically testable proposition, and one I took up with Rob Simmons and David Forrest, who are perhaps the leading exponents in the UK on the measurement of the demand for league sports. In 'Broadcasting, Attendance and the Inefficiency of Cartels' we found that showing a game live on TV had only a small effect on the attendance, and given the significant sums of money that broadcasters such as Sky would be willing to pay to show more games, we concluded that the Premier League was giving up a substantial amount of revenues. The theme that cartels are not just acting as a monopolist, but tend to be an inefficient monopolist, is the one that Steve Ross and I have explored more fully in our joint work.

Racism is an issue that has bedevilled sports across the world. It is not surprising that an activity which is so bound up in our own sense of personal identity can become as much a means of social *exclusion* as it is of *inclusion*. Racism in English football has been aimed mainly at players of Afro–Caribbean descent, many of whom were the children of immigrants who were invited to the UK during the 1950s and 1960s. Until the 1970s there were very few black players who had ever played in the English leagues, but by the 1980s they were coming to represent a significant fraction of the players on the field, although a much smaller fraction of the crowd. Moreover, although many played the game, few people of Asian descent (whence there had come a significant number of migrants over the same period) were to be found either on the terraces or the pitch. Numerous testimonies from non-whites affirm that you were unlikely to be welcome at an English football ground, while the taunts, chanting and missiles thrown at black players (the favourite object was usually a banana), did not leave much room for doubt. On the field, some coaches also developed racial stereotypes about the capabilities of black players, even after it had become apparent that much of the best domestic talent was of Afro–Caribbean descent. The first step in dealing with racism is recognition of the problem, and by the end of the 1980s the clubs themselves began reluctantly to accept that they had a responsibility to stamp out racial abuse. As the clubs supported anti-racist campaigns the scale of the problem in England diminished, although it has not been entirely eliminated.

Few clubs have ever acknowledged that they have contributed to the problem through racist policies of their own, yet it was well known in the 1980s that some clubs appeared averse to hiring black players. However, the consequences of such a policy in a competitive market where talent is easily recognised are not simple. In essence, discrimination by some clubs presents an opportunity to non-racist clubs to hire those facing discrimination at a discount to their market rate. In other words, black players would be paid less than equivalently talented white players because their job opportunities were narrower. My paper 'A Market Test for Discrimination in the English Professional Soccer Leagues' demonstrated statistically that this was precisely what was happening in the 1980s, by showing that teams with an above average proportion of black players performed better, after taking into account wage spending, than teams with a below average proportion.[5]

While football income across Europe continued to grow in the new millennium, concerns about financial problems continued unabated. The collapse of broadcast contracts in England and in Germany, a general economic crisis in Italy and a number of corruption scandals surrounding football, and a sense that smaller leagues were suffering because of the growing economic power of the big five (England, France, Germany, Italy and Spain) produced widespread calls for reform. FIFA and UEFA warned that the free market for players in Europe was contributing to the perceived problem and that reform was necessary. Against this background I helped to organise, together with Umberto Lago and Rob Simmons, a meeting of economists in Rimini, sponsored by the University of Bologna, to present information on the football crisis in 11 UEFA nations. 'The Financial Crisis in European Football: An Introduction' summarises our findings. In general it was perhaps surprising to find that the economists were sanguine about the prospects in most countries, and the extent to which there was a crisis, it was largely centred on the smaller clubs. The paper 'English Football', co-authored with Tunde Buraimo and Rob Simmons, examined the extent of the financial crisis in England.

Arguably the most important policy issue in any sport, including football, has always been competitive balance. To my knowledge, however, the concept was seldom, if ever, mentioned by the football authorities before the 1990s, even though it had long been the case that most national competitions were dominated by a small number of teams.

The influx of large sums of money into football in the 1990s gave the game an economic dimension that attracted the interest of governments and competition authorities across the European Union (and inside the European Commission). When policies were challenged, the football authorities responded by claiming that their policies were intended to promote competitive balance.[6] Here is an issue where economists should have much to say. What is the evidence that a balanced competition is attractive to fans? What measures promote competitive balance? In 'Income Inequality, Competitive Balance and the Attractiveness of Team Sports: Some Evidence and a Natural Experiment from English Soccer', I examined the issue of competitive balance by comparing attendance at games between the same teams playing in different competitions. In each season English league teams compete against the other teams in their own division, but also against all other league teams in the FA Cup. Over time the income inequality between divisions has grown much faster than income inequality within divisions. As a result, the FA Cup has become a much more unequal competition than the league competition. In each season teams from the same division may be drawn against each other in the Cup, and therefore by comparing the attendance in each competition format it is possible to identify the effect of increasing imbalance. The data show that attendance at Cup games has declined relative to League games between the same teams, suggesting that the growing inequality of the FA Cup has adversely affected demand.

In 2002 I was promoted as full professor, and I gave as my inaugural lecture at Imperial College the paper that was later published as 'The Champions League and the Coase Theorem'. As is customary the paper reviewed what I thought was some of my most important work. One of the most important questions to me was how redistributive policies would affect competitive balance. The league organisers had always assumed that revenue sharing would improve competitive balance; research by the American School of Sports Economics claimed that redistribution would make no difference – a version of the Coase Theorem known in the literature as the 'invariance principle'. My own research had shown that certain types of revenue sharing could actually make a competition more imbalanced, and that this apparently perverse result made sense because it would attract more fans.[7] In this chapter I considered the imbalances in the Champions League, and whether negotiation among the clubs would enable efficient bargains to be realised.

The last chapter in this volume is concerned not with league policy, but government policy towards hosting major sporting events. It is usual for governments to claim that hosting major events will generate a substantial economic stimulus. 'The Economic Impact of the World Cup 2002' surveys some of the evidence that economists have produced on the subject and applies it in the context of the Japan–Korea World Cup in 2002.

3. The context in 2010

At present there remain a great many policy questions that are unanswered. The financial crisis that drove the world economy into a deep recession at the end of 2008 has significant consequences for football. Consumer spending on entertainment such as sports is closely correlated with changes in consumer income, so it is only reasonable to expect a slump in football club income. By the same token, once a recovery starts, consumer expenditure on football will start to grow again. Nonetheless, a financial crisis will inevitably lead to calls for tighter regulation, and the backlash against free market policies will further strengthen the claims of would-be regulators. Economists must surely have a role to play in setting out plausible welfare functions for football and evaluating policies against these yardsticks. Specific policies that are being proposed to regulate labour markets, such as FIFA's '6 + 5' rule and home-grown player proposals of UEFA, would also benefit from careful economic analysis. The problem of dominance in Europe, its causes and consequences, remains a significant issue on which economists have written little. The issue of doping, already a major policy debate in the USA, also requires consideration, as does the appropriate balance to be struck in the 'club versus country' debate. If the application of economic analysis to football has come of age over the last decade, it is now time for economists to demonstrate to a wider audience the value of their thinking.

Notes

1. the UK government is quite explicit in using this approach, requiring all new policies to undergo a cost–benefit analysis with an explicit monetisation of all costs and benefits; see UK Treasury Green Book and BERR impact assessment website.
2. A lot of it is sensationalist (e.g. *Broken Dreams* by Tom Bower), sentimental (e.g. *The Football Business* by David Conn) or even Marxist (e.g. *Regulating Football* by Steve Greenfield and Guy Osborn). My own views can largely be found in *Winners and Losers: The Business Strategy of Football* (co-authored with Tim Kuypers).

3. The standard method of identifying a relevant market in antitrust cases is the SSNIP test – a market is defined as the smallest collection of products such that a hypothetical monopolist controlling the pricing of all the products would be able to profitably impose a small but significant, non-transitory increase in price. The idea is that products outside this collection do not offer a significant competitive threat to those products inside the collection, and are therefore not part of the market in question. See Gregory Werden, 'The 1982 Merger Guidelines and the Ascent of the Hypothetical Monopolist Paradigm', *Antitrust Law Review*, 71, 2003, pp. 253–269.

4. The possibility that in fact there is reverse causation (from success to wages) was considered and rejected statistically in 'Testing Causality Between Team Performance and Payroll: The Cases of Major League Baseball and English Soccer' (with Stephen Hall and Andrew Zimbalist), *Journal of Sports Economics*, 3, 2, 2002, pp. 149–168.

5. A companion paper co-authored with Ian Preston, 'Race and English Football Fans', *Scottish Journal of Political Economy*, 47, 4, 2000, 342–363, examined the geographical basis for this discrimination.

6. The judgment of the European Court of Justice in the Bosman case explicitly recognised the legitimacy of competitive balance as a policy goal of the football authorities, but denied that the existing restraints on player mobility materially advanced that goal.

7. See, 'Competitive balance and gate revenue sharing in team sports' (co-authored with Stefan Késenne) and 'Professional team sports are only a game: The Walrasian fixed supply conjecture model, Contest-Nash equilibrium and the invariance principle' in *The Comparative Economics of Sport*.

1
The English Football Industry: Profit, Performance and Industrial Structure

Stefan Szymanski[a] *and Ron Smith*[b]

[a] *Imperial College Management School, London*
[b] *Birkbeck College, London University, London*

Abstract

The English (Association) Football League is a long-established industrial cartel selling a highly popular product with only imperfect substitutes. Despite that, the majority of its member clubs lose money and the industry has faced successive financial crises over the last decade. This chapter develops an empirical model of the financial performance of English League clubs using a high-quality data set of 48 clubs over the period 1974–89. The underlying model explains how rents are competed away through the maximising behaviour of club owners subject to production constraints. This model is parameterised by a system of equations which describe the behaviour of a maximising owner subject to demand and production constraints. The model is then used to examine the coordination failure which lies at the heart of the English Football League's decline and to assess the prospects for the Premier League.

1. Introduction

The idea of an industry, a set of competing specialist firms within a well-defined market, is little more than a metaphor in most of the economy,

We are grateful to Sean Wilkins for excellent research assistance in collecting the data and to two anonymous referees for constructive comments. The chapter was written while the second author was visiting the Centre for Economic Forecasting, London Business School.

but in the area of professional team sports it represents a very precise description. This chapter analyses the structure of the English Football industry. Despite what is generally perceived to be a very high and price-inelastic demand for the services of professional football teams, the clubs themselves seldom make money. In many other industries we see firms engaging in tacitly collusive behaviour in order to mitigate the impact of competition; in football we do not see such behaviour, at least in aggregate. In this chapter we present a theoretical model of the behaviour of football club owners which rationalises the observed intensity of competition. We then fit that model to the data for 48 English Football League Clubs over the period 1974–89. Thus we model the period before the changes during the 1990s, which we discuss below.

There is a large literature on the economics of professional team sports, which is surveyed in Cairns *et al.* (1986). Most of this literature has been concerned with one of two issues: first, estimating the demand for professional team sports, and second, trying to identify the objective function of professional clubs. However, few papers have attempted to marry the analysis of supply and demand conditions in order to derive an equilibrium model of team performance. We attempt to develop such a model using accounting data as well as League performance data. The analysis highlights a coordination failure which encourages club owners to neglect the infrastructure of League Football whilst concentrating on short-term playing performance. Given that in most cases English clubs neither are the recipients of open-ended financial backing from industrialists nor receive significant support for the upkeep of stadia from municipal authorities, as is common in other countries, most clubs live on the brink of financial failure. Whilst these problems have been pointed out by previous research [see, for example, the Chester Reports of 1968 and 1983 (commissioned by the Football League); Jennett & Sloane, 1985; Arnold & Beneviste, 1987; and most recently the Taylor Report, 1989], there have been no previous attempts to model the economic problem systematically and confront it with the data.[1] The data set combines information on League performance and attendance with accounting data on revenue, wage and transfer expenditure.[2] The sample means are given in Tables 1.1a and 1.1b.

The broad structure of the model, which is set out in detail in Section 2, is as follows: Football skills are bought on a competitive market for players, with the quality adjusted wage being determined as a Nash equilibrium between the clubs. The amount of skill a club purchases determines its position in the League. This corresponds to the production function of the industry which we estimate. Position in the League determines the revenue a club earns from gate receipts, television

Table 1.1a   Average annual performance by club, 1974–89 (£000)

	League position	Turnover	Gate receipts	Wage spend	Net transfer spend	Pre-tax profits	Number of major cup games
Liverpool	2	3592	3208	1630	617	172	14
Everton	7	2943	2263	1486	416	25	10
Arsenal	7	921	2206	1493	307	205	10
Manchester United	8	4653	4340	1700	493	−17	10
Tottenham Hotspur	11	3337	2868	1695	501	20	10
Aston Villa	14	2368	1593	1049	285	59	10
Coventry	14	1416	1050	963	152	33	8
Southampton	15	1470	1113	817	312	−110	9
West Ham	16	2144	1980	1135	276	38	9
Leeds	18	1649	1604	1039	251	−379	8
West Bromwich Albion	19	1560	1191	919	−53	19	8
Newcastle	20	1810	1810	950	60	−64	7
Luton	21	1546	1392	845	30	−18	8
Leicester	21	1343	976	758	−73	−11	7
Chelsea	22	2530	1964	920	−82	−182	7
Birmingham	23	1167	947	886	−68	−96	7
Sheffield Wednesday	33	1271	1009	734	35	65	7
Oldham	35	638	368	412	−93	−28	6
Blackburn Rovers	35	586	421	465	−85	7	6
Sheffield United	39	894	758	512	0	−258	6
Bolton	42	803	510	566	41	−317	5
Shrewsbury	44	353	251	315	−31	−55	5
Hull City	46	482	293	401	−17	−81	5
Bristol Rovers	47	523	394	310	−64	−126	5
Carlisle	49	436	308	342	−48	−13	5
Burnley	49	652	506	607	−312	−96	6
Plymouth	50	1026	411	425	−38	18	5
Barnsley	50	445	387	391	−2	−82	5
Preston	54	565	331	395	−101	−34	4
Gillingham	55	494	473	336	−4	−153	4
Walsall	55	375	246	310	−11	−4	5
Huddersfield	56	519	380	438	−91	24	5
Swindon	57	614	422	394	2	−50	6
Rotherham	58	422	239	318	−3	−156	5
Cambridge	59	468	181	294	−8	−14	4
Wrexham	60	543	266	342	−32	−42	5

Table 1.1a (Continued)

	League position	Turnover	Gate receipts	Wage spend	Net transfer spend	Pre-tax profits	Number of major cup games
Reading	62	606	367	372	−19	−1	4
Brentford	63	592	351	343	17	−32	4
Bury	66	325	184	301	−57	−19	4
Southend	66	436	245	258	−43	−70	4
Port Vale	67	425	186	322	9	9	4
Mansfield	68	352	216	317	−59	−67	4
Colchester	68	399	200	244	−18	−63	4
Lincoln	68	427	264	258	−24	−40	3
Peterborough	70	338	203	289	−4	−55	5
Northampton	77	317	181	255	−47	−38	3
Scunthorpe	81	348	201	259	−13	−67	4
Rochdale	86	205	152	171	−24	−126	3

Table 1.1b Summary statistics by year (1985 Prices £000)

Year	Position	Turnover	Gate receipts	Wage bill	Net transfer spend	Pre-tax profits	Average weekly League gate (000)
1974	44	872	729	500	−31	−90	14.5
1975	43	796	665	480	0	−87	15.1
1976	43	876	739	467	4	1	14.5
1977	41	912	751	454	20	31	15.1
1978	42	1075	862	508	53	33	15.0
1979	42	1059	834	564	103	−41	14.1
1980	44	1062	815	621	80	9	13.7
1981	43	1075	804	657	61	−114	12.4
1982	43	1064	779	686	104	−274	11.6
1983	42	1090	817	641	30	−54	10.8
1984	43	1206	924	639	25	9	10.9
1985	43	1265	965	684	21	−17	10.8
1986	43	1169	913	700	55	−123	10.2
1987	42	1314	1007	718	71	−9	10.6
1988	43	1378	1053	782	23	6	10.6
1989	44	1562	1147	892	42	−52	11.0

Net transfers means total expenditure minus total income from transfers. A negative figure means a net income for the club.

rights, sponsorship, etc., and this corresponds to the demand function of the industry which we also estimate. Combining the estimated demand and production functions with the budget constraint we derive the empirical trade-off that the club faces between profit and position in the league. This has a negative slope which indicates that increased spending on players is not self-financing through higher performance and revenue. The objective function of the owner of the club depends on both profits and position (see, for example, Sloane, 1971). Maximisation of the objective function, subject to the profit–position constraint, determines the optimal level of wages and, thus, the club's profits and position in the League. Whereas each individual club faces a negative trade-off between profit and position, between clubs profits and position are positively related. This is because clubs differ in their endowment – their inherent capability and revenue-generating potential – and these differences generate the observed distribution of profit and position.

The estimates of the model are presented in Section 3. Section 4 deals with some econometric issues, and Section 5 looks at some alternative specifications. Section 6 discusses some of the implications of the industrial structure and in particular how the interaction of non-profit objectives with the lack of an effective market for corporate control inhibits restructuring of the industry. This is discussed in the light of the changes introduced in the 1990s.

2. A model of the English Football League

The English Football League contained 92 clubs divided into four divisions.[3] We will consider a particular club i, which can be characterised by the quality of its performance, Q_i, a function of its position in the League. Most managers and owners seem to regard this as the most significant indicator of the performance of a club. Whilst success in cup competitions such as the FA Cup is highly prized, League position represents the outcome of sustained effort over an eight-month period, in which each club plays every other club in its division twice, without the random element introduced by the draw in a knock-out competition. In the empirical applications, to obtain linearity of the estimated relationships we used the negative of the log-odds (logit) of position: so quality is measured[4] as $-\log[\text{position}/(93-\text{position})]$.

In our model, clubs purchase players in a competitive labour market. In reality, prior to 1963 the clubs had an effective monopoly over the players on their own books, since a transfer required the consent of both clubs involved. Whilst a market for players existed in the sense that transfers did occur, the market was limited and likened to slavery

(Sloane, 1969). Until 1977 the 'retain and transfer' system imposed some restrictions on the freedom of players to move between clubs, but the market for players became much more active in the late 1960s and early 1970s. In 1977, the Professional Footballers' Association succeeded in establishing freedom of contract, and players are now almost completely free to accept the best contract on offer.[5] Each year several hundred players move clubs, although only a small fraction are transferred for the large sums advertised in the newspapers. The market leads clubs to bid against each other competitively to secure the services of the best players. The effort and performance of players is easily observed and monitored, thus skill is readily identifiable.[6]

One important piece of evidence which we believe supports our assertion that the market is competitive is the fact that the performance and the wage bill of a club are very highly correlated. This suggests that the payment to teams is closely related to output. Figure 1.1 plots the average value of our measure of quality over 1974–89 against the average of the logarithm of the wages paid by the club relative to average wages in the year over all clubs. The transformation seems to have induced linearity; the relationship is positive and fairly close.[7] The most noticeable outlier is Liverpool, the highest performing club, which spends considerably less on wages than one would expect from the average relationship.[8]

Whilst there have been some papers on the operation of the English soccer labour market (e.g. Ruddock, 1979; Carmichael & Thomas, 1992),

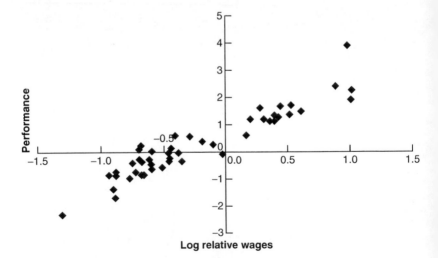

Figure 1.1   Wages and performance (averages 1974–89)

we know of no studies which have tested for the existence of a competitive labour market along the lines of US studies of the baseball labour market. This literature is surveyed in Cairns *et al.* (1986). These studies use data on individual salary levels and estimated marginal revenue product, which should be equal in a competitive market. They find that the system of labour contracts which prevailed prior to 1976 (which resembled English soccer's 'retain and transfer' system) was associated with salaries well below the estimated marginal revenue product, but after 1976 when freedom of contract was established, salaries rose considerably and were closer, if not identical, to marginal revenue product. Separate tests for racial discrimination tended to suggest that major league baseball was not a perfectly competitive labour market. Replication of this type of work is not easy for soccer, or most team sports, since disentangling the contribution of the individual from that of the rest of the team is problematic, whilst in baseball the contribution of the individual in terms of hitting and pitching is much easier to identify. However, if the baseball literature is relevant at all, it does suggest that freedom of contract enables one to treat labour markets as approximately competitive, as we do here.

In our model the wage bill of the club is $W = wL$, where w is the quality adjusted wage rate and L the quantity of playing skills the club employs. There is a limited supply of playing skills and the labour market clears when total expenditure of all clubs is equal to the total wage bill corresponding to this supply, giving a wage rate of

$$
w_t = \frac{\sum_{i=1}^{N} W_{it}}{\sum_{i=1}^{N} L_{it}} \tag{1}
$$

Thus, the expenditure of each club depends on the proportion of the total playing skill they demand and the total expenditure by all clubs. This formulation assumes the existence of a Nash equilibrium in wages, i.e. each club bids for players in such a way as to maximise its objective function (discussed below), assuming that all other clubs do likewise. Thus, the share of the available playing skill that a club commands is equal to its share of the total wage bill of all clubs

$$
\frac{L_{it}}{\sum_{i=1}^{N} L_{it}} = \frac{w_t L_{it}}{w_t \sum_{i=1}^{N} L_{it}} = \frac{W_{it}}{\sum_{i=1}^{N} W_{it}} \tag{2}
$$

We will characterise the technology of the club by two equations, corresponding to a production function and a demand function, the parameters of which will, in general, differ between clubs. The production function describes how performance is produced by the quality adjusted inputs of skilled players, purchased on a competitive market, relative to the inputs of other teams. Clubs differ in their inherent performance potential as a result of such factors as history and intrinsic management differences.[9] Relative inputs are measured by relative wages. In the empirical implementation we allow for variations in total expenditure on wages by all clubs, but treating this as fixed for the moment, we can write the production function in terms of a club's expenditure on wages

$$Q_{it} = c_i + dW_{it} \tag{3}$$

Each club faces a budget constraint that generates profits as a function of the set of decision variables that we model

$$P_{it} = p_{it}G_{it} + O_{it} - T_{it} - N_{it} - W_{it} \tag{4}$$

where upper case P refers to profit and lower case p refers to ticket price, G to gate attendance, O to other income sources, such as TV and sponsorship (discussed further in Section 6), T to transfers and N to non-wage expenditure. Each club faces a demand function from fans which specifies how gate attendances, for a given quality of a team, depend on ticket prices

$$G_{it} = f(p_{it}, Q_{it}) \tag{5}$$

In order to estimate these demand functions we assume that they are separable and linear in prices and quality. They differ between clubs because of the size of their catchment area, local population density, traditions, etc.[10] Each club is assumed to charge a price which maximises net gate revenue, so that price can be substituted out to give a reduced form function in which gate revenue depends on performance.[11] If, in addition, we assume that other revenue, from TV etc., also depends on performance, then total revenue becomes a function of the club-specific intercept, the performance of the team, which depends on its quality, and chance, captured by a stochastic error term. This ignores general shifts in attendance and revenue which affect all clubs, for example, the weather and the general decline in attendances, but we shall return to these secular trends in Section 6.[12] The systematic component of the revenue equation (conditional on gate prices) is thus

$$R_{it} = a_i + bQ_{it} \qquad (6)$$

We shall assume that non-wage expenditures, N, and net transfers T are linked to wage costs

$$N_{it} + T_{it} = \tau W_{it} \qquad (7)$$

As will be seen below, empirically this works quite well. Proper treatment of transfers raises inter-temporal aspects, which are a matter for further research.[13] Clubs acquire playing skills in one of the two ways. Through recruitment and training programmes directed at the young people in their locality they develop their own talent. Second, they purchase already developed talent through the transfer market. Overall this is a market for human capital. Some of this human capital is firm-specific, paid for by the club, so the club requires compensation when a player leaves to join another club. We can think of each club's investment programme generating a team with a value (wage cost) W^A. The optimisation, described below, generates a desired wage bill W^*. Transfers are determined as

$$T = v\left(W^* - W^A\right) \qquad (8)$$

a linear function of wages as we assumed above. Clubs with a high desired wage bill will buy players ($T > 0$) and clubs with a low desired wage bill will sell players ($T < 0$). This is broadly consistent with the data. Clubs lower down the League, whose training and recruitment may be very good, earn significant income by selling players to clubs at the top of the League whose demand for playing skills is so great that it exceeds their ability to generate them by their own local investment.

Profits are the difference between revenue and total expenditure, thus at any moment in time

$$P_i = R_i - (1 + \tau)W_i \qquad (9)$$

Thus the profit–quality trade-off the owner faces is

$$P_i = \pi_i + \phi Q_i \qquad (10)$$

where

$$\pi_i = (a_i d + (1 + \tau)c_i)/d$$

and

$$\phi = b - (1 + \tau)/d$$

In this simple model, profits are just a linear function of expenditure. If it were a positive function, then the owner faces no conflict, he can have both more profits and more quality by spending more. We shall assume that this is not the case (the estimates below confirm this) and that the owner faces a trade-off, summarised by equation (10). All clubs face the same price, given by the slope, but differ in their endowment, determined by the intercept. Intercepts differ because clubs differ in their inherent revenue potential and in their efficiency in converting player inputs into performance. In the empirical applications, this intercept will also be shifted over time by the total revenue and the total expenditure on wages of all clubs, and we shall assume an intertemporal objective function with quadratic costs of adjustment, leading to a partial adjustment model.

We assume that the owner cares about both quality and profits so that the owner's objective function can be written as

$$W = P_i - (\alpha/2)\, P_i^2 + \beta Q_i - (\gamma/2)\, Q_i^2 \tag{11}$$

The correct way to identify the objectives of a football club has always been a matter of some controversy. Since it is the owners who make all the key financial decisions, we have focused on owners. Sloane (1971) discusses this issue in some detail and argues that the objective of the football club is essentially to achieve playing success whilst remaining solvent. One reason why profit maximisation on its own is not a very plausible objective to assume is that unlike most large corporations whose ownership is embodied in shares, which are actively traded on the stock market, there is a very limited market for corporate control. Normally the market for corporate control imposes a constraint on those who control a company to maximise profits. The absence of a market in football club ownership is in striking contrast to the football, baseball and hockey franchises of North America. English clubs are usually tightly controlled by a small number of board directors (see for example, Jennett & Sloane, 1985, p. 47). However, whilst most football clubs repeatedly report financial losses being subsidised by their owners, these owners must place some limit on the extent of the subsidy. Our assumption is consistent with the idea that owners have some limit in mind, but that this differs between clubs. Welfare is maximised by quality

$$Q_i^* = [\beta + \phi(1 + \alpha \pi_i)]/(\gamma + \alpha \phi^2) \tag{12}$$

and the team will make profits (losses)

$$P_i^* = [\pi_i \gamma + \phi(1 + \phi\beta)]/(\gamma + \alpha\phi^2) \tag{13}$$

The team is more likely to make a profit if the owner puts less weight on quality relative to profits or if the team has a higher inherent endowment.

Although each individual owner faces a negative trade-off between performance and profits, over teams we will observe a positive association. As the break-even performance increases, an owner would choose higher levels of both profits and performance (assuming they are both normal goods) tracing out the equivalent of an income expansion locus. This is shown in Fig. 1.2. The more similar are the tastes of different owners, the closer will be the cross-sectional relation between profits and performance. Figure 1.3 plots the observed relationship over the sample between average performance and average profit margin (logarithm of the expenditure/cost ratio). As the theory suggests, the relationship is significantly positive although there is a considerable scatter,

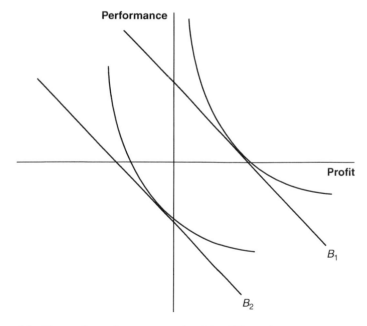

Figure 1.2 The profit–performance trade-off for differently endowed clubs

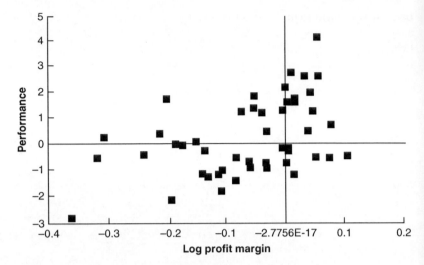

Figure 1.3   Profits and performance (averages 1974–89)

which would be consistent with preferences between performance and profits differing between owners.

3.   Empirical results

This section presents basic estimates for simple versions of the revenue, performance and total-cost functions. Extended versions are considered in the next two sections, but the basic estimates are robust to these extensions.

Above, we assumed that adjustment of revenue to quality and of quality to position was instantaneous. For empirical implementation, we allow for partial adjustment, because both success and failure generate considerable persistence. The data were transformed to produce linearity, and the transformed variables will be denoted by lower-case letters. As was explained in Section 2, quality was measured by the negative of the log-odds of position in the league N, which can run from 1 (top) to 92 (bottom). Thus, in our empirical applications $q = -\ln[N/(93 - N)]$. Labour input, w, was measured as the deviation of the logarithm of expenditure on wages by the club from its mean for that year over all clubs. Revenue, r, was measured by the deviation of the logarithm of revenue from its mean over all clubs.[14] These transformations induce a broadly linear relation between profit margin log(revenue/costs) and performance (the logit of position), as can be seen from Fig. 1.3. They also imply a relationship between the absolute level of profits and position that fits the pattern observed. Clubs high in the League make profits, clubs in the middle make large absolute losses and clubs at the bottom of the League make small absolute losses.

The estimated model for the revenue function is

$$(r_{it} - \bar{r}_t) = \lambda a_i + \lambda b q_{it} + (1 - \lambda)(r_{it-1} - \bar{r}_{t-1}) + \varepsilon_{it} \tag{14}$$

and for the production function is

$$q_{it} = \mu c_i + \mu d(w_{it} - \bar{w}_t) + (1 - \mu)q_{it-1} + \varepsilon_{it-1} \tag{15}$$

Both functions were estimated by OLS allowing for club-specific intercepts on pooled data [for the 48 clubs over 15 years (1974 was used for lags); 720 observations]. Wu–Hausman tests (using lagged revenue, performance and wages as instruments) indicated that both performance and wages could be treated as exogenous ($t = 0.56$ and 1.75, respectively).

The estimate of the revenue function is

$$(r_{it} - \bar{r}_t) = \lambda a_i + 0.134 q_{it} + 0.466 (r_{it-1} - \bar{r}_{t-1}) \qquad R^2 = 0.94$$
$$(0.012) \qquad (0.031)$$

and for the production function is

$$q_{it} = \mu c_i + 1.076 (w_{it} - \bar{w}_t) + 0.427 q_{it-1} \qquad R^2 = 0.85$$
$$(0.120) \qquad\qquad (0.057)$$

Standard errors are given in parentheses. Clearly there is substantial persistence, both in performance and revenue. The implied estimates of the long-run revenue and performance parameters (with standard errors in parentheses) are

$$b = 0.252 \qquad d = 1.894$$
$$(0.019) \qquad (0.178)$$

In the logarithmic formulation, the profit margin of the club can be written

$$(R/C) = ac(1 + \tau)^{-1} Q^{(b-1/d)}$$

where a and c are the antilogarithms of the intercepts in the revenue and performance functions. The slope of the budget constraint is $b - 1/d = -0.28$, which is negative as assumed.

The 48 club-specific intercepts in the performance function are of some interest. When transformed, they indicate the notional position the club would have had in the League had it spent the average amount on wages. If we imagine notional divisions divided at average positions 22, 44 and 68, our sample of 48 clubs would be divided into 14 First, 7 Second, 21 Third, and 6 Fourth division clubs on the basis of their average position over the 16 years. If we examine the intercepts, the notional average position they would have had, were they to spend average amounts on wages, we find only 1 First (Liverpool), 31 Second, 16 Third and no Fourth Division clubs. On the basis of the intercepts, all but five clubs would have average positions between 25 and 55. The two below 25 are Liverpool and Shrewsbury; the three above 55 are Scunthorpe, Rochdale and Burnley.

When estimated by OLS on the whole panel, the relation between the logarithms of total costs and wages is given by

$$c_{it} = 0.272 + 1.038w_{it} \qquad R^2 = 0.833$$
$$(0.099) \ (0.017)$$

The hypothesis that total costs are proportional to wages, over all clubs, would just be rejected at the 5% level, $t = 2.27$, but would be accepted if the significance level is adjusted to take account of sample size in the way explained below. If club-specific intercepts are included, the result is

$$c_{it} = \alpha_i + 0.922w_{it} \qquad R^2 = 0.88$$
$$(0.020)$$

which suggests that the club-specific intercepts in the total cost function are positively correlated with the level of wages a club chooses.

4.   Econometric issues

The results above are based on the assumption that the slopes are constant across clubs. If the slopes are not the same, then pooled estimators of dynamic models can give very misleading estimates, Pesaran and Smith (1995) discuss the issues. In dynamic heterogeneous models the appropriate estimator is the Swamy (1971) Random Coefficient Model

(RCM), which estimates the weighted average of the 48 individual time-series regressions for each club. In fact the RCM estimates of the long-run coefficients are almost identical to the panel estimates in this case: $d = 1.86$ (0.465) and $b = 0.28$ (0.048).

In testing for coefficient equality in large samples, it is inappropriate to keep the size of the test or significance level constant at the conventional 5%. As the sample size increases one would wish to use the extra information to reduce both type one and type two errors rather than just type two as would be implied by using a constant size. A consistent way of doing this is provided by the Posterior Odds Criterion;[15] see Klein and Brown (1984). The F statistics for coefficient equality (that is, testing 48 separate regressions against the fixed-effect pooled model) are 1.748 for the revenue equation and 1.586 for the performance equation, both with 94 and 576 degrees of freedom. The null would be rejected at the 1% level for the first and accepted for the second. However, if one uses the posterior odds criterion, which allows for the effect of sample size on model selection, the pooled model is clearly chosen in both the cases. Lagged exogenous variables were significant neither with the fixed-effect nor with the Swamy estimator.

The fixed-effect estimator is inconsistent (N going to infinity, fixed T) when lagged dependent variables are included. But the bias declines quite rapidly with T, and the fact that the fixed-effect and RCM estimates are so similar confirms that this is not a problem. Neither the random-effect nor the cross-section estimator would be appropriate in this case, since the effects are almost certainly correlated with the regressors: for instance, the intercept in the quality equation will determine the optimal expenditure on wages, which is the regressor in that equation.

5. Further issues

In this section, we present estimates of the demand function (Table 1.2) for attendance and an extended revenue function (Table 1.3) which allows for a number of other influences. The estimates above assume a homogenous competition. In fact League competitions are divided into four divisions.[16] Each year some clubs in each division get relegated to the division below and some clubs of the lower divisions get promoted to the division above; the number involved has varied over the sample. Thus, the division a club belongs to is a non-linear function of lagged position. If revenue depended on which division the club played in, rather than position as such, this non-linearity would bias the results.

Table 1.2   Demand equation. Dependent variable: log gate attendances (A)

Year effects	Excluded		Included	
	Coeff.	*t*-statistic	Coeff.	*t*-statistic
Price	−0.38	−8.05	−0.19	−2.01
Q	0.20	13.46	0.20	14.86
A(−1)	0.50	13.24	0.45	11.84
D2	0.10	2.19	0.09	1.96
D3	0.18	2.86	0.15	2.48
D4	0.41	4.96	0.38	4.88
P1	0.27	3.50	0.30	4.20
P2	0.30	4.97	0.33	5.83
P3	0.01	0.17	0.03	0.79
R1	−0.37	−4.58	−0.40	−5.29
R2	−0.11	−1.98	−0.13	−2.43
R3	−0.11	−2.62	−0.11	−2.95
CUP	0.01	2.55	0.01	3.61
R^2	0.95		0.96	

Table 1.3   Revenue equation

Variable	Coefficient	Absolute *t*-statistic
Q	0.11	7.76
R(−1)	0.46	14
D2	0.00	0.03
D3	0.02	0.41
D4	0.09	1.24
P1	0.21	2.82
P2	0.25	4.10
P3	0.06	1.47
R1	−0.42	−5.39
R2	−0.06	−1.14
R3	−0.08	−2.05
CUP	0.03	9.25
$R^2 = 0.95$		

To test for the effect of being in a particular division, three division dummy variables, D2, D3 and D4, were added for being in divisions 2, 3 and 4, respectively. To test for the effect of promotion or relegation, the changes in the division dummies were also added: P1, P2, P3 and R1, R2,

$R3$, where the former take a value of 1 if the club was promoted to the relevant division and 0 otherwise, and the latter take a value of 1 if the club was relegated from the relevant division and 0 otherwise.

Revenue also depends on performance in cup competitions since this generates extra games as well as (more speculatively) increased support for the club as a whole. We collected data on the number of rounds played in each year by each club in each of the FA Cup, The League Cup (variously known as the Milk Cup, the Rumbelows Cup and now the Coca-Cola Cup), and the various European club competitions, the European Cup, The UEFA Cup and the European Cup Winners' Cup. The variable CUP is the total number of games played in any of these cups. When entered separately, their effects were not significantly different, either in the demand function or the revenue function.

The demand function explains the logarithm of average annual gate attendance by the logarithm of price (gate revenue per person, deflated by the RPI). Our data on gate attendance refer to League games, whilst gate revenue covers all games played. In order to adjust for this in our price series we define this as gate revenue divided by average gate times the number of league games plus half the number of cup games all divided by the RPI.[17] Gate revenue was not available for all clubs, so that for this exercise our sample was reduced to 659 observations. Also included were performance, lagged attendance, the divisional, promotion and relegation dummies and the number of cup games played. Club-specific intercepts were included, and the equation was estimated with and without year-specific intercepts. In our study we have not attempted to capture the effect of uncertainty of outcome, which has been shown to affect demand (see, for example, Peel & Thomas, 1988) since our data are annual rather than match by match. The club-specific intercepts capture effects such as local population size, age and gender structure and wealth, which will influence demand for football. Given the severe difficulties in defining these variables properly,[18] we do not believe that using club-specific intercepts is in practice likely to involve much loss of accuracy.

The implied long-run price elasticity from the equation without time dummies for each year is -0.76, but this falls to -0.34 when time dummies are allowed (with a t-statistic of -2.05). This suggests that the price elasticity picks up the effect of the secular decline in the demand for football unless time dummies are included. The finding that demand is price inelastic is in line with earlier studies looking at the demand for football over the longer term.[19] If we suppose that football clubs are local monopolists, this implies that there is considerable scope to increase profits through higher prices. However, we believe there is reason to be sceptical about this conclusion. There are (at least) three possible approaches to interpreting these estimates:

(i) Misspecification induced by aggregating gate attendances. Suppose clubs set prices in such a way as to ensure that the ground is full for every game, taking into account the different attractiveness of each fixture. This would be consistent with a high elasticity of demand being rationally exploited by a price discriminating monopolist but would not show up in our estimates.

(ii) Misspecification of the production function. If attendances are an input into the performance of a team, then this consideration will feed through the objective function of the owner into the price setting decision, making it rational to charge low prices even though a pure profit maximiser might set higher prices.

(iii) Owners may not be monopolists at all. Even if other clubs are not good substitutes for the local product, other leisure activities may be. If clubs are competing against these activities, then their capacity to set higher prices may be limited.

It should be noted that the crucial parameter in our argument, the slope of the profit-position trade-off, does not depend on this elasticity. All the promotion and relegation dummies are significant, except for promotion from the Fourth to the Third division. They suggest that there is a one-off boost to revenue on promotion to the first and second divisions, which disappears in subsequent years, and also-that there is a one-off dip in revenues after relegation from the first, second or third divisions which also disappears in later years. These seem to be picking factors such as supporter morale. Promotion generates an enthusiasm which is not sustained in later years, whilst relegation creates an initial despair and loss of support which is partly recaptured once the initial depression has worn off.

The significant positive values of the lower-division dummies do not indicate that members of the lower divisions get larger attendances than first-division clubs, but that they get more than would be expected from extrapolating the relationships between attendance and performance, price, etc. of a first-division club. This might reflect the possibility that first-division clubs are capacity constrained.

As might be expected, cup performances increase gate attendances significantly, although it is perhaps surprising that the restriction that all cups increase attendances equiproportionately is accepted by the data. For the European club championships there are only a very small number of observations in our sample, but it is striking that the League Cup is apparently as popular as the FA Cup, since this competition was often criticised as being superfluous and uninteresting.

The revenue function was re-estimated including the additional variables (except relative price which was not significant in any case), and the results are given in Table 1.3. The long-run effect of performance on revenue is 0.21 (0.03), which is not significantly different from the earlier estimates without the additional variables. The divisional dummies are now insignificant. This means that for a given position in the League, being in a particular division exerts no additional effect on revenue, the positive relative effects of being in a lower division on attendance being offset by the negative effects on other revenues. By contrast, the promotion dummies are significant for the first and second divisions and the relegation dummy is significant for the first and third divisions.

6. Market structure

Conditional on the club-specific intercepts and the aggregate wages and revenues, the model described above explains the main features of the market: only the top clubs make profits and there is a high degree of concentration. The top five clubs in terms of average League position account for some 20% of all income over our sample period. Were club owners profit maximisers, the loss makers would be likely to exit, raising the profitability of those remaining and bringing the industry back towards an equilibrium where firms generate non-negative profits. But given the owners' objective functions, this does not happen, and given the lack of a market in corporate control, they are not constrained by threat of take-over. Jennett and Sloane (1985) also argue that the wider shareholding, which would be associated with a market for corporate control, would provide a source of capital for the improvement of facilities.

This leads one to ask if the observed market structure is efficient either in terms of the general interest or in terms of the joint interest of the owners. Football has aspects of a quasi-public good in that it provides entertainment to a fairly wide public of fans. This public good is produced as a joint product, with a private good, the personal interests of the club owner. The interests of the owner may differ from the general interest, particularly in relation to the setting of ticket prices. Clubs are generally thought of as local monopolists, and therefore pricing is likely to involve a dead-weight loss. Perhaps more interesting than this fairly standard economic problem is the issue of whether the manner of competition between club owners promotes either the joint interests of the owners or the broader general interest.

Competition between clubs on ticket prices is not likely to be a general phenomenon. Competition takes place for position in the League, and the medium for this competition is the market for playing talents.[20] Clearly the Nash equilibrium will not be the joint profit maximising one, since increased competition is a negative-sum game. Competing for position itself is a zero-sum game, but an owner who wishes to improve position spends money on players. But spending on players puts upward pressure on the quality-adjusted wage rate, increases the rent extracted by players and puts downward pressure on profits. The removal of what was effectively an indenture system in the early 1960s has provoked a spiral in players' wages which can be seen in Table 1.1b.[21] The clubs themselves are well aware of this phenomenon, but the scope for outright collusion is (now) limited by the law while the possibility of sustaining tacit collusion is limited by the improbability of credible punishment strategies.[22]

A consequence of this 'excessive' competition for players is that clubs have fewer resources available for the purchase of other inputs required to produce services consumed jointly with attendees at a football match: a safe, comfortable environment, refreshments and so on. During the 1980s a series of tragic accidents in football stadia highlighted the problem: English grounds were antiquated and dangerous, attractive to few other than hooligans, while the clubs had neither the means nor the will to change matters. Given that competition for players was also competing away all economic profit, the clubs had no incentive to improve the football environment since any extra profits generated would pass immediately to the players. Thus, not only was the structure of competition against the joint interest of the owners, but it also acted against the general interest.[23]

This story characterises English football up to 1989, the end of the period covered by our data set. Since then, however, two critical developments have helped to transform the picture: First, the implementation of the Taylor Report commissioned by the government after the Hillsborough disaster has obliged clubs to invest in all-seater stadia which has had the side-effect of modernising the facilities to make them more attractive to spectators. By obliging clubs to do something collectively, which it would not have been individually rational to do (for standard prisoner's-dilemma reasons), the government has helped to push the clubs towards an alternative to the low-quality equilibrium in which they were caught.[24]

Second, increasing competition among the television companies has increased the available funds for football clubs. In particular, competition from satellite broadcasting upset the pre-existing terrestrial 'duopsony' and brought about a tenfold increase in broadcast revenues. The most notable effect of this change was to cause the leading clubs to break away from the rest of the Football League to form the Premier League and so keep almost all the broadcast revenues for themselves. However, the Premier League has so far been little different from the old First Division. In the short term the extra funding has helped to pay for the rebuilding programme for the larger clubs. In the long term it has created a powerful vested interest, not in the performance of individual clubs, but in the attractiveness of football as a whole. This may act as a focus for coordination between clubs in the future.

Both of these developments have had the effect of providing a focus on the interests of the entire sport and so have helped to deal with the prisoner's-dilemma element in the owner's problem. Fortuitously, these developments seem to have coincided with a more general increase of interest in football. The post-war trough in League attendances occurred in the season 1985/86. Since then there has been a steady increase in attendances despite rising real ticket prices. This may be connected with increased effectiveness of policing at Football grounds leading to a lower incidence of hooliganism.[25] Overall, the future of English football seems brighter now than at any other time since the late 1940s.

7.   Conclusions

Over the period covered by our data, English League Football is an interesting example of a mature industry with a set of very characteristic problems. Like many old industries, it had to deal with declining demand and increasing competition from more technologically advanced leisure products. Most firms made losses, its plant was antiquated and grossly under-utilised, and heavy investment was required both to meet government mandated safety standards and to improve the quality of the product sufficiently to compete on modern markets. Firms in this industry have little control over their main input cost, players, which are traded on a competitive market. Of course, many mature industries are very profitable.

The interesting question is why market forces so often fail to restructure such industries. In this case, and perhaps others, the answer seems to lie in the failure of the market for corporate control. Obstacles to takeover and acquisition allow current owners to follow non-profit objectives, allow small groups to veto changes which might be in the general interest and inhibit the internalisation of the externalities inherent in adjustment. Only when external forces impose a coordinated strategy on the competing firms, is there any prospect of change. In the case of English Football, the Taylor Report and the TV companies have provided a focus for coordination.

Our model has a number of potential applications. It can be used to derive the required expenditure to raise a club from a low position to the top of the League. It is also possible to analyse the effect of the new League structure in England and Wales, which combines a Premier League of top clubs (organised by the FA) and a rump of Football League clubs. Finally, the model can be used to analyse the impact of other reforms which may be proposed for the organisation of English football in the future and to understand their chances of success by understanding the likely impact on the distribution of profits throughout the industry.

Notes

1. In fact the organisational structure of English League football is relatively easy to study since all clubs are independent limited companies whose annual accounts are lodged at Companies House. To the best of our knowledge, most economic research on football emanates from the UK, although there are some exceptions such as Gartner and Pommerehne (1978), Janssens and Késenne (1987).
2. We obtained all the accounting lodged at Companies House for the 92 clubs in the English League (in 1990). Since the accounts of some clubs were incomplete or did not break down the data in sufficient detail, we focused on the 48 with complete records for the period 1974–89. To check the representativeness of our sample we calculated its average position in each sample year. The highest was 41st and the lowest 44th (against a population average of 46th). Whilst there is some bias towards the top of the League, we do not believe this is significant.
3. Until 1992, these were the First, Second, Third and Fourth divisions. Since the start of the 1992/93 season, they are the Premier, First, Second and Third. The old first division left the Football League, to form the Premier Division, organised by the Football Association, mainly to avoid having to share TV revenue with lower-division clubs.
4. One advantage of this functional form is that it imposes reflecting barriers at positions 1 and 92. This is an approximation at the lower barrier

since there have been a small number of exits over our sample period. Treating the ranking as a continuous variable also introduces a small approximation.

5. After our estimation period the European Court judgment on the Bosman case further changed the position.

6. This means that the 'agency' problem common to many markets for highly skilled labour is not as pressing in the market for football players. An alternative view of the market for players is provided by Carmichael and Thomas (1992) who present a bargaining model of transfers. In their approach the transfer price of each player is the outcome of a bargain between clubs, the price being determined by the threat points and bargaining strength of each side. Where buyers and sellers have market power, transfers will not reflect the value of the individual's contribution to the team. Unfortunately measuring these individual contributions is problematic in football (unlike, for example, baseball, see Cairns et al., 1986), and the two approaches are difficult to distinguish empirically.

7. In particular, the fit is much better than comparable regressions of measures of corporate performance on payments to top executives, e.g. Smith and Szymanski (1995).

8. Another outlier of the same sort is Nottingham Forest whose accounts are only available from 1982 onwards and so are not included in the data set. These cases, which involve non-appropriable sources of competitive advantage, are discussed in more detail in dell'Osso and Szymanski (1991).

9. Strictly, this is an ownership rather than management difference, since managers can be hired on a competitive market and their wages will be included in the total payment for skill. The intercept captures a separate club-specific effect partly associated with the tendency of the owners to interfere. For instance, Brian Clough, probably the ablest English manager of his generation, was sacked by Brighton and Leeds partly because the owners could not get on with him.

10. Hart *et al.* (1975), Smart and Goddard (1991), Cairns (1987), Bird (1982), Jennett (1984), Walker (1986) and Peel and Thomas (1988) present estimates of football demand functions. Other studies have included variables such as population within a local catchment area, seats as a proportion of ground capacity and local unemployment rates. In our analysis these effects are picked up by year and club-specific intercepts.

11. This follows conveniently from our separability assumption as well as the fact that we ignore possible feedback effects from attendances to performance quality. Were such mechanisms allowed then there could be a trade-off between ticket prices and performance. Whilst our estimates reported below lead us to believe that any such effects are likely to be small in practice, we discuss their possible impact in Section 5.

12. For empirical implementation we shall proxy these by average revenue over all clubs, which will be added to the equation.

13. See also Carmichael and Thomas (1992).

14. Using deviations from year means is equivalent to including year-specific intercepts, given that q also has mean zero.

15. This chooses the model which has the higher value of a criterion calculated as the maximised log likelihood less the number of parameters times half the log of the sample size.
16. Up to 1987, the first two divisions had 22 clubs each, while the third and fourth divisions had 24. In 1988, the numbers were 21, 23, 24, 24; in 1989, 20 in the first, 24 in the other three.
17. This approximation is flawed in four possible ways. First, it assumes that half of all cup games are played at home, whilst the actual proportion depends on the draw. However, over time this should not induce any systematic bias in the estimates. Second, it ignores replays which will lead to slight overestimate of prices. Third, it assumes that gate attendances at cup games equal attendances at League games on average. Whilst attendances at particular cup fixtures may be much larger than average, we do not believe that this bias will be very great on average (one Arsenal fan told us that the largest gates of the season are for games against the other leading clubs: Manchester United, Liverpool, Tottenham, regardless of whether they are cup or league matches). Fourth, the estimate does not allow for the possibility that clubs raise prices for cup games. In fact the brisk business of ticket touts at popular games suggest that clubs are not varying their prices by enough to account for the differing attractiveness of different games.
18. For example, it is hard to choose the precise catchment area for a club and this is certainly not likely to be stable over time given factors such as increased car ownership. Wealth effects are likely to be important, but it is again hard to define the wealth of a potential catchment area precisely.
19. Bird (1982) estimates a price elasticity of −0.2 using data for 1948–80. A recent study by Dobson and Goddard (1996) using data for 1925–92 estimates an elasticity of −0.015. Our much higher estimate probably arises from the fact that the period covered by our data set was one of rapidly increasing real prices and, generally, falling attendances. Earlier periods had relatively stable prices and attendances (see, for example, Dobson and Goddard, 1996, Figures 1.1, 1.2 and 1.3).
20. The most famous recent example is Jack Walker, the owner of Blackburn Rovers, who raised the club from the bottom of the (old) second division to Premier League Champions by spending about £50m over a five-year period. However it must be admitted that attempts by sugar daddies to pull off similar feats at other clubs have often failed.
21. The average annual increase over the period was nearly 4% in real terms, which is a very high rate to sustain over such an extended period.
22. Tacit collusion would involve an unwritten agreement not to pay too much to players combined with the threat of some sort of punishment for clubs which cheated on the arrangement. The punishment would need to raise the costs of the cheater's strategy: it is not clear how this could work in practice.
23. More critical fans often blame the quality of the management that runs a club for failure to innovate, but a zero-profit industry is unlikely to attract the most talented (commercial) managers.

24. The government has also helped to fund these changes, but most of the burden is borne by the clubs.
25. In and around the grounds, at least.

References

Arnold, A. J. & Beneviste, I. (1987) Wealth and poverty in the English football league, *Accounting and Business Research*, 17, pp. 195–203.

Bird, P. J. (1982) The demand for league football, *Applied Economics*, 14, pp. 637–649.

Cairns, J. A. (1987) Evaluating changes in league structure: The reorganisation of the Scottish Football League, *Applied Economics*, 19, pp. 259–275.

Cairns, J., Jennett, N. & Sloane, P. J. (1986) The economics of professional team sports: A survey of theory and evidence, *Journal of Economic Studies*, 13, pp. 1–80.

Carmichael, F. & Thomas, D. (1992) Bargaining in the transfer market: Theory and evidence, mimeo, University of Aberystwyth.

dell'Osso, F. & Szymanski, S. (1991) Who are the champions? An analysis of football architecture, *Business Strategy Review*, 2, 2, pp. 113–130.

Dobson, S. M. & Goddard, J. A. (1995) The demand for professional league football in England and Wales, 1925–1992, *The Statistician*, 44, 2, pp. 259–277.

Gartner, M. & Pommerehne, W. (1978) Der Fussballzuschauer—ein Homo Oeconomicus? *Jarhbuch fur Sozial Wissenschaft*, 29, pp. 88–107.

Hart, R. A., Hutton, J. & Sharot, T. (1975) A statistical analysis of association football attendances, *Applied Statistics*, 24, pp. 17–27.

Janssens, P. & Késenne, S. (1987) Belgian soccer attendances, *Tijdschrifit voor Economie en Management*, 32, pp. 305–315.

Jennett, N. (1984) Attendance, uncertainty of outcome and policy in Scottish League Football, *Scottish Journal of Political Economy*, 31, pp. 176–198.

Jennett, N. & Sloane, P. J. (1985) The future of League football: A critique of the report of the Chester Committee of Enquiry, *Leisure Studies*, 4, pp. 39–56.

Klein, R. W. & Brown, S. J. (1984) Model selection when there is 'minimal' prior information, *Econometrica*, 52, pp. 1291–1312.

Peel, D. & Thomas, D. (1988) Outcome uncertainty and the demand for football, *Scottish Journal of Political Economy*, 35, pp. 242–249.

Pesaran, M. H. & Smith, R. (1995) Estimating long-run relationships from dynamic heterogenous panels, *Journal of Econometrics*, 68, pp. 79–113.

Ruddock, L. (1979) The market for professional footballers: An economic analysis, *Economics*, 15, pp. 70–72.

Sloane, P. J. (1969) The labour market in professional football, *British Journal of Industrial Relations*, 7, pp. 181–199.

Sloane, P. J. (1971) The economics of professional football: The football club as a utility maximiser, *Scottish Journal of Political Economy*, 8, pp. 121–146.

Smart, R. A. & Goddard, J. A. (1991) The determinants of standing and seated football attendances: Evidence from three Scottish League clubs, *Quarterly Economic Commentary*, 16, pp. 61–64.

Smith, R. & Szymanski, S. (1995) Executive pay and performance, the empirical importance of the participation constraint, *International Journal of the Economics of Business*, 2, pp. 485–495.

Swamy, P. A. V. (1971) *Statistical Inference in Random Coefficient Regression Models* (Berlin, Springer-Verlag).

Taylor, Rt Hon Lord Justice (1989) The *Hillsborough Stadium Disaster* (HMSO) Cm962.

Walker, B. (1986) The demand for professional League Football and the success of football league teams: Some city size effects, *Urban Studies*, 23, pp. 209–220.

2

The Market for Soccer Players in England after Bosman: Winners and Losers

Stefan Szymanski

Imperial College Management School, London

Abstract

The Bosman judgement has changed the types of employment contracts which football clubs can write with players. This chapter analyses the effect of this on the equilibrium of the English football leagues. The English leagues are characterised by open entry and consequently intense competition in an economic as well as a sporting sense. While technology is expanding the size of the entire football market, the market for players is approximately efficient so that most of the football "rents" go to the players. If clubs already wrote contracts which were economically efficient, then Bosman would not affect the football league equilibrium. However, if some clubs are unable to write efficient contracts because of capital market constraints, then these clubs may be driven out of the market. The judgement is also likely to redistribute the rents among the players. The chapter discusses the financial impact so far using accounting data.

> *No system prevalent in modern football has aroused so much discussion than that designated the transfer system. There never was a more controversial matter in regard to which the evidence was of*

I would like to thank Steve Ross for a fruitful e-mail discussion and John Cubbin for some helpful comments.

*such conflicting character. Some men hate and abominate the trans-
fer system; others declare that it has been the salvation of the weaker
section of first-class football clubs.*

William Bassett, West Bromwich Albion, 1905

1. What they said

The Bosman judgement of the European Court in 1995 has thrown
English football into disarray. Big clubs have been forced to write down
the value of their assets; small clubs have claimed that the effect of
the judgement will be to drive many of them out of business. This
chapter is concerned with the relationship between the Bosman judgement and the wider economic context of English football. There can
be no doubt that in the view of most people involved with the game
directly, dramatic changes are anticipated:

**"I'm staggered and gob-smacked. This is going to send shock
waves through football"**

Graham Turner, manager of Hereford United on the League Transfer
Tribunal's decision to take the Bosman ruling into account for the
first time when valuing a footballer, cutting the club's asking price to
Orient of £200,000 to £42,500 for defender Dean Smith (26).

**"I don't know just what Gullit is being paid, but I should imagine
that when he joined Chelsea they took the view that under normal circumstances they would have paid £2 million for a player
of that age, and so they pay a large proportion of that to the
player himself in salary."**

Alan Sugar, Chairman and principal shareholder of Tottenham
Hotspur. Tottenham reduced the valuation of their players by a
third – almost £7 m – in the wake of the European Court of Justice
ruling.

**"This is the best news I've heard in 19 years in the game. Please,
please God, make this the final decision as well. Perhaps now
football chairmen will come into the real world. Having been
connected with showbiz for so long I have never understood football contracts. If you rent a television you can walk away when
the agreement is up. Footballers can't do that."**

Eric Hall, players' agent.

"If the transfer compensation system isn't allowed to continue in some form, the implications for the smaller clubs and the game as a whole will be very adverse."

Graham Kelly, Chief executive, FA.

"I am damned if I'm going to put my money into a youth system just to let the bigger clubs snaffle up the product. The fat cats may get fatter but the scrawny ones down this end will die of starvation. A lot more players are going to be out of work."

Mike Bateson, chairman of Torquay United, rooted to the foot of the Third Division.

To examine in more detail whether these views have any foundation in fact, this chapter will start by describing the formal rule changes that are anticipated. The following section will provide an historical overview of the structure of the English Football Leagues, and Section 4 will consider the main economic forces which drive the structure and conduct of the English football industry. Section 5 will then analyse both the short-run and the long-run effects of Bosman in the light of "industry conditions" as well as looking at some data from which we can evaluate the initial impact. The final section contains some conclusions.

2. The Bosman judgement and the conduct of English football

The Bosman judgement affects the way English football is organised in two ways. First, the general implication derived from the Court's belief that football is an economic activity and therefore falls within the scope of Treaty of Rome is that rules restricting the freedom of movement of players are inadmissible under Article 48. Consequently the rule which limited the number of foreign players appearing in European cup games to a maximum of three was scrapped, and a limitation on the incentive of English clubs to hire foreign players was removed. Second, the specific verdict of the court that denies the right of clubs to obtain transfer fees for players out of contract effectively outlawed the English transfer system which had operated since 1978. Under this system a club was entitled, if it chose, to demand a transfer fee for a player out of contract as long as the club had offered a new contract on terms no worse than the previous contract. The fee itself was a matter of negotiation, but in the event of disputes the Football League Appeals Committee (FLAC), consisting of club and player representatives, met to agree a fee binding on all the parties. Empirical work[1] has shown that such fees tended on average to be set below freely negotiated fees, and to relate in fairly predictable ways to characteristics of the player (e.g. age, indices of ability and so on). The ruling immediately freed foreign players whose contracts had expired to come to England without a transfer fee being paid. Until now (late 1997) the old system has remained in place for domestic players, and despite threats by some players, has gone unchallenged in court. In late 1997 the English Football Association agreed a new system with the English leagues. It is planned that no fees will be required for players over 24, although this will not prevent clubs demanding fees for players whose contracts have not yet expired. At the beginning of their careers players will sign training and development contracts up to the age of 21, and the contract will include wider education and vocational training. Any player who moves club between the ages of 21 and 24, having refused a new contract with the existing club, will only be transferred if a fee is paid reflecting the investment made by the club, and to be fixed in the case of disputes by the FLAC. The proposed system is due to be implemented from July 1st 1998 and is said to have already received approval from the European Commission.

3.   The professional english football leagues

Professional footballers appeared in England during the 1870s, about ten years after the foundation of the Football Association and at a time when there were relatively few football clubs. As the popularity of football grew, the major football clubs came together to create a league, guaranteeing regular fixtures and establishing a League competition. Unlike competition in many other professional sports leagues around the world, English professional football was by no means dependent on the existence of the League. The FA Cup, established in 1871, was long considered a far more prestigious competition, and still retains a certain mystique which the League competition cannot emulate. Nonetheless, the Football League, founded in 1888 with 12 member clubs, prospered and grew to 88 teams by 1923 and finally reached 92 in 1950. During the early years English football "clubs" were precisely that, "clubs" maintained by membership subscription and with limited financial powers. Between 1885 and the First World War most football clubs became "professional", employing only full-time professional footballers, and transformed themselves into limited liability companies. Limited liability was a means to greater financial freedom, but not a move towards

Table 2.1   Average annual profits (losses) as a percentage of total
sales

	Division 1	Division 2	Division 3
1907–15	8.6	10.6	
1922–29	11.5	0.3	1.3
1929–39	4.3	2.5	−3.6
1947–60	10.1	8.8	3.7
1961–70	9.1	−2.9	−9.9
1971–78	0.6	−6.1	0.7
1979–88	0.2	−11.2	−16.2
1989–96	−3.9	−14.2	−8.8

Source: Companies House, football club accounts

encouraging the pursuit of profit, which was generally frowned upon.
Furthermore, a founding principle of the Football League was to prevent
footballers themselves making too much money. At its foundation it
was a stated aim of the League to control players' freedom of movement
through the retain and transfer system (established 1890) and to impose
a maximum wage (achieved in 1900).

Up until the First World War the maximum wage was fixed at £4 per
week, about 50% more than an industrial worker might expect to earn.
Attempts by the players' union to challenge the system resulted in total
defeat for the players. The maximum wage (which remained in force
until 1961) ensured that it was possible for football clubs to generate
substantial surpluses (see Table 2.1).[2] Before 1914, in an era when 5%
returns were considered comfortable, football clubs were very profitable,
and out of these profits financed the construction of large and elegant
stadia. Investors received only their comfortable return, most clubs paying the maximum dividend permissible which had been fixed by the
Football Association in 1896 at 5% per annum.

Between the Wars first-division clubs continued to sustain healthy
profits of about 10% over sales on average, but in the second and newly
created third divisions (north and south) profits were closer to zero on
average. While successful clubs could generate a surplus, those competing below tended to invest heavily in transfer spending in order to try
and improve performance. After the Second World War football clubs
enjoyed a boom as attendances reached all-time highs and even third-
division clubs could make a small profit. Indeed, in 1948 when Notts
County bought Tommy Lawton for £20,000, breaking the English transfer fee record, they were a third division side. Meanwhile the minimum
wage had changed little in real terms since the First World War. Indeed
with the new prosperity of the 1950s the average footballer was little

better off than any industrial worker. By 1960 the maximum wage was £20 per week, less than any respectable profession would pay.

In 1960 the players, led by a revived union, the PFA (Professional Footballers' Association), threatened a strike unless the maximum wage was abolished. At the beginning of 1961 the clubs caved in, fearful that they would be unable to maintain wage restrictions in the light of the relatively recent legislation against restrictive trade practices. Between 1948 and 1960 football club wage bills had risen at around 6% per year, a little over the inflation rate. In 1962 the average club wage bill rose by about 50%. In 1963 the old system was dealt a further blow by the Eastham judgement which effectively abolished the retain-and-transfer system. Under the retain-and-transfer system a club was given the ownership rights over its players' registrations without which a player was unable to play for other member clubs. This effectively controlled the ability of a player to play professional football.[3] From 1963, under the new system, a club was still entitled to retain a player as long as it continued to offer a player terms as good as any offer made by another club. But despite the fact that a player might be able to negotiate better terms on this basis, and was entitled to appeal against a club's decision, it was still basically the club which determined the future of the player.

As wages continued to grow at 10% per year, club profitability collapsed. During this period most clubs ceased to pay any form of dividend, which had in any case become valueless because of the FA rule which took no account of inflation (being based on the nominal value of the paid-up share capital). During the 1960s the average second-, third- and fourth-division clubs registered an annual pre-tax loss, with only the first-division clubs being profitable. In the 1970s even the most profitable first-division clubs did little better than break even. Concern about the declining attractiveness of football, declining attendances, antiquated facilities, spiralling wages and financial crisis spawned a series of prominent inquiries, all recommending the restructuring of competition, all largely ignored. Meanwhile the PFA achieved its final triumph in 1978, effectively obtaining freedom of contract. This meant that players were entitled to move to any club they wished after their contract expired. Nonetheless, the clubs managed to retain one aspect of the old system: clubs would still be entitled to a transfer fee when a contract expired.

The immediate consequence of freedom of contract was an explosion of transfer fees as clubs competed to sign available players. In 1977, one year before free agency, Liverpool paid a record £440,000 for Kenny Dalglish. Two years later, the record rose to £1,469,000 paid by Aston Villa for Andy Gray. Between 1977 and 1982 the average club wage bill doubled while attendances dropped by around 25% thanks to the deep recession in the UK and the increasingly poor reputation of football for crowd trouble. Not surprisingly profits dropped; equally predictably there was another official inquiry, another set of recommendations to restructure competition, and another failure to reach agreement. Despite the parlous condition of the game as a whole, the top English clubs were in fact in quite a healthy state. Liverpool dominated domestic competition as well as winning four European Championships during this period. Nottingham Forest also won this competition twice and Aston Villa once during this era. Thus in a ten-year period English clubs won this most prestigious of European competitions on seven occasions. Most of the top clubs also managed to make a small profit on their activities. To these clubs the problem was obvious: too many teams in the Football League. Although there was no revenue sharing from attendance money in League competition, the top clubs became dissatisfied with the collectively negotiated TV contract which shared the money much more evenly than the actual coverage. In the mid-1980s the formation of a breakaway League by the top clubs was just avoided. Meanwhile the clubs started to believe that they could get a lot more money out of TV contracts.

In the early years of football broadcasting the BBC and ITV, the two terrestrial stations, acted together to keep the contract price down so that at the beginning of the 1980s the TV rights for the entire Football League were sold for just over £2.5m per year. A result of the clubs' increased expectations from TV rights was a dispute in 1986 during contract negotiations which led to a TV blackout for the early months of the 1986/7 season. An exclusive deal with ITV signed in 1988 gave the League £44m over four years. Finally the pressure from the top clubs combined with the introduction of satellite TV into the UK. In 1992 the FA organised a breakaway Premier League, consisting of the old First Division, and signed a TV deal with BSkyB worth £214m over five seasons (to be divided among 22 clubs as opposed to the 92 members of the old Football League).

English football reached its nadir around 1985. Following the earlier wage and transfer escalation most clubs were forced to slow down their spending and rebuild their balance sheets. Supporters continued to drift away from the game while violence on the terraces worsened. In 1985 Liverpool reached the final of the European Cup against Juventus. Fighting broke out on the terraces before the match began. Terrified Juventus fans tried to escape and 38 died in a crush caused by the collapse of a wall. As a result English clubs were banned from European football for the next five years. However, from this time onwards football began to recover. Perhaps because the police had developed better methods to control crowd trouble, attendances at matches started to increase in the late 1980s. As a consequence of two further football disasters, the Bradford City fire (55 deaths) and above all the Hillsborough Stadium disaster (95 deaths), a government inquiry led to legislation obliging football clubs to build all-seater stadia. The government diverted taxes raised from football betting in support of rebuilding. As a result of the resurgence in the popularity of football more money started to come into the game, both from TV and from sponsorship. Football clubs still existed on the edge of profitability but one exception showed the way.

In 1991 Manchester United Football Club floated itself on the stock market. For the most widely supported club in England, the flotation coincided with a dramatic improvement in playing success which led to the club winning four out of the first five Premier League Championships. By early 1997 the club had a market value of over £500m, greater than the annual turnover of all professional English clubs combined. Indeed the club's annual profit was greater than the turnover of all but one or two clubs. Following the signing of a further four-year TV contract with BSkyB and the BBC for £670m in 1996 the stock market became enthusiastic about the prospects of football clubs as investments, and by late 1997 more than a dozen clubs had introduced themselves to the market in one way or another. Ironically, faced with the obstacle of the FA's maximum-dividend rule, football companies had to be created parallel to the existing club structures, but there can be little doubt that clubs have been driven towards a more profit-oriented outlook.

4.   The economic fundamentals of English football

There are three fundamental characteristics of the English football leagues which drive both their behaviour and the outcome of competition:

(i)   Free entry

Unlike closed leagues where the member teams are guaranteed continuing membership, at least during the life of a franchise, in English football existing clubs can always drop out of the leagues due to poor team performance and new clubs can always enter. The most spectacular case of new entry in recent years is that of Wimbledon FC. An amateur team outside the Football League until 1978, the club rose rapidly on admission to the fourth division and reached the first division in 1986, since when it has never been relegated and has generally achieved positions mid-table or higher. The rise (and fall) of clubs is usually less dramatic than this, but the threat of entry constrains the actions of clubs, particularly at the bottom end of the leagues.

(ii) Revenue is driven by viewing technology

Changing technology not only drives the total available income for the football industry, but also tends to concentrate the revenue on a smaller and smaller number of clubs. Technology has enhanced the possibilities of viewing top-class football for a wider class of consumers. This has tended to reduce the attractiveness of talented teams in lower divisions. As a result the ratio of income of, say, first-division to third-division clubs has grown from about 2:1 in the early 1950s to in excess of 10:1 by the mid-1990s.

(iii) Player market efficiency

Market efficiency means that all the predictable factors which affect player performance are captured by the wage bill. A club's wage bill is much more important financially than its transfer expenditure. Most clubs' transfer expenditure over a period of years is approximately zero, while the wage bill is a substantial cumulative net expenditure.[4] Prior to the advent of free agency in 1978 the market was inefficient because clubs could obtain rents from the players on their books thanks to their rights in relation to player registrations. Before 1961 the efficiency of the market was constrained by the maximum wage. However, since 1978 the wage bill has been a highly efficient predictor of performance.[5] For example, in Fig. 2.1 the relationship between wage expenditure and league position is illustrated for the 1994/95 season. Wage expenditure can explain over 80% of the variation in the position of teams. Other factors that affect performance, such as player quality measured by international appearances, do not constitute distinct explanatory variables once the impact of wages (which tend to be higher for internationals) is included.

These fundamentals drive both the potential revenue and the costs of football clubs. A great deal of British ink has been spilt discussing the underlying objective of football clubs.[6] Most writers have agreed that the behaviour of the clubs has seemed to be more consistent with max-imising objectives such as league position and other measures of league success rather than profits. Given the growing exposure of football clubs to the stock market and professional investors this view will have to be revised. However the economic fundamentals mean that the objective makes little difference to the outcome. Clubs with the greater revenue generating potential will attract the better players whose wages will be

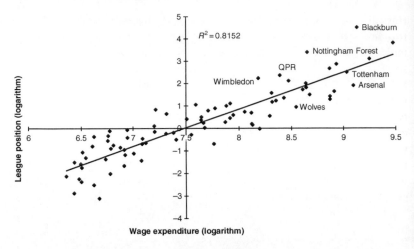

Figure 2.1   League position and wage expenditure 1994/95

bid up to slightly over the value that the second highest bidder would be prepared to pay (just as in an auction the winning bid need only be slightly over the maximum bid of the second highest bidder). This will occur regardless of whether the club maximises position or revenue. Given a very large number of clubs, the difference between the valuation of the highest and second highest bidders is likely to be small, and this will ensure that the market is (approximately) efficient.

The free-entry condition will ensure that clubs with smaller revenue generating capabilities will compete to hire players to the point where profits are the minimum feasible for survival. Competition at the upper end of the leagues will drive down profits for all but the clubs which are endowed either with some special capability (e.g. the ability to make players achieve a higher level of performance than they would be capable of in other teams) or with significantly greater revenue generating capabilities than other clubs.[7] Technology may affect the total amount of money coming into the game, but the free entry and market efficiency will ensure that virtually all this money goes to the players.[8]

5.   The Bosman judgement and the economics of English football

(a)   Bosman in the short run

It is clear from the comments quoted in Section 1 and made elsewhere that the Bosman judgement came as something of a shock to many in the game. The judgement undoubtedly gave rise to unexpected opportunities. First, the bigger clubs were able to acquire top foreign players (such as Gullit) for international competitions and so improve their squad strengths. Many managers have complained about the shortage of available English talent, and hence the widening of the market represented an important new opportunity. Any player near the end of his contract was also given the unexpected opportunity to move to a new club and obtain a higher wage than would otherwise have been possible under the old system, since the club could save on the transfer fee. Given the competition in the market, these players received an unexpected windfall. Against this, clubs which held players expecting to make a substantial profit on contract expiry suffered an unexpected loss (e.g. Tottenham and Hereford United). Tottenham, together with a number of other clubs, treats players' registrations as assets on the balance sheet, and hence the club was obliged to write down the value of the registrations to reflect the elimination of their "redemption" value. Thus, overall the winners were the clubs that had access to a wider market and the out-of-contract players who obtained a windfall salary increase, while the losers were the clubs holding players close to the end of their contracts.

Tables 2.2–2.5 give some indication of the financial changes which have occurred comparing the years immediately before and after the Bosman judgement. Most of these changes may have little to do with the Bosman judgement itself.

Table 2.2 illustrates the massive increases in revenues which have occurred thanks primarily to the TV contracts which have benefited all the divisions, not merely the Premier League. Table 2.3 shows the changes in employment costs which can be broken down into changes in employment and changes in average wages. Again, although the changes have been most noticeable in the Premier League, the percentage changes in employment and wages have been similar in all the

Table 2.2 Comparison of revenue before and after the Bosman judgement

Revenue £m	1994	1996	Change
Premier League	241.5	346.2	43%
Division 1	95.8	103.9	8%
Division 2	29.9	41.7	39%
Division 3	19.9	25.4	28%

Table 2.3 Comparison of employment cost before and after the Bosman judgement

Wage bill £m	1994	1996	Change
Premier League	116.9	172.7	48%
Division 1	62.6	79.1	26%
Division 2	21.7	29.0	34%
Division 3	12.7	16.9	33%
Employees			
Premier League	2552	3133	23%
Division 1	2190	2416	10%
Division 2	939	1438	53%
Division 3	686	839	22%
Average wage (£000)			
Premier League	45.8	55.1	20%
Division 1	28.6	32.7	15%
Division 2	23.1	20.2	−13%
Division 3	18.5	20.1	9%

Table 2.4 Comparison of transfer spending before and after the Bosman judgement

Net transfer income £m	1994	1996	Change
Premier League	−25.1	−105.6	−80.5
Division 1	0.9	6.6	+5.7
Division 2	5.2	2.3	−2.9
Division 3	2.0	3.2	+1.2

Table 2.5 Comparison of profits before and after the Bosman judgement

Operating profit £m	1994	1996	Change
Premier League	40.8	51.9	+10.1
Division 1	−10.0	−28.4	−18.4
Division 2	−4.0	−8.0	−4.0
Division 3	−2.3	−5.8	−3.5

Source: Touche Ross annual football surveys

leagues. The big difference between the Premier League and the rest is illustrated in Table 2.4, which shows transfer spending. Most of the money coming into the Premier League has been spent on overseas players; very little has trickled down into the English leagues. However, the Bosman ruling certainly does not appear to have had any restraining effect on transfer activity at least in the short run. In the 1996/97 there were 132 foreign players in the English football leagues (excluding Scots, Welsh and Irish players), and a transfer fee was paid in all but 16 cases (12% of the total). Finally, Table 2.5 illustrates the changing profit position of the divisions. Despite the massive outflow of transfer spending, Premier League clubs have managed to increase their operating profits. Meanwhile the financial position of the lower divisions has deteriorated yet further.

(b) Bosman in the long run

To calculate the impact of Bosman in the long run one has to imagine the career of a player starting from the beginning and consider the interaction between the post-Bosman rules and the economic fundamentals. The Appendix presents an economic model of the transfer market, which captures the impact of the Bosman ruling. The rest of this section puts into words the implications of the model.

Under 24s

Under the proposed rules a club will be entitled to sign a player and demand a transfer fee up to the age of 24 leaving the player in a situation little different to that which obtained pre-Bosman. On reaching 24 the player will expect to obtain a much larger salary if he is a player of high talent, given that he will move to the club which bids the most and no transfer fee will be paid. In this case the club which initially held the registration will be worse off than under the old system. However, this situation is unlikely to arise in practice as long as a player's talent is apparent before reaching 24. Any club in possession of such a talent will engineer a transfer well in advance of his 24th birthday and thus secure a transfer fee. The issue then is the time gap between recognising the talent of the player and his 24th birthday. If the gap is two years or more, then the player can be sold in much the same way as pre-Bosman. If, however, the player's talent is only recognised very close to the age of 24 then the selling opportunities for the club will be limited. Cases of late recognition/development of talent do arise from time to time (Ian Wright is a famous example) but they are relatively rare. Exceptional talents have usually been recognised by the age of 20, leaving plenty of time for a profitable sale. Moreover, not all professional players have exceptional talents. Perhaps the majority of footballers are "journeymen", average talents who are readily swapped for similar players with similar talents. For these players little will change with the approach of their 24th birthday, since the player can expect to be paid the going rate for their talent. Thus the new rules imply only marginal changes in the treatment of under 24s and the potential for clubs to profit from their sale.

Over 24s

By the age of 24 a player of exceptional talent may already have been sold by his original club and be on a contract with a new club. Pre-Bosman contract lengths varied, but a typical contract length would have been around three years. A five-year contract would have been exceptional. It is now widely argued that clubs will write much longer contracts in order to retain the possibility of selling the player before the contract expires.[9] It is perhaps useful to ask why such contracts were not written before. It is a fundamental proposition of labour market economics that it is efficient for firms (which are approximately risk neutral) to insure employees (who are risk averse) by giving them long-term contracts, which guarantee a relatively stable income.[10] Firms effectively charge for this insurance by paying lower wages, but employees are prepared to accept this because of the benefits of a stable income flow. Few businesses employ workers on contracts as short term as football clubs. In many cases such contracts are difficult to sustain because the fixed payment limits the incentive of the employee to contribute effort which is often hard to observe. However, this is not the case in football, where effort is readily observable on the pitch every week. Furthermore, clubs themselves are able to insure against risks relating to injuries and so on, so that the extra risk associated with a long-term contract may be partly re-insured.

Given that such contracts would have been attractive to players and cheaper for clubs (on average) in the pre-Bosman world, we must look for some constraint in the system which prevented them from being written. The most likely explanation is the financial constraints faced by clubs. Most clubs, even relatively large ones, have lived on the edge of financial viability for at least 30 years. This is a consequence of the excessively competitive nature of the English leagues and the continual threat posed to club survival by the free-entry condition. Any club that fails to spend on players is threatened with long-term decline and may ultimately drop out of the league. In a normal business environment many of these limited companies would have gone into liquidation, leading to a less crowded market place and increasing the potential for survival of the remaining few. Grimly many clubs have hung on in the face of financial ruin hoping for some unexpected saviour to emerge.[11]

Financing efficient long-term contracts would have required a degree of financial backing which simply was not available to these clubs. Most clubs exist on an overdraft from the local bank and with some voluntary contributions from local businessmen. In some cases the cash for monthly wages only becomes available at or around the date they have to be paid. Banks may underwrite these payments based on short-term beliefs about attendances and money coming into the club, but they would be unlikely to sanction long-term employment contracts. Any bank that agreed to finance such a contract would be committing itself to supporting a business entity in danger of collapse. Of course, long-term support from the bank might improve a club's chances of survival; however, it may be that banks can earn greater profits from short-term loans at high interest rates than they might earn from more risky long-term loans.

Short-term employment contracts were sustainable for many clubs under the old transfer system because clubs could obtain transfer fees even at the end of these contracts, which gave the banks a further element of security for lending to the clubs. The removal of this source of security is likely to diminish the willingness of banks to finance overdrafts. But as long as the number of professional clubs remains unchanged, the banks will also refuse to secure the additional borrowings which may be required to finance a long-term contract. The smaller, less financially secure clubs will find themselves in a Catch-22 situation. If only they could write long-term contracts they would be able to earn transfer fee income in the future, but because of the limitations of their sources of income the banks will not finance them to do this. To see that this must be so it is sufficient to realise that long-term contracts would have been beneficial for the clubs even before the Bosman ruling.

In this sense, then, it would appear that Graham Turner is indeed correct. The Bosman ruling is likely to deprive clubs of income, but only because they are, and have always been, unable to write efficient contracts, because they face liquidity constraints, and because they are not financially viable. This analysis suggests that the consequences of Bosman will be the demise of at least some clubs, which are not financially viable. Alternatively, some clubs which are currently marginal as professional clubs might have a healthier future as semi-professional clubs. This might mean abandoning the ambition of growing to become the next Manchester United, but such an ambition is in any case unrealistic for all but the biggest clubs. Whatever be the case, the result for the remaining clubs will be a greater degree of financial stability and the ability to write more efficient contracts so that all players, not just those who turn out to have higher ability, will end up better off.

However, it would be foolish to predict too easily the demise of small English clubs given that they have managed to stave off financial disaster for so many years. It may be that the rules for under 24s will be sufficient to keep the banks happy, and that in practice income from the sale of over 24s is not significant. If so, the Bosman ruling's principal effect will be to diminish the earning power of younger players. Pre-Bosman, clubs would invest in many players with a view to recouping their investment on one or two stars. While clubs will still invest in the hope of finding a star (youth policies are extremely unlikely to be terminated),[12] the amount they will pay will be diminished by the extent of the expected profit on selling stars. This would be a perverse outcome for the players, and one which arises only from the inability of clubs to write efficient contracts.

6. Conclusions

The Bosman ruling may significantly affect the structure of English football, but these changes will also depend on the broader economic structure of the leagues. For example, Bosman will not affect English football in the same kind of way as free agency has affected US sports leagues, because they are structured so differently. The extent of competition and "free entry" into the English football leagues mean that the labour market is approximately efficient, in the sense that player earnings generally reflect the expected value of player abilities, while all but the top clubs earn negligible profits. In this context Bosman will affect league outcomes only to the extent that pre-Bosman contracts were inefficient due to financing constraints faced by the smaller clubs. The effect of Bosman may be to drive some of the smaller clubs out of the market, but if that is the case, the primary cause will be their inability to finance efficient contracts, rather than the judgement itself.

Appendix: An equilibrium model of transfer fees

The model forms the basis for the descriptive analysis of transfer fees in Section 5. The model is a simple two-club, two-player, two-period model, while there exists the threat of entry from a fringe football club.

Model Assumptions:

1. There are two players, indexed a and b
2. There are two clubs, indexed i and j
3. Players have careers for two periods, indexed 1 and 2, and then retire
4. Neither clubs nor players discount the future
5. The talent of player b is constant and common knowledge, with value x_b
6. Player a has known talent $x_a < x_b$ in period 1. In period 2 player a's talent is $x_a + \varepsilon$, where $\varepsilon = p\varepsilon^h + (1-p)\varepsilon^1$. Call these values y_h and y_1, with $y_h > x_b > x_a > y_1$.
7. Players have strictly concave additively separable utility functions $u(w_1) + u(w_2)$ where w is the wage paid in each period. In a stochastic framework concavity implies risk aversion. Utility is unaffected by the club played for and there is no disutility associated with playing football.
8. Clubs are risk-neutral profit maximisers and have strictly concave revenue function $r_k(m)$ where m is playing talent. Assume $r_i(m) > r_j(m)$ for all m. Thus club revenues depend on the talents employed, although clubs differ in their revenue generating capacities. There are no competitive balance effects.
9. Contract transparency: any contract between clubs and players is fully verifiable and enforceable in court.
10. In cases where the player is indifferent between two options, it is assumed that players are willing to accept the decision of the clubs.
11. Free-entry condition: There exists at least one potential entrant with a potential revenue function identical to that of club j.

In the model the free-entry condition is the basic rule that determines the equilibrium.

The following equilibria are compared:

(i) Each club can only sign-one period contracts but selling clubs are entitled to demand a transfer fee (the right to demand a transfer fee for players out of contract characterises the system which operated in the English leagues between 1978 and 1995. Therefore call this an "English contract")
(ii) Each club can sign only one-period contracts with players, no transfer fees payable for out-of-contract players (post-Bosman rules on

transfers, although the English leagues still plan to charge fees for out-of-contract players under 24)

(iii) Both clubs can sign two-period contracts

Case (i) "English contract"

It is assumed in this model that each club can only offer single-period contracts. At the end of the first-period contract the players may be transferred, although under the pre-Bosman rules considered here the selling club will still be entitled to a transfer fee. To solve the two-period problem we need now to work backwards from period 2. This is because the wage settlement and any transfer fees paid will affect the wage offer in the first period. Period 2 contracts will depend on the realisation of ε.

(a) if $\varepsilon = \varepsilon_1$

$$w_{2a} = r_j(y_1)$$
$$\pi_{2j} = 0$$
$$w_{2b} = r_j(x_b)$$
$$\pi_{2i} = r_i(x_b) - r_j(x_b)$$

Thus player b (the better player in this case) is paid his opportunity cost, which is what he would have earned playing for club j. By the free-entry condition club j must pay out all its revenue in the form of wages. Club i can make a profit based on the difference between the opportunity cost (wage) of player b and the revenue generating capacity of player b at club i.

(b) if $\varepsilon = \varepsilon_h$, now club i will want to hire player a but must pay a transfer fee to club j.

$$w_{2a} = r_j(y_h),$$
$$T = r_i(y_h) - r_j(y_h) - [r_i(x_b) - r_j(x_b)]$$
$$\pi_{2i} = r_i(y_h) - r_j(y_h) - T = r_i(x_b) - r_j(x_b)$$
$$w_{2b} = r_j(x_b)$$
$$\pi_{2j} = T$$

The transfer fee reflects the incremental profit associated with having player a instead of player b. The solution of the period 1 contracts must ensure that all the profits that club j earns in period 2 (in expectation) are dissipated in period 1, otherwise the free-entry condition will be violated. Thus

$$w_{1a} = r_j(x_a) + pT$$

$$\pi_{1j} = -pT$$

$$w_{2b} = r_j(x_b)$$

$$\pi_{li} = r_i(x_b) - r_j(x_b)$$

Thus in period 1 player a is paid for his expected improvement in period 2. In expectations

$$Ew_a = r_j(x_a) + p\{r_i(y_h) - r_j(y_h) - [r_i(x_b) - r_j(x_b)]\} + pr_j(y_h) + (1-p)r_j(y_l)$$

$$w_b = 2r_j(x_b)$$

$$\pi_i = 2r_i(x_b) - r_j(x_b)$$

$$E\pi_j = 0$$

Under the "English contract" player a is the beneficiary of the incremental profit (rent) associated with the transfer of player a when $y = y_h$. Player a benefits regardless of whether he actually turns out to be a better player. In other words, the "English contract" shares the rents derived from exceptional talent among the players by giving them a higher wage in period 1 than their currently observed talent warrants. Club j will *ex post* earn profits or losses depending on the realisation of ε. However *ex ante* its expected profit is zero. Club i earns the same profit regardless of the realisation of ε.

Case (ii)   One-period post-Bosman contracts

In the post-Bosman world there are no obligations remaining once the first-period contracts end and so there is no need to work backwards to solve for the contractual outcomes. Thus

$$w_{1a} = r_j(x_a), \qquad \pi_{1j} = 0$$

$$w_{1b} = r_j(x_b), \qquad \pi_{1i} = r_i(x_b) - r_j(x_b)$$

Clearly the club with the superior revenue generating function (namely, i) hires the better player (namely, b) and pays him his opportunity cost (playing for a club identical to club j) while club j must pay its entire revenue to player a.

Period 2 contracts

(a) if $\varepsilon = \varepsilon_1$

$$w_{2a} = r_j(y_l), \qquad\qquad \pi_{2j} = 0$$
$$w_{2b} = r_j(x_b) \qquad\qquad \pi_{2i} = r_i(x_b) - r_j(x_b)$$

(the only difference with period 1 is that player a faces a wage cut and club j generates smaller revenues)

(b) if $\varepsilon = \varepsilon_h$, now club i will hire player a, so
(a) if $\varepsilon = \varepsilon_1$

$$w_{2a} = r_j(y_h), \qquad\qquad \pi_{2i} = r_i(y_h) - r_j(y_h)$$
$$w_{2b} = r_j(x_b), \qquad\qquad \pi_{2j} = 0$$

Compared to period 1, both players have moved clubs, player a has a higher wage, player b is paid the same and club i's profits have increased. In this post-Bosman world, no transfer fees have been paid since both players were out of contract. Thus in expectations

$$Ew_a = r_j(x_a) + pr_j(y_h) + (1-p)(y_l)$$
$$w_b = 2r_j(x_b)$$
$$E\pi_i = r_i(x_b) - r_j(x_b) + p[r_i(y_h) - r_j(y_h)] + (1-p)[r_i(x_b) - r_j(x_b)]$$
$$\pi_j = 0$$

In the post-Bosman contract, player a is paid his opportunity cost at all times. In the "English contract" player a benefited from the bargaining power of club j which was able to extract all the rent from club i, and the competitive mechanism ensured all this rent went to player a (at least in expectation). Player a is worse off in a post-Bosman world because, in this model at least, he has less bargaining power. If we were to suppose that player a had all the bargaining power, then he could extract all the rent in the second period $\{r_i(y_h) - r_j(y_h) - [r_i(x_b) - r_j(x_b)]\}$. In such a case player a would earn more if he turned out to have high ability than under an "English contract", but the expected utility of this outcome would be lower since

$$U[r_j(x_a)] + pU\{r_j(y_h) + r_i(y_h) - r_j(y_h) - [r_i(x_b) - r_j(x_b)]\} + (1-p)U[r_j(y_1)] <$$
$$U[r_j(x_a) + p\{r_i(y_h) - r_j(y_h) - [r_i(x_b) - r_j(x_b)]\}] + pU[r_j(y_h)]$$
$$+ (1-p)U[r_j(y_1)]$$

This is a consequence of the assumption of risk aversion (concavity of the utility function). *Ex ante*, risk-averse players will prefer to be insured against the risk that they turn out not to have high ability. Thus the losers from post-Bosman contracts are the players, although players of high ability with strong bargaining power will be able to obtain more in the second period than they could under "English contract". The winners are the bigger clubs, which are able to extract larger rents than in a pre-Bosman world, because they do not pay transfer fees. Small clubs are unaffected since they remain constrained by the free-entry condition.

However, in general single-period contracts are inefficient and will be dominated by two-period contracts, as will now be demonstrated.

Case (iii)   Two-period contracts

Even though club j offers a two-period contract to player a, in period 2 if $\varepsilon = \varepsilon_h$ then club i will want to purchase the player. To buy out player a's contract it must now compensate club i for its payment under the two-period contract. Thus a two-period contract will offer a wage to player a in period 1 equal to

$$w_a = r_j(x_a) + p[T + r_j(y_h)] + (1-p)r_j(y_1)$$

The maximum transfer fee club i would pay is

$$T = r_i(y_h) - r_j(y_h) - [r_i(x_b) - r_j(x_b)] + r_j(y_h)$$

The transfer fee is the same as under the "English contract" except that the last term compensates club j for the wages already paid under the contract. Player b writes the same contracts in periods 1 and 2 as in both post-Bosman and "English contract" cases, and in fact formally all three cases are indistinguishable. The main difference with the two-period contract is that player a is now better off. In the "English contract" case his expected utility was

$$U(w_{a1}) + EU(w_{a2}) = U\{r_j(x_a) + p[r_i(y_h) - r_j(y_h) - [r_i(x_b) - r_j(x_b)]]\} +$$
$$= pU[r_j(y_h)] + (1-p)U[r_j(y_1)]$$

While with a two-period contract his expected utility is

$$U(w_a) = U\{r_j(x_a) + p[r_i(y_h) - r_j(y_h) - [r_i(x_b) - r_j(x_b)] + r_j(y_h)] + (1-p)[r_j(y_1)]\}$$

which by concavity yields a higher expected utility. Note that in the event of a transfer player a is paid nothing by club i, since club j effectively sells the contractual obligations of player a. However, this does not imply indenture. Player a is actually indifferent between playing for club i and j, and therefore by assumption 10 is willing to move clubs. Another way of thinking about this would be that the period 1 contract involved a severance payment of $r_j(y_h)$ payable to club j by player a in the event of a transfer offer by club i, which is then reimbursed by club i paying a wage $r_j(y_h)$ (this would also render the transfer payment the same as in the "English contract"). In the long-term contract club i now makes a larger loss if player a's ability is low which is matched by a higher profit if his ability is high. Thus profits are more variable than under the "English contract", although the profits of club i will be identical in each state.

The fact that player a is better off with a long-term contract is a standard result from the contracts literature. Club j effectively offers full insurance for player a against his career risk. Given club j's risk neutrality it is willing to bear the extra variability in profits. However, competition ensures that the club obtains no benefit (no premium) for bearing the risk.

Implications of the model

1. In an efficient market long-term contracts would dominate. Therefore the Bosman issue would not even arise. Clubs would write career contracts with players and transfers would only occur for within-contract players.
2. The fact that such contracts were not written in the past suggests that there is some market inefficiency operating. The most likely candidates are:

(i) Asymmetric information
     Information asymmetries will obstruct the signing of efficient contracts if, for example, a player is better informed about his underlying abilities, or can take actions which affect his future abilities but which cannot be monitored or controlled by his employer. A classic example would be substance abuse. A player on a long-term contract might have less incentive to keep bad habits under control.

A contract might be written which required the player to reimburse his employer for such actions, but either this might prove difficult to enforce or the player might have limited assets with which to pay any fines for breach of contract. However, it is possible to imagine ways around these problems. Thus a portion of a player's wages might be held in trust during his playing career. Monitoring is generally a problem in employment contracts, but it might be argued that in the sports business it is less of a problem since the actions of players (both on and off the field) often are widely observed and reported on.

(ii) Credit rationing

The efficient contract required the marginal club to incur possible substantial costs in terms of initial wages based on expected performance. In practice such clubs may have limited access to capital markets. This problem may be exacerbated by the threat of moral hazard on the part of the directors if they cause the club to borrow on the capital markets and defraud the company which then goes into liquidation. In the post-1978 era the Football League imposed the rule that 50% of any transfer fee must be paid immediately, indicating that credit constraints have been a problem.

Competitive balance

The model presented here defies the established sports literature by ignoring the issue of competitive balance. According to this notion, a given team will be more able to generate revenues if it has successful competitors. Whilst in principle this may be true (although it will inevitably depend on the precise model of competition specified), effective tests have proved hard to construct and the results from the models which have been produced have been inconclusive. It may seem obvious that a close competition is more entertaining than an unequal one, but to present this as an axiom is to impose preferences on consumers. In fact unequal competitions are often quite popular with spectators (recall the Christians against the Lions). It is a noticeable feature of the English FA Cup that often the most popular televised fixtures are those between a Premier League Goliath and a non-professional David. Spectators can enjoy the vicarious thrill of a massacre or the shock of an upset. Schadenfreude should not be underestimated as a source of revenue generation. Strong rivals may also diminish the revenue generating powers of a given club by providing an alternative object for the affection of potential supporters. Even if clubs colluded, strong competition will diminish the potential market for one club; if strong competition leads to intensive rivalry, then there may be a deeper erosion of the club's revenue base.

In the two-club model presented here, it is clear that at least some form of competition is required. If competitive balance affected revenue generating capabilities in the sense that more equal teams could generate more income than unequal teams, the clear implication is that the value of player a in the event of transfer would be lower than that suggested here. However, the basic mechanism which determines equilibrium would be unchanged. Club j (the weaker club) would still make choices consistent with the free-entry condition, while club i could generate rents as a result of its superior bargaining position with players.

Notes

1. Speight and Thomas (1997).
2. Between 1911 and 1914, Aston Villa, a leading first-division club, reported cumulative profits of £19,897 on a turnover of £69,662, an average return of 29. Even a team consistently placed at the bottom of the first division, such as Tottenham Hotspur, could register exceptionally high returns: £22,524 on sales of £104,425 (22%) over the period 1909–14.
3. This system was often subject to arbitrary and callous abuse by the clubs. For instance, Bill Shankly played professional football for Preston North End before and after the Second World War. Reaching the end of his first team career, he asked to be transferred. The club fixed the fee it required at such a high level that there were no bidders and to his great dissatisfaction he was never able to play professional football again.
4. See Szymanski and Smith (1997) for some empirical evidence.
5. See Szymanski (1997) for a more detailed analysis.
6. See e.g. Sloane (1971, 1980), Dabscheck (1975), Arnold and Webb (1986), Carmichael and Thomas (1993), Szymanski and Smith (1997), Dobson and Gerrard (1997), Kuypers (1997).
7. For a discussion of these special capabilities see dell'Osso and Szymanski (1991).
8. One of the most important changes in English football in the 1990s, the upgrading of football stadia to make them more attractive to fans, has only been achieved through government intervention following the Taylor Report (1989) on the Hillsborough disaster. For a long time clubs neglected necessary improvements due to the imperatives of competition for players.
9. See Simmons (1997) who cites evidence that such contracts are already being written in Italy and the Netherlands.
10. See, e.g. Lazear (1995).

11. This may be an entirely rational event since saviours are not unknown in football e.g. Elton John at Watford and possibly Mohamed Al-Fayed at Fulham.

12. Antonioni and Cubbin (1997) show in a formal model that the Bosman judgement will have no effect on a club's decision to invest in a player.

References

Antonioni, P. & Cubbin, J. (1997) 'The Bosman ruling and the emergence of a single market in soccer talent', Mimeo, City University.

Arnold, A. & Webb, B. (1986) Aston Villa and Wolverhampton Wanderers 1971/2 to 1981/2: A study of finance policies in the football industry, *Managerial Finance*, 12, 1, pp. 11–19.

Carmichael, F. & Thomas, D. (1993) Bargaining in the transfer market: Theory and evidence, *Applied Economics*, 25, pp. 1467–1476.

Dabscheck, B. (1975) Sporting equality: Labour market versus product market control, *Journal of Industrial Relations*, 17, 2, pp. 174–190.

dell'Osso, F. & Szymanski, S. (1991) Who are the champions? *Business Strategy Review*, 2, 2, pp. 113–130.

Dobson, S. & Gerrard, B. (1997) 'Rent Sharing in the English Football Leagues', Discussion Paper, Leeds University Business School.

Kuypers, T. (1997) Unpublished PhD Thesis, University College, London.

Lazear, E. (1995) *Personnel Economics*, MIT Press, Cambridge, MA.

Simmons, R. (1997) Implications of the Bosman ruling for football transfer markets, *Economic Affairs*, 17, 3, pp. 13–18.

Sloane, P. J. (1971) The economics of professional football: The football club as a utility maximizer, *Scottish Journal of Political Economy*, 17, 2, pp. 121–146.

Sloane, P. J. (1980) 'Sport in the Market?' Hobart Paper No 85, IEA, London.

Speight, A. & Thomas, D. (1997) Arbitrator decision making in the transfer market: An empirical analysis, *Scottish Journal of Political Economy*, 44, 2, pp. 198–215.

Szymanski, S. (1997) 'Discrimination in the English soccer leagues: A market test', discussion paper, Imperial College Management School, London.

Szymanski, S. & Smith, R. (1997) The English football industry: Profit, performance and industrial structure, *International Review of Applied Economics*, 11, 1, pp. 135–153.

Taylor, Rt Hon Lord Justice (1989) *The Hillsborough Stadium Disaster* (HMSO) Cm962.

3
The Americanization of European football

Thomas Hoehn[a] *and Stefan Szymanski*[b]

[a] *LECG Limited and Imperial College Management School, London*
[b] *Imperial College Management School, London*

Abstract

Will European football keep leagues open, or adopt the American system of closed leagues? Would this reform be to the benefit of consumers? This chapter develops a framework to analyse the consequences of the structure of competition – whether teams play in both national and international competitions or not – and the effects on performance of revenue sharing among teams within the same league. The authors argue in favour of the creation of a European Superleague and against teams playing both in the Superleague and in national leagues. They derive a number of policy conclusions and examine various regulatory issues in European football.

1. Introduction

> Le football est le seul facteur de mondialisation qui échappe à la tutelle américaine. Si le monde de l'image est dominé par Hollywood et celui de l'argent par Wall Street, la planète foot est très peu nord-américaine.[1]
>
> (Vallet, 1998)

European football as we know it may soon be a thing of the past. Six years after the completion of the Single Market programme, one of

We thank Kai A. Konrad, Carmen Matutes, Paul Seabright and Panel members for helpful comments. We also acknowledge with thanks the helpful assistance of Ghantelle Bramley, Alan Castle, Martin Schimke and Anna Smith.

the major remaining segmentations of national markets in Europe is under threat. National championships organized under the auspices of national football associations and European cup competitions organized by UEFA, the federation of national football associations, are being challenged by private interests that seek to break up the old order. Over the summer of 1998 Media Partners, Milan, were actively courting the top European football clubs. They tried to persuade them of the attractions of a European Superleague and the viability of their proposals to set up a new league by the year 2000. In the event, a compromise was reached by the dozen clubs that had been openly toying with the idea of joining a Superleague outside the established structure (see *Financial Times*, 15 October 1998). As of the 1999/2000 season, the UEFA Champions League will be vastly expanded and offer more matches at the European level than ever. For the leading countries, the qualifying opportunities will be enhanced, allowing several clubs to participate, not just the domestic-league champions and the runners-up, as at present.

The fundamental question is whether this compromise represents an equilibrium or whether tensions in the present system of open multiple league structures will continue to drive clubs towards a true European Superleague, possibly with a hermetic structure. European competition authorities have become increasingly interested in the commercial organization of sports, and of football in particular (Wachtmeister, 1998). The European Commission has queried the arrangements between governing bodies and external marketing organizations, broadcasters or sponsors several times over the last year. Formula One, sponsorship agreements of the Danish tennis federation, and the allocation of tickets to the 1998 Football World Cup are just three examples of cases where the Commission has launched major investigations or made high-profile interventions (Ratliff, 1998).

This chapter develops a framework to analyse the role of European competition policy in sports. We start with the basic model of a hermetic league that represents essentially the structure of American sport leagues. We then consider the current European structure of multiple leagues, where the top clubs participate in both domestic and international competitions. We can then assess how international competition affects the competitive balance between clubs at the domestic level. The comparison between US-style hermetic and European systems offers an insight into the advantages of controversial redistributive measures that are typical in team sports.

In American sports, each league governs its own competition but has no jurisdiction over rival leagues. From time to time, new leagues may be created to compete with existing leagues, but there is no mobility within American leagues – no promotion and demotion. In contrast, the essentially European character of football organization is its unitary structure within a hierarchy of governing bodies and leagues. Governing bodies license all forms of football and in addition administer their own competitions (e.g., the FA Cup or the UEFA Cup). Clubs compete simultaneously at many levels and are subject to rules of promotion and demotion that permit mobility within the hierarchy.

The American model may represent a natural equilibrium for European football. Most researchers have argued that leagues that are more balanced, in the sense that competition results in a more even distribution of winning records, will be more attractive to consumers (El-Hodiri and Quirk, 1971; Jennett, 1984; Peel and Thomas, 1988). We show how the interlocking nature of European competition has created an unbalanced system and that a stand-alone Superleague is likely to sustain a more balanced competition.

This chapter addresses the following three policy issues: First, should the European Commission attempt to protect the existing fragmented structure of European football – with its traditions and its strict hierarchy of national leagues controlled by self-regulated governing bodies – when a transnational league system appears the most plausible market solution? Second, if a dominant European Superleague were to emerge, should UEFA control the governing body or would it be in the public interest to maintain a separate organization entrusted with the commercial administration of the sport? Third, what stance should the Commission take towards redistributive measures of the Superleague that may enhance the competitive balance between the participating teams, but may also act as a coordination mechanism for extracting monopoly rents?

The chapter is structured as follows: The recent commercialization of and the main policy interventions in European football are reviewed in Section 2. Section 3 compares the current structure with American sports leagues. Section 4 analyses competitive balance under American and European conditions to illustrate the fundamental policy issues. In section 5, we consider in detail the policy issues raised above.

2.   Recent trends in European football

2.1.   Increased commercialization

UEFA, the European governing body of football, estimated that the 1996 Champions League, the premier club competition in Europe, attracted 3.5 billion viewers in Italy, France, Germany, the UK, Spain and the

Netherlands, including an audience of 60 million for the final. Association football was invented in English public schools in the early nineteenth century and had spread around the world by the end of the century (see, e.g., Walvin, 1994). Football clubs have existed since the 1850s, and most of the major European clubs are around 100 years old. As a legal entity, a club is usually an association of members who pay an annual subscription and are entided to vote on policy at an annual general meeting (AGM). A club's day-to-day business is run by a club committee appointed at the AGM, whose members must accept financial liability in raising funds or borrowing for club activities. As football attracted spectators and footballers became paid professionals, the clubs evolved into businesses as well as being sporting organizations. To facilitate the raising of capital and avoid the difficulties associated with unlimited liability, English clubs started to incorporate as limited liability companies in the late nineteenth century. By the 1920s, almost all the professional clubs in England had converted to limited liability status.[2]

In other parts of Europe, the legal structures have been more varied. Some clubs have been run as members' clubs, with ownership spread out among a large number of supporters and with limited financial powers. Typical of this have been the German clubs, which have maintained the traditional legal structure of a *Verein* (social private club). This is explicitly recognized in law as a non-profit-making entity and combines the football club with other sporting activities (Galli, 1998). Alternatively, clubs have been owned by industrial enterprises (e.g., PSV Eindhoven) or controlled by wealthy industrialists (e.g., AC Milan by Silvio Berlusconi). Other examples of such close relationships include Fiat and Juventus, Peugeot and Sochaux, Bayer and Bayer Leverkusen, and Volvo and Gothenburg. In Spain, the dire state of management and the excessive degree of indebtedness of Spanish clubs led to legislation in 1990 that reformed the legal nature of football clubs.[3] Most clubs are still associations whose members are mostly fans (e.g., Barcelona has 104,000 members).[4] In France, clubs are able to choose from a variety of legal structures, which include a 'corporation with a sporting objective', a 'mixed economy company' and an association (club) (see, e.g., Bourg and Gouguet, 1998). These differing legal structures effectively restrict the ability of owners and directors in terms of their objectives, and are often viewed as important restraints on the commercialization of the game.

It is only in the last decade or so that European football has become a commercially significant operation. For example, in 1986 the combined annual turnover of the 22 First Division clubs in England was

£50 million. Since then football has enjoyed an economic boom that
has turned it into a significant business. Increasingly, football has been
'gentrified' – transformed from an essentially working-class pastime sold
at commodity prices into a middle-class entertainment. The quality of
stadium accommodation has improved, clubs have developed their merchandising arms, and the value of broadcasting rights has increased
dramatically. A rough indication of the economic magnitude of the
clubs is given in Table 3.1. Revenues vary even among the top teams
in each league. If the more lowly ranked clubs were included in this
table, the disparities would become much more pronounced.

Table 3.1   Football club finances

Club	Year	Total revenue (£m)	Wages/ revenue (%)	Wage bill (£m)	Profit
England					
Manchester United	1997	87.9	26	22.6	27.6
Newcastle	1997	41.1	43	17.5	8.3
Liverpool	1997	39.2	38	15.0	7.6
Tottenham	1997	27.9	43	12.1	7.6
Arsenal	1997	27.2	56	15.3	−1.6
Chelsea	1997	23.7	63	14.9	−0.4
Aston Villa	1997	22.1	46	10.1	−3.9
Leeds	1997	21.8	57	12.3	−9.7
Everton	1997	18.9	58	10.9	−2.9
Germany					
Bayern München	n/a	57.0	23	13.1	5.2
Borussia Dortmund	n/a	44.7	31	13.8	0.2
Italy					
Juventus	1997	51.9	56	29.1	0.7
AC Milan	1997	46.3	74	34.3	−9.6
Inter Milan	1997	38.1	47	17.9	−7.6
Roma	1997	26.3	52	13.7	0.2
Parma	1997	27.9	55	15.3	−9.0
Lazio	1997	27.3	56	15.3	0.1
Fiorentina	1997	25.8	69	17.8	−3.7
France					
Paris Saint-Germain	1996	28.4	43	12.1	2.5
Bordeaux	1996	14.5	42	6.1	0.2
Spain					
Barcelona	1996	41.3	42	17.5	n/a

Sources: Deloitte & Touche (1998a,b); SID Sport Informationsdienst.

Clubs have increasingly looked to the financial markets to supply investment capital. In the mid-1990s, football clubs in the
UK discovered the stock market as a source of finance and today there
are 23 clubs listed on either the London Stock Exchange or the AIM
(20 in England and 3 in Scotland). In the summer of 1998, the Italian club Lazio Rome floated on the Milan Stock Exchange, and Ajax
of the Netherlands, floated on the Amsterdam Stock Exchange. A number of other major European clubs, such as Juventus, AC Milan, Borussia
Dortmund, Atlético Madrid and Marseille, are said to be seeking a listing
or considering share issues. Flotation has in many cases involved a significant organizational restructuring. In 1997 the members of Borussia
Dortmund voted to transform the mutually owned club into a shareholding company.[5] In other countries, the transformation has required
a change in the law. Italian clubs have been able to adopt limited liability status like their British counterparts following the enactment of a
series of laws relating to the treatment of sporting enterprises (see Lazio
Offering Circular, 1998).

Television has played a significant role in the commercialization of
European football. In the 1960s, broadcasting rights for league matches
generated a few million US dollars of income for the game. By the 1990s,
the development of pay-TV, satellite, cable and pay-per-view increased
the revenue generation into the hundreds of millions. In 1997 the
annual value of league TV contracts in the UK, France, Italy, Spain and
Germany combined was in the region of $1 billion (see Table 3.2). In
1996 FIFA sold the world commercial rights (excluding the USA) for the
2002 and 2006 World Cups to the Sporis/Kirch group for $2.5 billion.

Table 3.2   Annual revenues from domestic TV rights to domestic
league games (£m)

	Free-to-air TV	Pay-TV/PPV	Total
England	18[a]	168[b]	186
Germany	52	27	79
France[c]	31	75	106
Spain[c]	–	130	130
Italy[d]	32	38	70

[a] £73 million paid by the BBC over four years for Saturday evening
highlights.
[b] £670 million paid by BSkyB over four years for 60 live matches per
season.
[c] Bourg and Gouguet (1998).
[d] Deloitte and Touche (1998b).

However, the significance of TV income should not be overstated. For example, Manchester United currently generates about 15% of its revenue from TV contracts, far less than from selling tickets to matches or from merchandising, catering and conferences.[6] In the case of Bayern München, the top-rated German football club, merchandising is said to be worth 50% of its total revenues of DM165 m (see Sport Informationsdienst). The excitement surrounding TV contracts has as much to do with the remaining potential for enhancing this source of income as with their current value.

Perhaps even more fundamental to the long-term structure of European football has been the developing trend towards ownership of clubs by media companies. In Italy, Silvio Berlusconi added AC Milan to his media empire in 1986. In the mid-1990s, Canal Plus bought Paris Saint-Germain. In September 1998 the UK satellite broadcaster BSkyB made a bid of £625 million for Manchester United Football Club. Other UK broadcasters are considering similar investments for top clubs, such as Newcastle and Arsenal. The media companies are likely to provide the strongest backing for a Superleague. Indeed, Berlusconi was attempting to create a Superleague in 1988. The proposals that emerged in the summer of 1998 were simply the latest in a long line of attempted breakaways.

The commercialization of football has gone hand in hand with an increased involvement of the law in the business of sport. In particular, the current labour market arrangements of clubs have been significantly affected by the Bosman judgment of the European court, while recent competition law cases in Germany, the Netherlands and the UK have challenged the legality of selling broadcasting rights collectively through the leagues.

2.2. Policy interventions

The trends described above raise major questions of public policy. In the near future, the new Champions League proposals agreed by UEFA in the autumn of 1998 will need to be cleared with the Competition Directorate of the European Commission, DG IV. So far, football has faced limited intervention from antitrust authorities largely because of the relative economic insignificance of sports. This has changed in the 1990s. A number of major cases dealing with the sale of broadcasting rights and the promotion of football have been investigated by national and European competition authorities (Temple Lang, 1997; Ratliff, 1998). In various official pronouncements, the Commission has made it clear that it now wants to treat sport like other businesses for the application of European competition law. Before this more recent development, the increased commercialization of sport and, in particular, the emergence of the professional athlete in individual (tennis) and team (football) sports led to a number of employment issues coming to the fore at the national level.

In the past, the governing bodies of football in Europe maintained a number of labour market restrictions. The effect of these restrictions was in general to hold down the wages paid to players and, so the clubs claimed, to redistribute income to weaker teams in the leagues. The main labour market restriction has been the payment of transfer fees. Most European countries operated a version of the 'retain and transfer' system. At the end of each season, a club would assign a player to the 'retained' list, which would make him unavailable for transfer to any other club; alternatively, they would place him on the 'transfer' list, setting a price that they would be prepared to accept in exchange for permitting the player to move to another club. If no club was willing to pay the fee, then the player could not move, even if the current club had no use for his services. This system, and its variants, was finally outlawed by the Bosman judgment of the European Court of Justice in 1995 (Court of Justice of the European Communities, Case C-415/93).

The Bosman case challenged two elements of the player transfer regime: first, the right of clubs to demand a transfer fee for players out of contract; and second, the right of UEFA to impose limits on the number of 'foreign' players appearing for a team in any competition. These restrictions were held in contravention of Article 48 of the Treaty of Rome, which guarantees freedom of movement of labour within the European Union. The ruling did not outlaw the payment of transfer fees for players within contract, which even before Bosman accounted for the majority of actual transfers. The Bosman ruling provides clubs with incentives to write longer-term contracts with players in order to protect any investment they may make in a player. Three-year contracts were the norm before Bosman. Contracts as long as five or even ten years are becoming increasingly common now. UEFA and the national associations have consulted with the Commission and a new system is being introduced that will entitle clubs to receive transfer fees for players under the age of 24 in recognition of a club's investment in a player's development. However, this ruling might still run foul of European competition law.

In the aftermath of the Bosman ruling, many clubs and football officials argued that the ruling would weaken the poorer clubs while strengthening the big city clubs.[7] In the Bosman ruling, Advocate-General Lenz made it clear that football clubs may be entitled to enter into restrictive arrangements if they promote competitive balance. Thus agreements necessary 'to ensure by means of specific measures that a certain balance is preserved between the clubs' were lawful (Bosman, 734). However, the specific restrictions dealt with by the courts were deemed neither strictly necessary for competitive balance nor in proportion to that legitimate aim. This is a view that has been emphasized by the Commission. It is too early to detect any long-term shifts caused by the Bosman decision, but there has not as yet been a significant run of bankruptcies.

On the product market, the application of competition law, both national and European, has focused on the way football and other sports are marketed. In Germany, the Bundeskartellamt (German Cartel Office) successfully challenged the centralized sale of broadcasting rights of the domestic games in two UEFA competitions, the UEFA Cup and the Cup Winners' Cup. Its decision in 1994 to block an amendment of the rulebook of the German Football Association (DFB) which would have transferred rights away from clubs was taken on appeal to the Supreme Court, which upheld its initial decision in the court's ruling of December 1997 (BGH, Beschluss v. 11.12.97-KVR 7/96). In its decision, the German Supreme Court argued, among other things, that the German football clubs are entities that are subject to the provision of the antitrust legislation. Without the amended rule granting the DFB exclusive rights to the domestic games in the two UEFA competitions, the German clubs would continue to sell these rights on an individual club basis, as is the case in other European countries. The DFB, the court argues, adds nothing in terms of the organization of the game or the broadcast itself. The only purpose of the amended rule is to increase the revenues from a centralized sale. Thus, the court argued that the challenged rule restricted competition without any compensating benefits to the consumer or the sport itself.

In the Netherlands, Feyenoord attempted to negotiate its own TV contract following the collective sale of rights by the Dutch Football Association (KNVB) to a pay-TV channel called Sport 7. Feyenoord's case was upheld in court and the Dutch Minister for Economic Affairs wrote to KNVB stating that collective selling of rights was in breach of competition law. The competition authority has also challenged the collective sale of highlights, arguing that even these could be sold on a club-by-club basis. In the UK, the Office of Fair Trading has brought a case in the Restrictive Practices Courts challenging the collective sale of Premier League rights.

Both the Dutch and UK cases are analogous to the German case, but go further. Both the KNVB and the FA Premier League are arguably involved in the organization of their league championships and cannot be dismissed as not adding but simply appropriating value in the same way as DFB in the case of UEFA broadcasting rights. The extent of interdependence between clubs has led some US observers to argue that clubs cannot properly be thought of as economic competitors at all. The economic unit can be thought of as a league itself, and any restraints imposed by a league organization on member clubs are not vertical restraints, but simply internal organizational devices. Accordingly, there is no more relevance to the antitrust authorities in an agreement made between member clubs than there is in the internal allocation of responsibilities between subsidiaries of a large corporation. Examples of syndicated leagues, in which competition between teams is coordinated and financed centrally are not unknown in team sports and this method of organization bears some relation to the organization of individualistic sports such as tennis, golf and even Formula One, where centralized selling of broadcasting rights may be deemed acceptable. On the other hand, football clubs in Europe are genuinely independent entities, responsible for their own financial policies. Furthermore, in Europe, where teams are often located in close proximity to each other and compete to attract both players and fans, the restrictions implicit in collective selling can go beyond the mere coordination required to produce an attractive product and can lead to cartelization and rent extraction. When clubs are viewed as producers of substitutable brand identities, rather than merely complementary producers of a competitive match, market restrictions require much closer scrutiny.

These challenges to the existing organization of the marketing of football in Europe are having an effect on the behaviour of clubs. The potential freedom of clubs to sell rights to their home games individually is partially responsible for the investor interest of media companies in football clubs. At the moment, the European Commission is holding back intervening in the affairs of the Premier League. However, with the reform of the Champions League, the competition watchdogs in Brussels will no doubt get involved in a major way. In the words of Commissioner Van Miert (1997)

> Special features of the sporting world place restrictions on the production and organization of sporting events which would be inadmissible in other sectors of the economy ... if the spectator is to enjoy an interesting and high-quality event, the outcome of the competition must be uncertain. For this reason there must be a balance of

strength between the opponents... since the interests of the various clubs are intertwined, the market is intrinsically unstable whenever there is a financial imbalance between the clubs. This imbalance must therefore be corrected... I have always argued for solutions based on a solidarity fund between clubs (a percentage of earnings should be shared)... the league would then function as a body responsible for the redistribution of income... the question which still has to be solved in this connection is how far the establishment of such a fund would enable joint sales of broadcasting rights to qualify for exemption.

The implication here is that the Commission may be willing to look favourably on collective selling if it is a means for redistributing income and effectively promotes competitive balance.

3.   America versus Europe

There are two main differences between the structure and organization of sporting leagues in the USA and Europe. First, the US leagues are generally 'hermetic'. New teams are seldom admitted to a league, and there is no annual promotion and relegation between junior leagues and senior leagues. Expansion franchises are admitted on agreement between existing league members and the entry fee is divided among them. They are also closed, in the sense that member teams do not compete simultaneously in different competitions; nor, with occasional exceptions, do teams release players to compete for national team competitions (one exception being the 1996 Olympic basketball team). US leagues approximate quite closely a joint venture. In the extreme, some leagues, such as the current US soccer league, are syndicated: ownership is pooled and players can be allocated centrally to different teams to maintain competitive balance. Clubs easily perceive their joint interests. They can expect to be competing together in more or less the same format from year to year. In Europe this sense of solidarity is undermined by the fact that the composition of each league division changes from year to year and that the set of competitors differs in different competitions. While the US system sounds far less competitive from the point of view of the clubs, more competition emerges at the level of the league. Since the Second World War, for example, there have been four attempts by new leagues to enter the American football market. Three of these failed and one was absorbed by the NFL. Arguably, the threat of entry imposes some competitive pressure on the activities of the leagues.

Entry is also made feasible by the much lower density of top clubs. Thus with only 30 Major League baseball franchises for the whole country, many cities lack a major team. By contrast, in European football most major cities can boast at least one major team, and sometimes more than one.

Second, US league authorities have tried to maintain a competitive balance between the clubs through intervention in the labour market or redistribution of club revenues. The main intervention in the player market has been the 'rookie draft' system. When players finish college or high school and enter professional sports, the clubs within the league take turns to pick players, with the first pick being awarded to the team that finished last in the previous season's competition, the second pick to the second last team and so on. Poorly performing teams can acquire the best young talent and therefore improve their standing in the following year. The system also limits the ability of players to market themselves, and a number of legal challenges have led to some amendments of the system. Player contracts are typically longer in US sports than in European football. For example, in baseball five- or six-year contracts are common, compared to a more typical three-year contract in Europe. Other restrictions imposed by US leagues include salary caps on the overall wage bill of clubs. These were introduced through a process of collective bargaining in the NBA in 1984 and the NFL in 1994.

The main vehicle for redistribution in US leagues has been the sharing of national broadcast revenues. The Sports Broadcasting Act of 1962 exempted collective selling of national broadcasting rights by the members of leagues from antitrust scrutiny,[8] in direct recognition of the redistributive function of such revenues. Typically, these are shared equally among the clubs. Broadcast income is typically a much greater share of total income in the USA than it is in Europe, averaging 32% of income in baseball, 34% in basketball and 63% in American Football (Sheehan, 1996). By contrast, for most European clubs, television income has been negligible up until the 1990s. In Europe, broadcasting agreements typically include a performance-related element and a fixed share. For example, the Premier League contract shares half of the contract value equally among the teams, 25% on the basis of league performance and 25% on the basis of the number of games televised. In Italy, income from free-to-air broadcasts is shared equally and pay-TV income (including pay-per-view) is distributed on the basis of performance. In Germany, clubs receive a fixed share plus a fixed amount for every home game and a lesser amount for every away game broadcast. In the USA, the club itself retains local broadcasting income.

Some US leagues also redistribute gate income. In the NFL, 40% of net gate receipts go to the visiting team, leading some US critics to describe the NFL as 'socialist'. In baseball, revenue sharing is less pronounced (20% to the visiting team in the American League, 10% to the visiting team in the National League), and in basketball there is no gate sharing. Gate sharing arrangements have been limited in European football. In England, an agreement used to set minimum admission prices, and on this basis awarded up to a 20%

Table 3.3   Differences in structure of US and European sports leagues

	US sports	Football in Europe
League system	Closed, no promotion or relegation Teams compete in single league competition	Open, annual promotion and relegation Teams may compete simultaneously in many competitions
League functions	Collective sale of TV rights Centralized marketing	Collective sale of TV rights
Competition between clubs	Limited substitution by consumers	Significant potential for substitution
Competition between leagues	Numerous cases of entry by rival leagues	All leagues contained within the established hierarchy
Player market	Rookie draft Salary caps (NFL, NBA) Collective bargaining	Active transfer market
Revenue sharing	Equal division of national broadcasting income Gate sharing (NFL 40%, baseball average 15%, NBA 0%)	Sharing of television income Little or no sharing of league gate revenues Some sharing of gate from cup competitions
Competition policy	Antitrust exemption for baseball Sports Broadcasting Act exempts national TV deals from antitrust	Centralized sale of TV rights under attack Selected interventions (ticket allocation FIFA)

share of gate income to the visiting team, but this agreement was abolished in 1983. Since the creation of the Premier League in 1992, all gate receipts have been retained by the home team. In the FA and League Cups, the home and away clubs receive 45% each of the gate, while 10% is divided equally among all entrants of the competition (except in the semi-finals and the final of the FA Cup, where the clubs receive less and the FA receives a share). In Italy, there is no league gate sharing except for the top Italian clubs, which get a small percentage (less than 5%) of the ticket revenues at away matches. In cup competitions, the same rule applies in Italy as elsewhere in Europe, with both teams sharing the net receipts. In Germany, 6% of league gate revenues is paid to the DFB and the rest is kept by the home team, while in cup competitions a 10% share goes to the DFB and the clubs split the remainder 50:50.

In Europe-wide competitions, teams have kept their gate receipts while paying a small share to UEFA (except in finals, where the authorities have taken a larger share and the remainder has been split between the teams). In the Cup Winners' Cup and UEFA Cup, UEFA has left it to the national associations to determine how broadcasting contracts should be negotiated.

Table 3.3 summarizes the main differences described in this section.

4. Contests in hermetic and open leagues

The comparison between league structures in the USA and Europe suggests a fundamentally different approach to the organization of league competitions. These differences revolve around the mechanism through which competitive balance between clubs is promoted by the leagues and their stand-alone nature, in contrast to the open multi-league structure of European football.

4.1. Some fundamentals

Teams involved in league competitions effectively operate as collections of talent. A description of league structures is based on two fundamental hypotheses:

- For each team, increased wage expenditure leads to better performance on the pitch.
- For each team, improved performance on the pitch leads to increased revenues.

Each of these relationships is a consequence of the operation of markets. Teams consisting of better players generally perform better than their rivals. In the market for players, clubs must pay the going rate to attract stars. The talent and ability of individual players is, by comparison with most labour markets, readily apparent, and hence sellers can demand what they are worth and buyers can expect to achieve a given level of performance given what they spend. The outcome of league competition is not entirely predictable, and chance plays a significant role in the outcome of competition. However, the dominant factor in explaining performance is wage expenditure. Improved performance on the pitch generates increased revenue because at the margin fans are attracted by success, and advertising, television and sponsorship income tends to be highly sensitive to success.

The validity of these hypotheses can be confirmed using accounting data from English football. Figure 3.1, taken from Szymanski and Kuypers (1999), illustrates the relationship between wage expenditure and league position for a sample of 39 clubs, between 1978 and 1996. Figure 3.2 illustrates the relationship between league position and revenue. The financial data are taken from the published company accounts and wages refer to the total wage bill of the club. For

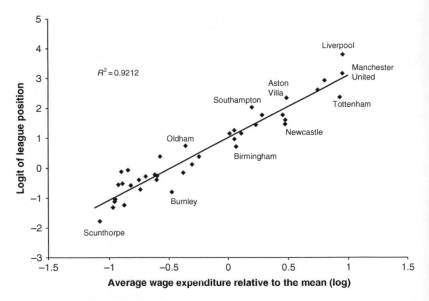

Figure 3.1   Wage expenditure and league position, 39 clubs, 1978–96

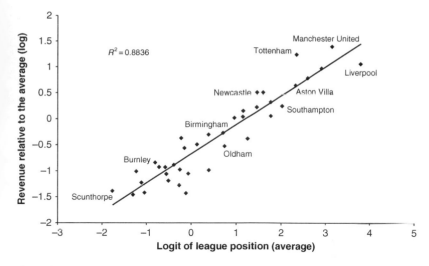

Figure 3.2 League position and revenue, 39 clubs, 1978–96

each club, performance was measured as an average of league position. Wage expenditure was measured as a ratio of wage spending in one year to the average of all other clubs in that year (what matters for league performance is not absolute expenditure on players, but spending relative to your rivals). For the graph, relative wage spending was averaged over all years in the sample. The same transformations were made to club revenue data. What is striking is the power of these relationships, illustrated by the R^2 of these simple regressions. Szymanski and Smith (1997) adopted a more sophisticated approach to the estimation of these relationships, but confirmed the relationships found here.

4.2. Contests in a hermetic league

We now analyse more formally some of the policy dilemmas, borrowing from the literature on contests and tournaments, similar to that used in the US team sports literature.[9]

We consider first a closed American-style league. For simplicity, suppose there are just two clubs that hire playing talent and compete against each other in matches. Success on the pitch depends on outspending your rival. On-the-pitch success is measured by win percentage (the percentage of matches won in a season) as is conventional in the US literature (see, e.g., El-Hodiri and Quirk, 1971; Fort and Quirk, 1995).

We adopt a special case of a contest success function that has been introduced and axiomatized in other areas of economics to describe the win percentage w_{12} of team 1 when playing team 2, as a function of the relative quantity of playing talent (t) on each side:[10]

$$w_{12} = \frac{t_1}{t_1 + t_2} \tag{1}$$

We assume that team revenues depend on three factors: success on the field, drawing power and attractiveness of the league competition. Success is expressed in win percentage. Drawing power depends on a team's location, history, reputation and so on. Well-supported teams, such as Manchester United, Bayern München and Barcelona, have higher revenues than their domestic rivals given the same league position. An important factor for the attractiveness of the league may be how balanced competition is. More balance, measured by the success of the teams participating in the league, may enhance overall demand for matches (either in the form of attendance at games or in terms of broadcasting). To capture these three sources of revenues, we specify a revenue function, which depends on the success of the team, its drawing power and the balance of competition.

$$R_1 = \mu_1 \left[\phi w_{12} + (1 - \phi) w_{12} w_{21} \right] \tag{2}$$

In this function μ_i represents the drawing power of team i, and ϕ represents the balance in the revenue function between the demand for 'own team winning' and the demand for a competitive balance. When $\phi = 1$ revenues depend only on win percentage, while when $\phi = 0$ revenues depend only on the degree of competitive balance. We assume that there is a competitive market for talent, which can be bought at a constant marginal cost per unit. Profit π_1 of team 1 is therefore the difference between revenue R_1 and expenditure t_1 for talent.

As a benchmark, we assume that each club maximizes its own profits. This is the view that has generally been adopted in the US literature (e.g., Noll, 1985; Quirk and Fort, 1992). In the European literature (e.g., Sloane, 1971) it has been conventional to assume that clubs are 'utility maximizers', where utility may incorporate factors such as success on the pitch, popularity of the club and profit considerations.

The equilibrium of simultaneous choice of expenditure for talent for $\phi = 1$ is well known from the contest literature. If both teams have the same drawing power, each wins with probability 1/2 and each spends

1/4 of the total revenue on talent expenditure. If the contest becomes less even, for example, because one team's drawing power is higher than that of the other team, this team chooses higher expenditure, wins with a higher probability and has a higher payoff than the other team in the equilibrium. Intuitively, as the drawing power of team 1 relative to team 2 increases, its marginal revenue of talent increases for all levels of talent, so that team 1 invests more than team 2, achieving a higher win percentage and profit. Team 2 anticipates this increase in team 1's investment and actually decreases its own investment. Thus when winning matters, the investments of teams in playing talent are strategic substitutes, in the terminology of Bulow *et al.* (1985).

Suppose now that there is a demand for competitive balance: $\phi < 1$. Let team 1 have a greater drawing power than team 2's. Revenues for each team are enhanced when the other team is more evenly matched. This introduces an element of strategic complementarity between the teams. In other words, each team has an incentive to match its opponent's investment in talent, in order to generate the maximum feasible profit in the market. Furthermore, in the absence of any outside competitive pressure, each team will recognize its complementarity and seek to reduce its investment in talent. Simulations show that, as ϕ falls, both teams reduce their investment in talent, but the team with greater drawing power does so proportionately more, so that competitive balance improves.

We now consider the effect of revenue sharing. Suppose a percentage α of each club's income is retained, with the remainder being shared out among its rivals. This might be thought of as a situation where the visiting team at each match receives a fixed share of the gate revenue. Team 1's revenue becomes $\alpha R_1 + (1 - \alpha)R_2$, and analogously does team 2's. While revenue sharing is generally justified by league authorities in terms of enhancing competitive balance, it is also a mechanism for internalizing the effects of competition. Reduced competition may be desirable from the point of view of team owners, but not desirable from the point of view of consumers. Suppose teams had equal drawing power ($\mu_1 = \mu_2$) so the league starts out in competitive balance. Revenue sharing will not alter competitive balance, but reduce investment in players. This reflects a wider point: any agreement to share out the prizes in a contest undermines the incentives for contestants to try and win. Fort and Quirk (1995) argue that

gate sharing has no effect on competitive balance in a league. Instead, an increase in α (more liberal gate sharing) has the effect of lowering player salaries... looking into the effect of gate sharing on league-wide profits, the answer is unambiguous in the case where there is no local TV. Gate sharing has no effect on competitive balance, and hence no effect on league-wide revenues. Further, gate sharing leads to lower talent costs; league wide profits go up with more gate sharing.

In fact, gate sharing will affect competitive balance, but in general the effect will be adverse. Consider an unbalanced league where only own team winning matters. When there is no revenue sharing, each team competes to attract talent. When revenue is shared, both teams want to invest in such a way as to maximize total returns of both clubs. Since the bigger club has the greater marginal income from success, it makes sense to engineer a reduction in competitive balance. Even if competitive balance matters, if some extra value is attached to own team winning, sharing will always lead to a reduction in competitive balance. This is illustrated by the simulation results in Table 3.4.

The finding is in contrast to conventional explanations, but may depend on the particular sharing rule. To see the problem with gate sharing, consider its effect on the incentive to win matches. Under gate sharing, teams playing away from home want their opponents to win (so long as own team winning increases home team revenues). Gate sharing thus appears like a tax on winning. Redistribution mechanisms that tax clubs on a lump-sum basis will avoid these kinds of disincentive effect, and if lump-sum taxes are then redistributed on the basis of performance, they may tend to improve competitive balance by equalizing opportunities to generate revenues. It is possible that collectively negotiated broadcasting contracts could satisfy these requirements. However, if collective selling is used as a mechanism for cartelizing the market, any

Table 3.4 Win percentage, investment in talent and profits as the revenue sharing grows

α	w_{12}	t_1	t_2	π_1	π_2
1.0	0.551	0.17	0.14	0.43	0.21
0.9	0.556	0.13	0.11	0.44	0.26
0.8	0.563	0.10	0.08	0.45	0.32
0.7	0.572	0.07	0.05	0.46	0.37
0.6	0.584	0.03	0.02	0.47	0.42

Note: Assumptions: $\mu_1 = 1.5$, $\mu_2 = 1$, $c = 1$, $\phi = 0.5$.

benefits for competitive balance may be outweighed by the dead-weight loss from higher prices and restricted output.

Given the theoretical prediction that revenue sharing will adversely affect competitive balance and investment incentives, it is perhaps surprising that the NFL in the USA manages to maintain both a relatively balanced competition and a high level of playing investment. One explanation might have to do with the objectives of owners. If owners were interested in maximizing success on the pitch rather than profits, then all redistributed income would go into player investment and the disincentive effects of revenue sharing would disappear.

Another explanation for the competitiveness of US team sports, such as the NFL, might be the array of alternative restrictive devices, particularly in the player market, outlined in Section 3. Those mechanisms resemble a system of handicapping, which is a frequently used method for inducing more effort in asymmetric contests. Handicapping, while potentially limiting the incentive to invest, does not create the same kinds of incentive to collude. One factor that has facilitated the creation of widely accepted handicapping systems is the unionization of team sports in the USA. Thus mechanisms such as salary caps have been negotiated through the unions, which have in return secured agreements on *minimum* as well as on maximum wages. It is perhaps ironic that in Europe the significantly lower level of unionization and the relatively low influence of player unions have prevented the development of potentially beneficial handicapping systems.

4.3. Competitive balance and income redistribution in multiple open leagues

In European football, the top clubs usually compete simultaneously in one of the three UEFA competitions and in the domestic league. UEFA competitions have always been a significant potential source of income. For example, appearance in the 1996/97 UEFA Champions League was worth around £4 million per club in broadcast revenues alone, compared to an average Premier League income of £17 million in that year. In the autumn of 1998, Media Partners, the promoters of the breakaway Superleague, were suggesting that the top European clubs could be paid £20 million per year for their broadcast rights. Appearances in European competitions are not evenly distributed among the clubs.

Table 3.5 shows the number of clubs that appeared in the top division in four countries over a ten-year period, and the proportion of European appearances of the biggest clubs (the data only run from

Table 3.5   The dominance of the top clubs

	Italy	Germany	Spain	England
Period	1988–96	1988–98[a]	1988–97	1991–97
Number of places in top division	18	18	20	20
Number of clubs appearing in top division	35	35	38	31
Number of European competition places	56	64	55	32
Number of clubs in European competition	14	23	16	13
Share of top 7 clubs (%)	80	73	75	81
Share of top 3 clubs %	43	39	47	48

[a]Excluding 1997.

1991 for England, since in the previous five years English clubs were banned from European competition). In each case, the three biggest teams account for between 40 and 50% of all competition places won (the teams were AC Milan, Inter Milan, Juventus, Bayern München, Borussia Dortmund, Werder Bremen, Real Madrid, Barcelona, Atletico Madrid, Manchester United, Liverpool and Arsenal). The seven largest teams (roughly 20% of all top-division participants in each country) accounted for roughly 80% of all European places. Taking into account that the bigger teams tend to survive more rounds in the competition, their share of all European matches played is even greater.

For simplicity, let there be two national leagues, each composed of two teams, and one team from each league also competes in an inter-league competition. This situation is represented schematically in Fig. 3.3.

Revenue in the Euroleague (the inter-league competition) depends on own-team winning and competitive balance in the same way it did in the hermetic context. For simplicity, we suppose that teams have the same potential drawing power, but the relative value of the Euroleague can vary. Clearly the value of European competition relative to domestic competition has grown significantly in recent years. Even though the drawing power of clubs is equal, the existence of an elite international competition automatically creates domestic competitive imbalance. We label clubs 1 and 3 the teams that compete in both domestic league and inter-league competition, while clubs 2 and 4 compete in the domestic

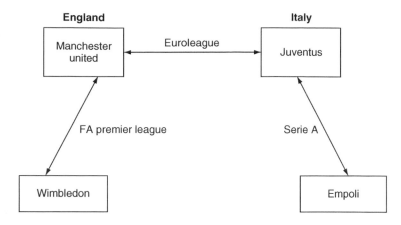

Figure 3.3 Schematic representation of European soccer leagues

competition only. Thus clubs 2 and 4 have revenues as in equation (2) for playing clubs 1 and 3, respectively, whereas clubs 1 and 3 have revenues as in equation (2) from playing clubs 2 and 4, respectively, plus the additional revenue of $\vartheta[w_{13} - (1 - \phi)(w_{13})^2]$ and $\vartheta[w_{13} - (1 - \phi)(w_{31})^2]$ from playing against each other. The parameter ϑ denotes the relative importance of the inter-league competition in terms of revenue generation. The main proposition of this chapter – that a European Superleague will become like an American sports league, with its members not competing in other competitions – can be shown by considering the effect of the parameter ϑ. As ϑ grows, the investment of the Euroleague teams in talent also grows. While this maintains competitive balance in the Euroleague, the smaller teams in national competition are left behind and domestic competition becomes more unbalanced. The more the competitive balance is valued, the faster the value of domestic competition is eroded. This is illustrated in Table 3.6.

Here the two countries are assumed to be symmetric. Hence, the outcome for team 3 is the same as for team 1, and the outcome for team 4 is the same as for team 2. As the value of the Euroleague increases, the investments of the competing teams grow. Given that team 2 (the purely domestic team) is always a strategic substitute for team 1 unless competitive balance is the only source of income ($\phi = 0$), the increased investment of team 1 will lead to falling investment on the part of team 2. Thus competitive balance in the domestic league falls. As long as the two Euroleague teams have equal revenue-generating capacities, competition remains balanced. While total revenue in the domestic

Table 3.6 Win percentage, investment in talent and profits as the Euroleague grows

ϑ	w_{12}	t_1	t_2	π_1	π_2	R_{12}	R_{21}
1	0.60	0.22	0.144	0.58	0.17	0.42	0.32
2	0.68	0.32	0.148	0.88	0.12	0.45	0.27
3	0.75	0.42	0.141	1.17	0.08	0.47	0.22
4	0.81	0.53	0.125	1.45	0.05	0.48	0.17
5	0.86	0.64	0.102	1.72	0.03	0.49	0.13

Note: Assumptions: $\phi = 0.5, c = 1$.

league falls, team 2 is more adversely affected than team 1. As a result, team 2's profitability is driven towards zero. Assuming that clubs have some fixed costs (which are not modelled here), then purely domestic teams will incur financial losses. Furthermore, we have not modelled here the additional costs, both fixed and variable, of the Euroleague teams competing in their domestic leagues, but if these costs are substantial, they may cause participation in the domestic league to be unprofitable. From this we conclude that single-league competition for the top clubs is the most plausible equilibrium for European football.

Could revenue sharing help to preserve the participation of the top teams in the domestic leagues? Our discussion in the previous section suggests that this is unlikely. International competition is like having a larger revenue base. When domestic teams share revenues, they are likely to want to concentrate talent in the stronger club for the same reasons as in the hermetic context. This will, if anything, lead to a less balanced domestic competition. We illustrate this in Table 3.7 with simulations of a contest in which there is domestic revenue sharing

Table 3.7 Win percentage, investment in talent and profits with increasing revenue sharing in a multiple league structure

α	w_{12}	t_1	t_2	π_1	π_2	$R_{12} + R_{21}$
1.0	0.60	0.22	0.14	0.58	0.17	0.739
0.9	0.61	0.19	0.12	0.60	0.20	0.737
0.8	0.63	0.17	0.10	0.61	0.23	0.734
0.7	0.64	0.14	0.08	0.63	0.26	0.730
0.6	0.66	0.11	0.06	0.64	0.29	0.725

Note: Assumptions: $\vartheta = 1, \phi = 0.5, c = 1$.

(we assume that teams will not share Euroleague revenues with their domestic rivals).

Domestic revenue sharing works in the same way as it did in the hermetic league model where one team had more power, although the reason is slightly different. Revenue sharing reduces the incentive of each team to invest in talent, but the effect on the Euroleague team is mitigated by its incentive to preserve its revenues from that competition. This means that the purely national team reduces its investment by more than the team playing internationally as well, and hence competitive balance deteriorates in the domestic leagues. While this serves to reduce the revenues in the domestic league, profits increase because the lower-investment effect dominates.[11]

4.4. Extensions

Our analysis in this section suggests that the interlocking system of leagues that currently operates in Europe is untenable because of the increasing dominance of competition in a Euroleague. Members of a Euroleague invest more in playing talent than the remainder of clubs, causing domestic leagues to become increasingly unbalanced. The most natural solution to this problem is for the Euroleague members to cease playing in the national leagues, thus making those competitions more balanced. The forces driving this change may be even greater than our analysis suggests. First, if there are fixed costs associated with operating in a league, then as domestic competition becomes unbalanced, the smaller clubs will be driven into losses and will want to quit the domestic competition altogether. Second, there are additional costs, both variable and fixed, for the Euroleague teams involved in participating in two leagues simultaneously. Under the current plans, Euroleague clubs will be playing two matches a week. Most players will be unable to play in both fixtures, and hence teams will need larger squads. While in our analysis revenues increase marginally for the Euroleague clubs as they dominate the domestic competition, we believe that this effect is likely to be more than offset by the cost of participating in two leagues.

In the new equilibrium, the relationship between a European Superleague and the domestic leagues would be analogous to that between the major and minor leagues in American baseball or that between the NFL and college football. This leads naturally to a set of policy questions, including the desirability of encouraging this transformation, the role of the football authorities, particularly UEFA, in promoting rival competitions, and the scope for redistribution mechanisms and 'solidarity' between the clubs.

5.   Conclusions and policy implications

The proposals for a European Superleague presented by Mediaset in the summer of 1998 have served to focus minds. At once UEFA and the national associations have been forced to reconsider the existing structure of competition and make significant concessions to the top clubs in the form of a revamped Champions League, with many more matches being played between European clubs. In due course, the Competition Directorate of the Commission in Brussels will be asked to approve the new arrangements proposed by UEFA. This comes at a time when Brussels is in the process of formulating its general policy on sport. This will mean making a number of policy decisions with far-reaching consequences.

Some commentators have argued that the revamped Champions League is the culmination of developments and already represents a European Superleague. This argument seems fundamentally to miss the point. The attraction of a Superleague for the top clubs lies in their ability to increase income by playing significantly more games against their larger European rivals. The new Champions League achieves this, but the leading clubs will be required to participate simultaneously in an extended mid-week European competition while competing with equal vigour in the domestic league at weekends. This solution seems out of touch with reality. The oldest league rule in football is that teams should field their strongest team in league matches.[12] It would be physically impossible for the best 11 players in a squad to play a domestic season of around 34 matches combined with a similar number of mid-week matches over a 40-week season. In practice, players would have to be rested, and clubs would have to allocate priority to different competitions (as in fact they tend to do already). The domestic competition will come to be seen as the 'reserve' tournament for the top clubs, downgrading national leagues to the status of second-team competitions. A proper European Superleague will have to break this historic link with domestic league competitions and become truly pan-European in structure.

5.1.   Welfare implications

Assessing the welfare implications of changes in the structure of football (and sports in general) is notoriously difficult. The appropriate measure of welfare is the sum of firm profits and consumer surplus, just like in any other industry. However, measuring both profits and consumer surplus are difficult. Few clubs report profits in their accounts. If clubs are not profit maximizers, then it is the 'utility' generated for the owners of the club that should be measured, and this is even more problematic. As far as consumers are concerned, it may be useful to differentiate committed fans from less committed 'armchair supporters'. This distinction is implicit in the revenue function of our contest analysis, where the committed fan might be thought of as caring only about his or her own team winning, while the armchair fan cares mainly about a well-balanced contest (although in practice there is probably a complete spectrum of preference). Committed fans are rather like long-term investors, or *noyaux durs*. They spend both time and money on supporting their club in the expectation of long-term sporting success. By contrast, the armchair fan wants to be entertained and considers only the immediate return on consuming a match. Each type of fan's welfare may be affected quite differently by club policies.

5.1.1. Towards a US-style superleague

Moving from the current European system to a more American structure should be beneficial for clubs. The big clubs will be able to focus on the competition that generates the greatest proportion of their income. Smaller clubs in the top domestic league would lose by no longer competing against Superleague teams that may bring with them large groups of supporters, but this loss is likely to be offset by the improvement in competitive balance in the domestic competition. In the long term, it may be more profitable to be a leading club in a second-rank competition than a no-hoper in the top competition.

For consumers, the effect on the *noyaux durs* will be analogous to that on the clubs, since these supporters are, properly speaking, stakeholders in the club. Armchair fans gain unambiguously because there will be a greater supply of well-balanced contests. However, this happy story depends in part on the long-term relationship between the Superleague and the domestic leagues. In particular, will there be promotion and relegation, or will the Superleague become truly hermetic like the American leagues? A closed Superleague benefits the incumbents and represents a welfare loss for the outsiders, who lose the option that they might one day reach the Superleague.

In practice, this distinction may not be as stark as it first appears. Even if the league were closed, the Superleague would almost certainly permit the creation of expansion franchises. This would mean less frequent entry than what occurs under the current system, and would restrict entry to those clubs large enough to benefit the entire league and provide balanced competition. The sale of expansion franchises is a mechanism by which the externality created by the quality of entrant teams is internalized. The shift to a franchise system would enhance the welfare of the incumbent teams and maximize the attractiveness of the Superleague, while diminishing the welfare of the excluded outsiders. The other potential effect of 'closure' is to reduce incentives. This effect has been widely commented on in the press (incumbents will not try so hard because there is no threat of demotion), but seems fairly implausible when one considers the highly competitive nature of closed US leagues. One reason that this may not be a real problem is that, even if a league is closed, there will always be the threat of entry by rival leagues if competition in the Superleague is not effective.

5.1.2.   Promotion and demotion

If promotion and demotion are preserved as of right, then the likely impact on the competitive balance of the Superleague will be adverse compared to a system where entry is restricted on the basis of available resources. It will always be the case, even in a league system based on a large number of matches, that relatively weak teams will occasionally be promoted. Such teams seldom fare well in a higher division and are usually demoted in the following season, having provided a relatively low standard of competition. However, even if it is true, it is not clear whether this effect will reduce welfare. While consumers may value competitive balance, there is also the possibility that they enjoy unbalanced 'David and Goliath' contests that will occasionally produce surprise results.

Perhaps more worrying from a welfare point of view is the possibility that the very largest clubs may be demoted. The effect of such demotions is clearly adverse for the supporters, who in themselves are a significant fraction of consumers, but such demotions also tend to affect adversely interest in the competition as a whole. Moreover, once demoted, such clubs are usually promoted back up with ease in the following season, thus diminishing the uncertainty associated with the outcome of the junior championship. Despite the increased welfare associated with fans of lesser clubs being able to see their team compete against a major, this effect seems unlikely to offset the adverse effects.

It seems clear that the proposals of Media Partners for a hermetic Superleague were aimed specifically at preventing this outcome, rather than limiting the access of the smaller clubs. It might therefore appear that an ideal compromise would allow permanent membership for big clubs while preserving promotion and demotion for weaker clubs. Unfortunately, as well as the fundamental problem of defining the 'big' and the 'small', such a system would be widely viewed as unfair, and this would in our view significantly undermine the attractiveness of the competition. Level playing fields matter.

It seems, therefore, that there is a straight choice between a promotion and relegation system and some kind of a franchise system. A franchise system, so long as it provided clear rules for the access of clubs, would be a better system because it enables teams to internalize the effects of unbalanced competition. This would also be fairer than the current system, which discriminates against moderate-strength clubs in strong leagues in favour of weak clubs in even weaker leagues.

5.2. Policy issues

We believe that a European Superleague in soccer that resembles Major League Baseball or the National Football League in the USA represents a market equilibrium. However, the competition authorities or even the member states have significant powers to block such an outcome or to limit its viability. For example, if Brussels were to accept the collective broadcasting arrangements of the current system, while indicating that if the Superleague members tried to break away entirely they would not be permitted to enter into such arrangements, that would have the effect of supporting the current system. We do not believe this is in the best interests of the clubs or the consumers (committed or otherwise), mainly because of the likely increase in unbalanced competition as the Superleaguers increasingly dominate domestic competitions.

There are policy dilemmas in endorsing the shift towards a hermetic Superleague. The most prominent are issues concerning (1) access, (2) redistributive measures and (3) the scope for inter-league competition and the role of UEFA.

5.2.1. Access to the Superleague

While there might be some political benefits in a European Superleague, promoting the notion of a European identity, the impact on member states would vary widely. Core countries such as Italy, Spain, England and Germany would be very well represented in any Superleague competition, given the strength of their top clubs. Some major European footballing nations such as France (World Cup holders, after all) might be less well represented, given the relative weakness of their clubs and the tendency for their top players to play overseas. Some smaller nations might be well represented because of the disproportionate strength of their clubs (e.g., the Netherlands with Ajax, PSV and Feyenoord). Other smaller nations with strong footballing traditions (e.g., Norway) might tend to suffer little representation, again because their top players play overseas.

A Superleague will offer only restricted access to the weaker clubs, as has always been the case with the European competitions. In the traditional cup structure of European competitions, weaker clubs that were strong in weak leagues (e.g., top clubs from Iceland) gained access to European competition through the qualifying rounds. Such access might be justified on regional-policy grounds, even if the system discriminated against second-rank clubs in strong leagues. The access of these weaker teams will decline in the absence of intervention (and we believe that such intervention would be unworkable and largely ineffective).

This suggests a regional-policy dilemma. Even if a Superleague remained open to promotion and relegation, some nations or regions (e.g., Wales) might never be represented in a Superleague. In our view, this is not a problem that can be solved by enforced maintenance of the status quo. Since weaker clubs do not enjoy much success in the top European competitions as it is, there is little to be gained by preserving unbalanced competition. We believe that policy makers should focus more on entry conditions and redistribution of income.

5.2.2. Redistribution

Our analysis suggests that the competition authorities should approach redistribution mechanisms in dominant sports leagues with a healthy degree of scepticism. Redistribution among the clubs is essentially a way of softening the effects of competition. Rather than promoting competitive balance, certain mechanisms may reduce the incentive to compete and worsen competitive balance. The trick is to design forms of redistribution that avoid or limit the adverse effects on competition. Alternative mechanisms for balancing competition are those that have been widely used in the USA such as the rookie draft and salary caps. If these mechanisms are not used simply to raise profitability, they will tend to increase the competitive balance of the league and can allow consumers to enjoy the same quality of competition at a lower cost. Any kind of restriction will create an incentive for avoidance, and the effectiveness of any scheme will depend on the ability of authorities to enforce it. However, a closed Superleague may create a better chance to do this than does the existing system. It is hard to imagine how a rookie draft system would operate in a system of open leagues with promotion and relegation, since the whole system is predicated on a recognized career progression from minor to major leagues. A closed Superleague would overcome this problem. Salary caps are also more likely to be implementable among a closed set of Superleague teams with more or less equal resources. Such a system could be consistent with EU laws on the freedom of movement of labour as well as the articles on competition, as long as the system was perceived to provide a clear benefit to the players (as it does in the USA). A natural corollary of a European Superleague would be a European players' union that might negotiate on salary issues and other relevant issues such as health and safety.

There seems to be greater potential for redistribution among the leagues. This may happen anyway as the big clubs move to buy up the smaller clubs and use them as farm teams. A system such as this seems to have operated for some years in Spanish soccer without any obvious adverse effects on the quality of competition among the top clubs, and a similar observation can be made about competition in the USA. However, there is also a case for a system of redistribution from the senior leagues to the junior leagues. Again, such a system might be difficult to implement within the existing structure where the beneficiaries are potential future competitors of the top clubs, but might be more acceptable within a closed Superleague.

5.2.3.   The scope for inter-league competition and the role of UEFA

The continuing role of UEFA is problematic. As the organizer of the Champions League, UEFA is likely to continue to be the promoter of the dominant European competition while acting as regulator of all competitions. As the Superleague evolves, it will increasingly face a conflict of interest between its promotion of its main product and the interests of the national leagues that it regulates.

One problem is the coordination of the fixture list for the expanded Champions League. Currently UEFA decides when fixtures in its own competitions are played and determines the permissible 'windows' for broadcasting matches within Europe. UEFA has an incentive to ensure that its own fixtures make use of the most attractive slots, and as a result of expansion will remove some available slots for the national leagues. Through its regulation of broadcasting windows, it also restricts the ability of leagues and clubs to generate broadcasting income. While this restriction has traditionally been imposed with a view to promoting lower-level national competitions, there is also a potential conflict of interest with UEFA's promotion of its own league. Thus while it may be revenue maximizing to create a Superleague, if UEFA is perceived to be coordinating the commercial development of football through its power as the governing body, it is likely to face investigation for abuse of its dominant position.

UEFA can defend itself against such charges by demonstrating that its actions promote the sport as a whole rather than the interests of the elite clubs. But this becomes a difficult line to hold if the top clubs are hermetically sealed in a dominant league. UEFA might use a significant proportion of the income to fund the development of the game, but in this case the clubs might feel they could do better by going it alone and keeping all the money for themselves. So UEFA appears to be caught in a catch-22 situation: as a promoter, it is liable to find itself either subject to an antitrust suit or deserted by its teams. In this situation it may be that UEFA has to choose between its roles as regulator and promoter. It would appear that there is growing scope for UEFA to exercise its regulatory functions.

5.3. Prospects for a true Superleague

Our final comments concern the prospects for a Superleague. A long-term solution must be both commercially viable and DG IV compatible. Our analysis suggests that the revamped UEFA Champions League has several major flaws. So what do we think would be a viable structure for a true European Superleague?

The structure outlined in Table 3.8 is purely hypothetical in its composition of teams and regional organization. We are not central planners and do not claim to know what is best for the European public. Nevertheless, the desirable features that could represent an equilibrium structure for European football can be spelled out. Top clubs are attracted by the possibility of repeated encounters with the top clubs and stars from rival leagues. In this way the top clubs can enhance the level of opposition and therefore enhance their own revenue-generating potential. Many of the top clubs would also like to abandon fixtures against much weaker clubs that tend to be found at the foot of the domestic leagues, since these matches generate less income while involving significant injury risks for top players. However, the problem for clubs wanting to create a Superleague is that, while they want more regular competition with top international rivals, they also want to preserve valuable domestic rivalries. For example, in Germany, Bayern München might want to play Juventus, Inter Milan, Barcelona, Real

Table 3.8 Possible structure and organization of a European Football Conference

South West League 4 countries, 15 clubs			Northern League 7 countries, 15 clubs		
Paris Saint-Germain	Fra	8717	Ajax	Ned	7858
AS Monaco	Fra	5764	Feyenoord	Ned	6208
Girondins Bordeaux	Fra	4917	PSV Eindhoven	Ned	4833
FG Nantes	Fra	3875	Manchester United	Eng	6617
Olympique Marseille	Fra	1500	Aston Villa	Eng	4375
FG Barcelona	Esp	7381	Arsenal	Eng	4167
Real Madrid	Esp	5951	Liverpool	Eng	3875
Atlético Madrid	Esp	4000	Newcasde United	Eng	3500
Deportivo La Goruna	Esp	3833	Chelsea	Eng	3264
Real Zaragoza	Esp	3333	Rosenborg BK	Nor	5458
FG Porto	Por	6538	Brondby IF	Den	5250
Benfica	Por	6458	Celtic	Sco	3250
Sporting GP Lisbon	Por	5667	Glasgow Rangers	Sco	2167
Club Brugge	Bel	4750	AIK Solna Stockholm	Swe	3167
Anderlecht	Bel	3858	MyPa-47	Fin	1000
Average UEFA ranking coeff.		5103	**Average UEFA ranking coeff.**		4333
Competitive imbalance		34%	Competitive imbalance		39%

Eastern League 14 countries, 15 clubs			Central League 3 countries, 15 clubs		
Spartak Moscow	Rus	7158	Juventus	Ita	8265
Lokomotive Moscow	Rus	3000	LazioRoma	Ita	7193
Slavia Praha	Cze	5483	AC Parma	Ita	7139
Panathinaikos	Gre	5350	Inter Milan	Ita	6735
Galatasaray	Tur	3833	AC Milan	Ita	6303
Steaua Bucuresti	Rum	4833	Fiorentina	Ita	1375
Ferencvaros	Hun	4083	Napoli	Ita	1167
Dinamo Kiev	Ukr	3375	Borussia Dortmund	Ger	7716
Rapid Wien	Aut	3417	Bayern München	Ger	6825
Dinamo Tbilisi	Geo	3000	Bayer Leverkusen	Ger	4600
Croatia Zagreb	Cro	3000	Werder Bremen	Ger	3217
Slovan Bratislava	Svk	2750	l.FC Kaiserslautern	Ger	3000
Legia Warsaw	Pol	2250	Eintracht Frankfurt	Ger	2750
Dinamo Minsk	Bis	2500	Hamburger SV	Ger	1167
Lokomotiv Sofia	Bui	1000	Grasshopper Club	Sui	3167
Average UEFA ranking coeff.		3669	**Average UEFA ranking coeff.**		4708
Competitive imbalance		40%	Competitive imbalance		53%

Madrid, Ajax, Arsenal and Manchester United more often, but they do not want to surrender regular fixtures against Kaiserslautern, Borussia Dortmund, Borussia Mönchengladbach, FG Köln, Bayer Leverkusen, Hamburg, Werder Bremen or Eintracht Frankfurt (and possibly others). The same argument would apply *mutatis mutandis* in every country. Thus a breakaway has to enrol a large number of clubs from the start in order to achieve critical mass.

Accommodating both national and international rivalries would require a league with at least 60 teams. This would not be feasible under a conventional football system where all play all twice, home and away. A hierarchical system would not be attractive either, given that one of the reasons for putting together a Superleague is to play more often with other top European teams, not avoid them. An alternative to this might be a US conference system where teams are organized in subgroups. Each season a club plays all the members of its own conference and in addition a limited number of teams from outside the conference, chosen on the basis of historic performance (to maintain a rough competitive balance). Such a system based around, say, four regional conferences of 15–20 teams might enable clubs to preserve domestic competition while enhancing international competition. If each conference contained 15 teams, then each team would play 28 matches against teams from its own league and in addition would play 6 teams from each of the other conferences (once only) over the course of the regular season, bringing the total number of games to 46. The selection of opponents would be based on past performance, so as to create a more balanced set of matches and to give the weaker teams a better chance in the championship. At the end of the regular season, a play-off system would involve, let's say, the top two teams in each league, with three rounds leading to the final and the status of European football champion.

We have constructed a hypothetical Superleague, primarily to illustrate the way in which a competition might operate. The conference members are listed in Table 3.8. The composition of a Superleague would be subject to negotiation, but we have adopted some simple rules of thumb. For the larger footballing nations, such as England, Germany, Italy, France and Spain, five, six or seven clubs have been selected first on the basis of their respective UEFA rankings. For another category of countries, two or three clubs have been selected. Smaller countries have one club to represent them. The decision as to how to group the teams has been made primarily on the basis of geography. In addition, countries have been grouped together where regional or historic rivalries are strong or the style of football is similar. A special league has been created to accommodate the countries of eastern Europe, with one team for each country except Russia. This is for two reasons: Income differentials between these clubs are less than that between other European clubs. Second, the attractiveness of matches with eastern clubs is generally lower for the top European clubs, and including them as part of other leagues would undermine the league's attractiveness in the short term. In the longer term, however, eastern European clubs can be expected to benefit from inclusion in the European Superleague and be able to develop strong teams of their own.

Table 3.8 also lists the 1998 UEFA rankings for each team. This allows the calculation of two indicators: the average ranking points of the teams assembled in the league; and the inequality of teams in terms of their respective UEFA ranking points. In our example, the South-Western League scores highest in terms of average UEFA rankings, combining the top clubs from France, Spain, Portugal and Belgium. The Eastern League scores lowest in terms of average rankings, but is quite evenly balanced.

Participation in domestic league competitions would not be permitted for teams playing in this European Superleague because a combined fixture list would be impossible to manage for even the largest teams and there would be a negative effect on competitive balance modelled above in Section 4. This does not mean that Superleague clubs could not compete in domestic cup competitions, which are played in a different format. Promotion opportunities and threats of relegation are other possible features that could be incorporated in a European Superleague, but perhaps only with difficulty.

Supporting measures to maintain the attractiveness of domestic competitions could be introduced along the lines of the rookie draft in the USA. For example, clubs participating in the European Superleague could agree among themselves a rule whereby no player under the age of 20 would be played in conference matches. This would give clubs involved in the domestic league competition *de facto* exclusivity for competitive matches involving emerging stars of the game. This may sound like a significant restriction on the free movement of players in the European Union and likely fall foul of the Bosman ruling. But this is not necessarily the case. First, it is arguable that in the wider market for players, the hiring restraint of 60 clubs is not a major distortion. Second, the wider benefits to European football are potentially substantial. Domestic league competitions would be more attractive than without such a restriction. Intense interest would be focused on the performance of those players who will become eligible to play in the European Superleague, creating an additional spectator interest in domestic league games. And third, there is the income redistribution effect between leagues, benefiting clubs that have on their books a promising young player under long-term contract, from which they can release him at the age of 20 for an appropriate consideration.

Discussion

Carmen Matutes

Institut de Anàlisi Econòmics, CSIC
This is a very interesting chapter, very informative and thought provoking. Among other achievements, the chapter is a step forward in understanding how departing from an American-style, closed league may change the implications of revenue sharing.

Let us take the following extension to the model, which, like the authors', incorporates the fact that increased wage expenditure leads to better performance on the pitch, and improved performance on the pitch leads to increased revenues, but allows for more teams and concentrates on demand[13] as the relevant payoff variable. Modelling demand as opposed to the profit function of two teams is important because only then can one take into account the fact that a team can be a 'complement' or a 'substitute' for the league or the remaining teams as a group, in the sense that if it hires additional talent, it increases or decreases, respectively, the sum of the revenue of all the matches where the team does not play. Demand should depend positively on the drawing power of clubs, on talent t_i, and on how important it is for either one team or both to win the match: for instance, because of the possibility of demotion if they do not win or the possibility of playing in a foreign competition if they do.

The role of a team's position in the league, or how likely the team is to win it, is less clear. Demand may increase with both teams' winning probabilities. Alternatively, if competitive balance is important, the absolute value of the difference in winning probabilities may matter. Finally, demand might increase with both winning probabilities if their difference is not too large, but when this difference exceeds a certain critical limit, demand goes up only when the chances of the weaker team go up.

Consider how an increase in the talent of team x affects the sum of the revenues of all the matches where x does not play. Let w_i be team *i*'s probability of winning the league. An increase in talent of team *x* diminishes the probability of any other team (say, *y* and *z*) winning the league. If demand for any match between *z* and *y* increases with both w_y and w_z, then every team is necessarily a substitute for the league. However, as can be shown, an increase in t_x lowers more the winning probability of those teams with many chances to win. This has two implications. First, it suggests that as the talent of team *x* goes up, the remaining matches in the league become more balanced. To the extent that competitive balance is desirable, the total demand for games in which *x* does not play may increase with team *x*'s talent, which means that demand for talent as a result of revenue sharing would not decrease by as much, or might even increase. Second, this should be so for weak teams in a league including very good teams. As a team hires additional talent, it decreases the chances to win of the remaining teams, but particularly so for the team with the highest chances to win in *that set:* the leader of the league, unless this is the team hiring extra talent. Thus, weak teams reduce their demand for talent by less or even increase it, as a result of revenue sharing. Likewise, to the extent that competitive balance is highly desirable,[14] a top team is a strong substitute for the league, and thus reduces by more its demand for talent as a result of revenue sharing. This is because its additional investment particularly reduces the chances of the second-best team winning and thus makes the league more unbalanced. Intuitively, the league becomes more balanced when the weak team increases its talent and less so if the team hiring additional talent is the top team. Thus, domestic revenue sharing of a closed league should result in a more balanced league. Sharing should have no impact on competitive balance when the league is balanced to start with.

Whether a team complements the league has consequences for evaluating the implications of measures when departing from a closed league. In a sense, the conceptual distinction between open and closed leagues is not as important: the impact of revenue sharing on the decision of one team to hire talent is similar whether the team is a top team playing in a foreign league or a 'complement' to the remaining teams in a domestic league. In both cases, revenue sharing induces the team to reduce its talent by less than other teams, and might even provide incentives to demand additional talent. On the other hand, to the extent that competitive balance is desirable, the teams that are more likely to be complements of the league are very weak teams: that is, at the other end of the spectrum from the teams that play in a foreign league. In this sense, participation in a foreign league acts as a countervailing tendency to the positive impact of revenue sharing on competitive balance. Whether this countervailing tendency is strong enough to reverse the impact of revenue sharing depends on how unbalanced the league is and how desirable competitive balance is. Hence, open leagues diminish the positive impact of revenue sharing on competitive balance, but it is unclear that they result in a more uneven domestic league if domestic competitive balance is very desirable and the original situation is highly unbalanced.

One of the main policy issues these days, as the authors argue, is whether the league itself or the individual clubs should negotiate the broadcasting rights. To capture the impact of TV income sharing, we should model the negotiations between TV stations and either the league or the clubs. Let us assume that there is only one TV channel and that many matches are to be played on a given day, but only one match at most will be broadcast. In this case, the maximum total surplus is the demand in the best match: that is, the match that has the highest demand. If the league and the TV station negotiate, the Nash bargaining solution is that each gets half of this surplus.

If, on the other hand, the TV channel can negotiate with the individual clubs, the channel can threaten to negotiate with the teams offering the second-best match, in which case the channel would get a larger share of the surplus. Indeed, even by negotiating with the teams playing the worst match, the TV channel would get half the surplus generated, and it could use this to negotiate with slightly better teams so as to get more surplus. And again, applying this logic recursively, the TV channel would get significantly more than half of the maximum surplus (particularly if we believe that competitive balance enhances demand and that the leagues are balanced). In brief, in negotiating TV rights, a more important issue than income sharing among teams may be dividing the pie between teams and the broadcasting stations.

The possibility that a cartel of teams might restrict TV broadcasting anti-competitively cannot be discussed without considering which type of contracts between the league and the channels are allowed. In particular, the league is subject to a dynamic problem of consistency: once one contract is signed, it has incentives to sign a new contract that satisfies the additional demand for TV viewing and so on. Thus important aspects of possible restrictions on broadcasting include whether contracts with one channel can be conditioned on other contracts that the league might sign, the possibility of exclusive broadcasting rights, and whether or not TV channels should be able to resell those rights.

The chapter does not treat the impact of buyout fees analytically, but points out that the received sports literature shows that it does not interfere with efficient allocation and hence has no impact on competitive balance. The Bosman case challenged the transfer system of players out of contract, but did not deem illegal the existence of buyout fees. So what is the rationale for these buyout fees? As the chapter explains, it is claimed that buyout fees are a way for the players to pay back to their club the initial investment in developing young talent (which is not club specific). In this way, clubs pool the risk, since the probability that they get a return is larger. In a paper on switching cost in the labour market, Burguet *et al.* (1998) show that, even without investments, buyout fees should be a feature of labour contracts for 'singular workers': those for whom there is uncertainty about their quality *ex ante*, but for whom *ex post*, once they have started working, there is a lot of transparency (not only the incumbent firm, but also outside firms learn a lot about the workers' performance). Soccer players are a good instance of this type of worker. The reason why buyout fees are a must when the market has so much information is that they maximize the payoff of the worker-incumbent firm: that is, they expropriate outsiders of all the rent from the efficient reallocation of the player. With *ex ante* competition among clubs to hire the player, he can appropriate all the surplus. In this case, ruling out buyout fees is detrimental to the player's welfare, since such a regulation results in short-term contracts that yield positive expected profits to the firms. On the other hand, if one club has *ex ante* market power, buyout fees allow the club to extend its power over time and are detrimental for the player's welfare.

Paul Seabright

University of Cambridge, Cambridge
This enjoyable and thought-provoking chapter provides a good illustration of the benefits of applying microeconomic analysis to a problem too often approached with slogans. As an armchair rather than a committed critic, I shall concentrate on asking: what is the good that football clubs supply and what differentiates the market in which they operate from markets for other goods? Football is like theatre in many ways. The players supposedly 'competing' are in fact collaborating to produce a show that satisfies the spectators who pay to see it.

One way of modelling the football industry might be to assume that the unit of competition is simply the league. The American-style hermetic league with its elaborate revenue-sharing arrangements and its expansion franchises fits this model best. It implies the scope for significant market power on the part of an individual league, constrained only by the threat of entry from rival leagues and the possibility of substitution to rival sports (or other leisure activities). So the antitrust exemptions enjoyed by league sports in the USA appear unjustified, to say the least. However, two considerations suggest that economic competition between individual clubs may after all provide a better model, though to a greater extent in Europe than in the USA. First, ticket prices are still set by individual clubs, and other decisions such as investment in players are made non-cooperatively (though they are subject to cooperative constraints in the USA, such as the rookie draft). Second, even if a particular match is a collaborative exercise between teams (which is to say that, for a given match, teams are suppliers of complementary rather than substitute products), different simultaneous matches are substitutes for each other, and teams also compete to attract loyal supporters who will follow them match after match. The process of competition is rather like that between airlines, which frequently collaborate to assure the different legs of a given journey, while competing against other suppliers of the same journey, and trying to ensnare frequent flyers into travelling with them again and again.

It would have been good to have in this chapter a more explicit analysis of the kinds of market failure to which this form of competition could give rise, and what might be the reasons (if any) for public intervention in this sport. After all, individual clubs' decisions give rise to significant externalities, which may be important in the aggregate even if the clubs' market power as conventionally measured is surely negligible. Separate issues arise about the implications for broadcasting, which is a different market that the authors do not analyse here. As it stands, the chapter confines itself to one explicit claim, namely, a European superleague composed of clubs that also play in their domestic leagues does not represent a stable equilibrium for the industry. I happen to think this claim is plausible, but the authors' model does not establish it convincingly. The simulations in Table 3.6 show that anything which encourages relatively successful clubs to invest more in talent will harm the profitability of relatively unsuccessful clubs, possibly leading them to close down altogether. But we knew this already from the way in which firms' revenues were assumed to depend upon win percentages. For instance, even when competitive balance is the only thing that matters, the derivative of revenue equation (2) with respect to t_2 will be positive if and only if

$t_2 < t_1$. So it is good for a strong team when a weak team invests, but not vice versa.

Is it good for the profitability of weak teams when strong teams play a larger proportion of their matches in a superleague? And can it be an equilibrium for strong teams to play only a proportion of their matches in a superleague, or will they wish to abandon their domestic leagues altogether? The analysis does not really answer these questions because it assumes (in a way that the text itself concedes to be implausible) that strong teams can play an unlimited number of matches in a superleague without forgoing revenue from domestic leagues.

Suppose that the profit function for superleague team 1 were equal to the average of the revenue R_N that this team earns if it plays only the national league and the revenue R_E that the team earns if it plays only the international league, with weights β and $(1 - \beta)$. Then it is easy to check that profits are increasing in the β only if $t_3 < t_2$ (that is, team 1 plays a team in the national league that has higher talent than the team it plays in the superleague – so the superleague is not really a superleague at all). This happens because increased profits from the superleague are offset by lost profits from the domestic league, and the former will exceed the latter only if the team's win percentage is higher in the superleague. In practice, of course, this formulation ignores the fact that superleagues are attractive because spectators want to watch talent as well as caring about the outcome. If they do, then there may still be a benefit to a domestic club from its rivals' participation in a superleague, since this improves the display of talent performing at its ground (also if rivals play less often in the domestic league, this may improve domestic teams' win percentages overall). Either way, this argument underlines the need for a clearer model of the precise reasons why teams want to play in a superleague and whether these would induce them to forgo participation in a domestic league altogether.

Although the precise model does not convince me, the chapter provides an excellent introduction to these complex issues, and a fruitful point of departure for further work.

General discussion

Philippe Aghion criticized the fact that the chapter takes the pool of talent as given. Talent in sports, however, is not exogenous because there are the important elements of selection and training. The problem here is that only part of the training is club specific and players may leave their team for another club. These spillovers of human capital have to be taken into account when designing the rules for a European league. To generate sufficiently high incentives for developing new talents, one could, for instance, think about limiting the mobility of players. Karl-Gustaf Löfgren argued that, if there is a potential market failure in developing new talents, the appropriate schemes for the distribution of talents, and for recruitment more generally, have to be included in the analysis. François Ortalo-Magné raised the question of whether teams should be allowed to get into talent-sharing agreements. This might be beneficial if it allows the farming of talent, which is an essential part of the US system. In basketball and football, the college system provides a good training period for young players. Baseball has the minor leagues for developing talents. Something comparable is needed in Europe if we want to implement a superleague successfully. Maybe the teams that are not admitted to the superleague can form such a basis for developing talents. The interesting question here is how to organize the minor league and its sharing of talents with the major-league teams. Samuel Bentolila felt that a European superleague should be complemented by national or minor leagues for an additional reason: namely, to create competition between the different leagues.

Kai Konrad noted that 50 years ago people also did sports and it was similarly exciting for the spectators, although the athletes might have been slower than nowadays. The reason why they were slower is that they put less effort into sports. Sporting contests tend to dissipate the rents they generate by the effort that is spent on winning the contest. Overall, too much effort may be spent on training. From a welfare point of view, it is therefore far from obvious that fostering competition and maximizing effort is appropriate. This is a straightforward implication from the theory of contests. There are further results from this theory that could be applied here. First, revenue sharing leads to less effort in the contest. And second, a handicap for the better team helps to increase the overall effort. If team A is stronger than team B, then the equilibrium outcome is that A is more likely to win, but that the equilibrium effort which both put into this contest is lower than if they were more equal. Hence, the trick is to handicap the more productive team. Many US sports take account of this effect by allowing the weaker participants the first choice in the rookie draft. David Begg added that horseracing provides a good illustration of the nature of demand in sports. Low-level horses take part in handicap races. The aim is to have a very close finish by handicapping. In the top horse races of the season, however, there is no handicap. Here people want to find out which is the absolutely best horse. There is an absolute standard, and spectators pay to be part, for example, of the race for records. However, when there is no absolute standard, people want to see a close finish. This aspect is particularly important for football games.

Paul Klemperer argued that it would be desirable to include a more explicit discussion of measures of welfare. Competitive balance might be desirable provided it was not driven by lack of effort by players. Spending on talent might also be desirable, especially if it improved national success. Should Europe also care about the success of European teams at world level? Do the same arguments justify efforts to promote more competitions at world level?

Samuel Bentolila thought that, from a technical point of view, the ups and downs of teams in a league show some similarities with the social mobility of households in income distribution. One could think of applying the technique of Markov matrices to compare the competitiveness of professional sports in the USA and Europe. Philippe Aghion wanted to know what kind of team production function is appropriate here. For instance, the output could be better if there were fewer superstars because this would strengthen the team element. The issue of how production takes place in football will be important for the optimal design of leagues. Furthermore, when trying to implement a new superleague, the success of such a reform will depend on who is involved in the decision process. Is it just the teams, or should broadcasters, the national football organizations and others also be included?

Notes

1. 'Soccer is the only contributor to globalization that has escaped American hegemony. The world of cinema may be dominated by Hollywood and that of money by Wall Street, but soccer is scarcely North American.'
2. All professional clubs in England are therefore subject to the commercial law and the statutes of the UK Companies Act.
3. In Spain, football clubs can form SAD, a special case of the more usual Sociedad Anonima (SA).
4. 'Barca' is an interesting example because the club seems as much a political symbol of Catalan nationalism as a sporting entity.
5. This change will also require the assent of the league authorities, but this is expected to be granted.
6. A similar story emerges for the top Italian clubs (see Deloitte & Touche (1998b).
7. Mike Bateson, then chairman of Torquay United, a minor English club, expressed a common viewpoint: 'I am damned if I'm going to put my money into a youth system just to let the bigger clubs snaffle up the product. The fat

cats may get fatter, but the scrawny ones down this end will die of starvation. A lot more players are going to be out of work'.
8. This is one of the main kinds of antitrust exemption granted to sports in the USA. The others are the baseball exemption granted by the Supreme Court in the 1920s, and the expiation for collective bargaining agreements between player unions and league authorities representing the clubs.
9. Contests of different kinds have been widely modelled in the economics literature. Examples include rent seeking in the public sector (e.g., Tullock, 1980), rivalry in R & D (e.g., Loury, 1979), competition for market share (e.g., Monahan, 1987) and labour markets (e.g., Lazear and Rosen, 1981). A useful review of the mathematical properties of these models is provided by Nti (1997).
10. In line with Atkinson *et al.* (1988), we assume that a team's playing talent can be approximated by a perfectly divisible aggregation over the different specializations within the team.
11. It might be argued that this result is an artefact of the effect that there is no specific demand to watch high levels of talent in its own right. This effect might be added by making revenue a function of total talent as well. While this would tend to diminish the effects somewhat, it would not change our qualitative results unless the 'own team winning' effect disappeared altogether.
12. This rule appeared in the original rules of the Football League in 1888 and, according to Inglis (1988), is the only rule not to have been amended.
13. As the revenue function of the chapter, this demand is not quite a demand function, since it does not include a price. Issues about pricing strategies will become relatively important because in the medium term they will have an impact on stadium attendance, which in turn will affect the willingness of TV stations to pay for broadcasting a match. So there is a full range of issues concerning pricing that may have important welfare consequences. Like Hoehn and Szymanski, I leave these potentially interesting issues aside.
14. An empirical study that investigates whether competitive balance is desirable should not be based only on whether the demand for a particular match increases when the two teams are equally likely to win the league. Demand for the matches of the league as a whole should be enhanced when the league is more balanced, and perhaps looking at individual matches underestimates how valuable competitive balance is. In particular, this suggests that when a traditionally small team increases its talent and thus its chances of success, all the matches of the league will have more viewers.

References

Atkinson, S., Stanley, L. & Tschirhart, J. (1988) Revenue sharing as an incentive in an agency problem: An example from the National Football League, *Rand Journal of Economics* 19(1), pp. 27–43.
Bourg, J.-F. & Gouguet, J.-J. (1998) *Analyse Economique du Sport*, Presses Universitaires de France.

Bulow, J., Geanokoplos, J. & Klemperer, P. (1985) Multimarket oligopoly, strategic substitutes and complements, *Journal of Political Economy* 93, pp. 488–591.

Burguet, R., Caminal, R. & Matutes, C. (1998) 'Golden Cages for Showy Birds: Optimal Switching Costs in the Labor Market', Mimeo, IAE, London.

Deloitte & Touche (1998a) *Annual Review of Football Finance 1997*.

Deloitte & Touche (1998b) *Financial Review of Serie A*.

El-Hodiri, M. & Quirk, J. (1971) An economic analysis of a professional sports league, *Journal of Political Economy* 79, pp. 1302–19.

Fort, R. & Quirk, J. (1995) Gross subsidization, incentives and outcomes in professional team sports leagues, *Journal of Economic Literature* xxxiii, 3, pp. 1265–1299.

Galli, A. (1998) Rechtsformgestaltung und Lizenzierungspraxis im Berufsfuss-ball: Die Situation in England, Italien und Spanien vor dem Hintergrund der Regelungen in Deutschland, *Sport und Recht*, 18.

Inglis, S. (1988) *English League Football and the Men Who Made It*, Willow Books, London.

Jennett, N. (1984) Attendances, uncertainty of outcome and policy in the Scottish football league, *Scottish Journal of Political Economy*.

Lazear, E. & Rosen, S. (1981) Rank-order tournaments as optimum labor contracts, *Journal of Political Economy*.

Loury, G. (1979) Market structure and innovation, *Quarterly Journal of Economics*.

Monahan, G. (1987) The structure of equilibria in market share attraction models, *Management Science*.

Noll, R. (1985) The Economic Viability of Professional Baseball, Report to the Major League Baseball Players' Association.

Nti, K. (1997) Comparative statics of contests and rent-seeking games, *International Economic Review*.

Peel, D. & Thomas, D. (1988) Outcome uncertainty and the demand for football: An analysis of match attendances in the English football league, *Scottish Journal of Political Economy*.

Quirk, J. & Fort, R. (1992) *Pay Dirt: The Business of Professional Team Sports*, Princeton University Press, Princeton, NJ.

Ratliff, J. (1998) 'EG Competition Law and Sport', paper presented at the British Association for Sport and the Law, London, October.

Sheehan, R. (1996) *Keeping Score: The Economics of Big-Time Sports*, Diamond Communications, South Bend, IN.

Sloane, P.J. (1971) The economics of professional football: The football club as a utility maximizer, *Scottish Journal of Political Economy*.

Szymanski, S. & Kuypers, T. (1999) *Winners and Losers: The Business Strategy of Football*, Penguin, Harmondsworth, UK.

Szymanski, S. & Smith, R. (1997) The English football industry: Profit, performance and industrial structure, *International Review of Applied Economics*.

Temple Lang, J. (1997) 'Media, Multimedia and European Community Antitrust Law', paper presented at the Fordham Corporate Law Institute, October.

Tullock, G. (1980) Efficient rent seeking, in J.M. Buchanan, R.D. Tollison & G. Tullock (eds), *Toward a Theoy of the Rent Seeking Society*, Texas A & M University Press, Austin, TX.

Vallet, O. (1998) Le football entre religion et politique, in P. Boniface (ed.), *Geopolitique du Football*, Editions Complexe.

Van Miert, K. (1997) Speech to the European Sport Forum, 27 November, http://europa.eu.int:80/en/comm/dg10/sport/nl/bnews5.html.

Wachtmeister, A.M. (1998) 'Broadcasting of Sport Events and Competition Law', Competition Policy Newsletter DG IV, no. 2.

Walvin, J. (1994) *The People's Game*, Mainstream, Edinburgh, UK.

4
Hearts, Minds and the Restrictive Practices Court

Stefan Szymanski

Imperial College Management School, London

1. Introduction

In footballing terms, the Office of Fair Trading (OFT) lost 5–1. Under the 1976 Restrictive Trade Practice Act (RTPA), the OFT can ask the Restrictive Practices Court to decide on whether a restrictive agreement between business organisations operates in the "public interest". When such cases come to court, the OFT on one side presents arguments as to why an agreement in question operates against the public interest, and the companies involved (the respondents) explain why it does not. In 1996 the OFT referred to the Restrictive Practices Court three agreements entered into between the Premier League and its member clubs, British Sky Broadcasting (Sky) and the BBC. These were

(a) Rule D.7.3 of the Premier League rule book that requires any club wishing to broadcast a match to obtain permission from the Premier League Board.
(b) Clause 2.2 of the broadcasting contract between the Premier League and Sky that gives Sky the exclusive right to broadcast 60 matches.
(c) Clause 2.3 of the broadcasting contract between the Premier League and the BBC that gives the BBC the exclusive right to broadcast a highlights programme (*Match of the Day*).

In practice, any request by a club under rule D.7.3 is refused as a consequence of the exclusive broadcasting agreements. The OFT claimed

---

I am grateful to Steve Ross, Martin Cave, Daniel Beard and Jon Turner for helpful comments. The views expressed, however, are entirely my own.

these agreements operated against the public interest because they restricted consumer choice to only 60 televised matches when in practice there would be considerable demand to watch the remaining other matches (currently 320 in a season). The OFT also argued that restricting choice raised the price of the rights by creating an artificial scarcity. Lastly the OFT argued that exclusivity restricted competition among broadcasters, since Premier League football is an important driver of demand for pay-TV services using new technologies.

The court ruled that the restrictions as a whole do operate in the public interest. The court identified five specific and substantial benefits flowing from the agreements:

The ability to market the Championship as a whole, not just parts of it	1–0
The ability to spend on players and stadia	2–0
The ability to share TV income fairly	3–0
The ability to subsidise non-Premier League football	4–0
The maintenance of competition in broadcasting	5–0

If one is charitable one might say that the OFT scored one goal:

The agreements did place some restriction on consumer choice	5–1

Overall the judgement represents a fairly thoroughgoing victory for the Premier League, Sky and the BBC.

In the rest of this chapter I will give my views as to how the OFT came to lose. I must at this stage declare an interest, since I was employed by the OFT in the case to analyse issues of football economics and appeared as an expert witness for the OFT on those issues. In my analysis I will concentrate mainly on the football issues as distinct from those issues relating to competition in the broadcasting market. These are dealt with by Martin Cave (the OFT's expert witness on broadcasting) in a complementary paper (2000, chapter 22).

My argument is that the OFT lost for two reasons. In legal terms, the OFT lost on a technicality. The judgement states the court must under the terms of the RTPA evaluate the benefits flowing from the agreements in comparison to a world where there existed no broadcasting restrictions of any kind. This, it was admitted on all sides, would lead to chaos. The court rejected the argument of the OFT that the relevant comparison was with a world where some restrictions exist, but do not have the adverse consequences identified by the OFT and recognised by the court. The current law is to be replaced on March 1st 2000 by a new

Competition Act whose interpretation may be more in line with the OFT's approach to the Premier League case. Having lost the away leg, the OFT might do better with the home advantage.

The second reason for the OFT's heavy defeat was the almost complete absence of any support for its action among the wider public. In particular, a number of football supporters' associations and most members of the Football Task Force as well as a majority of journalists in the national press argued that a victory for the OFT would not be in the interests of the game. Apart from the representatives of Premier League clubs and broadcasters who appeared as witnesses in the case the Premier League was able to produce a whole string of independent witnesses to support its case including Graham Bean, then chairman of the Football Supporters' Association, David Mellor, Chairman of the Football Task Force, David Elleray, the well-known referee, Bryon Butler, the journalist and even Kenneth Clarke, former Chancellor of the Exchequer. Such widespread support, coming as it did from those who might be thought to be the very consumers whom the OFT was trying to defend, clearly influenced the court's decision. However, in supporting the Premier League, many of these individuals expressed strong reservations about the way football has developed in recent years. Many expressed regrets about the commercialisation of the game and indicated support for root-and-branch reform of the game.

In Section 2 I will discuss the legal and economic reasoning that underlay the court's ruling, and in Section 3 I will discuss in more detail the tensions underlying the qualified endorsement of the Premier League by the supporters.

2.   The reasoning behind the Restrictive Practices Court judgement

The essence of the RTPA is the balancing of benefits and detriments arising from a particular set of restrictions, to determine the public interest. In the Premier League case the court decided that the five benefits mentioned above outweighed the three detriments which the court said could reasonably be said to exist (the three can more easily be treated as one, namely, the restriction of choice implied in the limitation on broadcasting).

The pivotal issue in the case turned out to be the way in which the balancing act is to be conducted. To say that a benefit arises from a restriction the court has to imagine what the world would be like if the restriction were removed. If the alleged benefit could still be produced in a world without the restriction, then the benefit cannot reasonably be said to be caused by the restriction. The court took a firm view on the limits to its imagination. "What the court has to compare is, on the one hand, a world in which the relevant restriction exists and is given effect to and, on the other hand, a world in which no restriction at all is accepted" (Ferris 1999 p. 136). In particular this would mean comparing the current state of affairs with one in which Rule D.7.3 was "abrogated and not replaced" (Ferris 1999 p. 139).

What this meant in practice was that if Rule D.7.3 were struck down by the court no collective agreement of any kind among the clubs to sell broadcast rights in the UK could be legally enforced. For instance if the clubs agreed to sell a package of 60 live matches over the season, to provide a broadcaster with a coherent series of broadcasts, then there would be nothing to stop a club offering to sell any of its matches that were part of the package to another broadcaster. Obviously no broadcaster would be prepared to pay very much for a package of matches that might end up being simultaneously broadcast on other channels. In all probability collective packages would not be sold in such a world.

It was as a result of this reasoning that the court identified its five benefits. For example, it is clear that many consumers would like to see not just one-off matches in the Premier League but a whole sequence of matches, following the ups and downs of the Championship leading to the end-of-season climax. Many of these people would be "floating voters", not committed to any particular team but interested in the competition as a whole. If the existing rules were abrogated and not replaced, it is hard to imagine a package of matches that a single broadcaster would be willing or able to provide. Not only would broadcasters be wary of buying rights to individual matches over which they did not hold an exclusive right, but the clubs themselves might sell their own exclusive packages (e.g. a club channel) so that certain clubs could be not covered at all in any collective package. It would be hard to imagine an attractive package that completely excluded, say, Manchester United.

This comparison was made even less attractive by the court's view that in the absence of Rule D.7.3 the court could not reasonably speculate on who might actually own the broadcast rights to individual matches. The court viewed a regime of "individual selling", the state of the world that would ensue on abolishing Rule D.7.3, as operating through "a series of trilateral deals between home and visiting clubs and particular broadcasters" (Judgement p. 101).

This was not the comparison which the OFT had in mind. It argued that the only obstacle to a new set of agreements which preserved any benefits found in the current arrangements, while enhancing consumer choice, would in practice be the continued opposition of the OFT, and that in practice the OFT would not obstruct a reasonable arrangement. The simplest example of such an alternative arrangement would be to continue with the existing Sky contract for 60 matches while permitting any remaining matches to be sold individually by the clubs. The current contract effectively gives Sky the first option on all the 380 matches played in a season – it can select any 60 subject to providing at least 6 weeks notice of the matches it intends to broadcast. Presently, when Sky does not exercise its option no one else can buy the rights instead. If Rule D.7.3 were rewritten so that clubs could not broadcast matches without prior permission of the Premier League, *but such permission could not be refused for matches not taken up under the option contract*, the most likely outcome would be that Sky or another broadcaster would be prepared to buy the option contract, while the remaining games could be sold on an individual basis or broadcast on club channels. The option contract would most likely be worth less to most broadcasters than the current contract, but this would also mean that a terrestrial broadcaster might be able to afford to compete, with obvious benefits to viewers, or the subscription for such a package on pay TV could be lower reflecting the lower cost of acquiring the rights. The main beneficiaries would probably be those fans interested in watching a club channel, mostly those committed fans who either could not afford a season ticket or were unable to travel to away matches.

Clearly, if one compares the existing arrangements with the kind of alternative world envisaged by the OFT the former yield far fewer benefits than they appear to generate when the alternative is the kind of chaotic world imagined by the court. From the legal point of view what matters here is what the law requires the court to imagine, and the court made clear its opinion. However, from a practical point of view it seems obvious that one should compare the current arrangements to the kind of regime that might actually exist in practice (indeed this is standard, applied by, inter alia, the US Supreme Court and the European Court of Justice). The chaotic world would not be likely to occur simply for the reason that all the parties to the case, including the OFT, said they would not wish for such an outcome and collectively they would have had it in their power to produce an alternative. Thus the one regime that the court considered was one that was unlikely to occur in practice. The kinds of alternative regime that would be likely to occur were simply not considered, or given any weight, by the court.

If a coherent series of matches could have been produced in the alternative world, then the existing arrangements produced no benefit on this count, removing entirely one of the five specific and substantial benefits identified by the court. As far as the remaining four are concerned, the effect of considering a plausible alternative world would not have eliminated entirely the benefits perceived by the court, but would have substantially reduced them in size. For example, in the chaotic world the income generated by TV contracts would have been substantially lower since broadcasters would have been unwilling to pay much for products (matches) that might end up being sold again by someone else. Furthermore, putting together a package of matches on the basis of tripartite agreements for every single match might be difficult and it might prove impossible to create attractive packages. With much less income there would be much less to spend on players and stadia, spending which the court considered to be an unmitigated benefit. In a more plausible alternative world the clubs might still generate less income than under the existing package, because there would be some competition between the clubs for the sale of rights, but the fall of income would be much less precipitous because it would still be possible to put together attractive packages.

The court also held that the best way to redistribute income is through collective packages. The existing agreements allocate the income from the collectively negotiated contracts on the basis of 50% allocated on an equal share to each club, 25% on the basis of merit (league position) and 25% in proportion to the number of televised appearances. If a collective package were still sold, then it would continue to be possible to redistribute income from this source (as well as redistributing income in other ways such as gate sharing and levies that have traditionally been employed in football). Finally, the court held that the Premier League would be much less likely to subsidise non-PL football if its collective-broadcasting income were lost. If the loss were less substantial in the real world, the potential loss of subsidy would also be smaller.

When the 1998 Competition Act replaces the RTPA on March 1st 2000 the OFT will be able to challenge restrictive agreements on the same basis as under European law. The Competition Act was modelled on Articles 85 and 86 of the Treaty of Rome (now Articles 81 and 82 of the Treaty of Amsterdam). The article that relates to restrictive agreements is rather different from the RTPA. It prohibits agreements between undertakings, unless such agreements provide benefits for the consumers *and are indispensable for the attainment of these benefits*. Indispensability implies that the same effect could not be achieved by a less restrictive set of agreements, rather than in the absence of any agreements at all. While not impossible, it seems much less likely that Premier League agreements would pass the test of indispensability. Whether or not the OFT does choose to challenge the broadcasting arrangements of the Premier League in 2000, it is widely agreed that the new Competition Act provides a much sounder basis for dealing with restrictive agreements. Indeed, this seems to have been the view of the court, which spoke at one point about "anomalies" created by the RTPA: "We think that these are the inevitable consequence of an attempt to promote competition by striking down commercial provisions which have to be identified by applying the highly technical provisions of the 1976 Act. No doubt this was one of the reasons why Parliament has now repealed the 1976 Act."

3. The fans

Few of those who applauded the outcome of the case were interested in the highly technical procedure that led to the court's decision. As far as they were concerned, the decision was victory for common sense, and that was all that mattered. The views expressed by the Football Task Force seem representative of a broad stream of opinion on this issue. Set up by the Labour government, it includes representatives not only from the Premier League and the Football League, but also from the Professional Footballers Association (PFA), the Sports Council, the League Managers Association, the Association of Premier League and Football League Referees and Linesmen, the Football Supporters Association, the National Federation of Football Supporters Clubs, the Disabled Supporters Association, the local government and the Commission for Racial Equality as well as Rogan Taylor of Liverpool University's Football Research Unit. One might have expected that such a disparate group of interests would find it hard to agree on anything, but in fact they managed to produce a unanimous denunciation of the OFT. In its report, "Investing in the Community", coincidentally published the day before the RTP court hearings began, it declared: "The Football Task Force is united in the belief that this outcome [victory for the OFT] would have a negative impact on English football." David Mellor QC, chairman of the Task Force, was even more direct and described the OFT's approach as "fat-headed".

The Task Force assumed that, had the court agreed with the OFT, it would have meant individual selling of *all* matches, rather than the ability to sell matches individually that had not already been sold through collective agreements. The Task Force argued against the OFT on two counts. Starting from the premise that there would be no collective income left to share out, they argued that if the OFT won its case "there is a strong chance that it would spell the end of re-distribution of income within football".

Second, they argued that clubs in the Football League might face bankruptcy because (a) there would be less Premier League income available as subsidies and (b) income from Football League collective agreements would also disappear. This second point seems completely erroneous since the Football League had been specifically left out of the OFT's reference, because the income generated by and the level of interest in live Football League matches was not great enough to warrant a challenge on grounds of the public interest. Thus Football League clubs would have become relatively better off compared to Premier League clubs whose TV income would be expected to fall somewhat.

As far as subsidies are concerned, the Premier League has since 1997 paid £20m per year to the Football League clubs for player development, equivalent to £280,000 per club (compared to an average turnover in 1998 of £7.3m for First Division clubs, £2.8m for Second Division clubs and £1.1m for Third Division clubs). Clearly such a subsidy could in some instances provide a substantial boost to some clubs. A further £5m a year goes to the Football Trust (although some of this may be retained for ground developments at Wimbledon and Southampton). Furthermore, the court pointed out that the Premier League has received far more in subsidy from the Football Trust (£88.5m) than the £12.7m it has far paid out. The Premier League also pays £7.5m a year to the PFA.

Perhaps more importantly, Richard Scudamore, then Chief Executive of the Football League and at the time of writing (9/8/99) expected to be appointed Chief Executive of the Premier League, stated in evidence to the court that the two Leagues were interested in jointly negotiating a broadcasting contract and sharing the income. If all Premier League matches had to be sold individually, a joint contract would no longer have been possible.

Once it is agreed that redistribution would end and smaller clubs would go bankrupt as a result of a ruling in favour of the OFT, it is not hard to reach the conclusion that it would be bad for football. However, even if the decision of the court had prevented any collective selling of Premier League rights, there are grounds for caution about the Football Task Force's conclusions.

First, it seems unlikely that redistribution would end if there were no collective sale of broadcast rights. Redistribution takes place in professional team sports because all the teams perceive that it is in their collective interests to ensure a degree of competitive balance. Where the players are hired in a competitive market each player attracts a salary that reflects his talents. Sharing income can promote competitive balance by equalising the purchasing power of the clubs. As long as shared resources are used to buy players (rather than to pay dividends to shareholders) redistribution will tend to create a balanced competition, and therefore a more interesting competition. The clubs support redistribution not out of their goodwill, but because of their regard for their own self-interest. During the case, all the club representatives that gave evidence were asked in court whether or not they would support income redistribution if collective selling of broadcast rights ended, and every one said that he personally would support it. If all the Premier League clubs supported redistribution then it would surely come to pass, and in fact under Premier League rules, a redistribution scheme would require the support of only 13 clubs to become compulsory.

Whether or not redistribution were to occur, it is wrong to exaggerate the benefits of income equality among the clubs. One of the notable features of the development of football over the last 30 years has been the growing inequality between the clubs. At every level the income gap has widened. For example, in 1967, compared to a fourth division club an average first division club generated nearly four times as much income, a second division club over twice as much and a third division club around 60% more. In 1997, compared to an average third division club, an average Premier League club generated 21 times the income, a first division club five times the income and a second division club more than double. At every level of the game, both within and between divisions, inequality has grown. The foundation of the Premier League has not stopped this trend. In the last year of the old First Division, Tottenham generated the largest turnover of any club (£19.3m), nearly six times as much as Coventry with the lowest turnover. In 1997, Manchester United generated an income of £88m, almost ten times as much as Southampton on the lowest income. Yet, despite this, the Premier League has been a success and top-division football in England has enjoyed unprecedented popularity. Match attendance has grown fairly consistently in all four divisions over the last ten years. If competitive balance were so critical to creating an attractive competition, we should have seen a declining interest in recent years, not the growing interest we have actually witnessed.

The second reason for being cautious about accepting the Task Force's apocalyptic scenario is that the Football League clubs would be unlikely to be bankrupted even if they received smaller subsidies from the Premier League. Football clubs are businesses, and have been so for over a century. They pay wages to players to entertain fans, who provide the club with income through ticket purchases and related expenditures. If clubs obtain income from an additional source such as a subsidy they may increase their expenditure on players. If the subsidy is withdrawn and the expenditure on players is maintained then the club may be bankrupted. But the directors of the company would be negligent if they allowed this to happen. Responsible directors would ensure that expenditure on players fell so as to bring expenditure in line with income. The highly publicised cases of club bankruptcy in recent times have had more to do with irresponsible behaviour on the part of club directors, in part fuelled by the lure of Premier League TV money, rather than inequality in income distribution.

Of course, many fans would argue that even if the loss of subsidies did not lead to bankruptcy, it would be regrettable if clubs in the lower divisions were less able to finance investment in players and therefore to compete with the Premier League teams. However, this view arises from a fallacy. If my team suffers a loss of income while the income of all the other clubs remains unchanged, then my team is disadvantaged. But if all the clubs suffer an equal loss of income, then no one team is disadvantaged relative to another. Assuming that the effect of lost income would be greater for the Premier League clubs than for the Football League clubs (since over 90% of the money goes to Premier League clubs), the relative position of the Football League clubs would actually improve.

The losers, of course would be the players, whose salaries would fall because there would be less money available to pay them. Partly this would make England less attractive to foreign stars. This argument was endorsed by the court but notably omitted by the Task Force, since most fans realise that for every £1m spent on attracting international talent, £10m has gone on paying the same old players more money.

In many ways this was the real issue in the case, at least from the footballing point of view. The spiralling cost of watching football, either at the ground or on TV, has financed staggering increases in the salaries of players. Whether one grudges the players their salaries or not, there is no obvious reason why clubs should be permitted to enter into restrictive agreements that simply have the consequence of fuelling player wage inflation. While it was reasonable for the clubs and the administrators to defend the positions that they have created for themselves, it is regrettable that so many of those who claim to represent the fans have refused to acknowledge the underlying economics of the situation. Many of these individuals bemoan the increasing cost of going to matches and the fact that many traditional fans have been priced out of the grounds. Some argue that player salaries are unreasonable and should be capped or taxed, or shared out in some other way, for the greater good.

Yet, had the OFT won its case, both the cost of watching football and player salaries would have been likely to fall. If clubs could sell individual matches not selected for a collective deal, there would certainly be more broadcasters and there would follow some competition on price, and possibly even a return of top-division live football to terrestrial TV. At the grounds, some clubs already discount tickets for matches broadcast live, and if more matches were broadcast this discounting would become more widespread. One wonders why supporter groups placed so little value on this probable effect, particularly given the fact that so many matches are sold out and tickets are so expensive. One reason may be that most of the supporter groups represent fans actually going to the matches. In many case fans who attend matches despise those who stay at home to watch, and certainly do not think that the interests of such people should be given any weight. "Couch potatoes" do not appear to have voice in football. This is unfortunate, given that, depending on the match, there are as many as 20 million couch potatoes in the UK interested in football.

Perhaps a second reason for the Task Force's view was that many of the supporter groups want a far more wide-ranging restructuring of football. Many of these groups have been calling for a regulator. For example Adam Brown, a member of the Task Force and member of the Football Supporters' Association, drafted a proposal to create a "semi independent regulator" who would "establish a code of conduct for football clubs; establish binding rules for clubs; set performance targets for football clubs on a variety of issues...call any club to account at any time for alleged breaches of the code or rules; gain access to any evidence from clubs, including financial and ticket records; carry out spot checks, issue reports on the performance of clubs in relation to the code of conduct and make recommendations, in conjunction with the clubs, for any failure to meet standards; undertake a series of measures where the regulator has the power to enforce rules, including imposition of new club governance structures, fines and points deductions" (Brown, 1999, p. 79).

These concerns go well beyond the notion of maintaining free and fair competition between the clubs. Because the OFT is only concerned with competition issues, rather than root-and-branch reform, many fans saw its action as at best irrelevant to the main agenda. The problem with this approach is that no government is ever likely to impose a regime as draconian as that suggested by Brown and others on what is, after all, a branch of the entertainment industry. Brown's catalogue of functions and powers is reminiscent of the kind of wartime restraints imposed on essential national industries. Even during the Second World War, when every aspect of national life was closely regulated, football was largely left to devise its own way of contributing to the war effort [Inglis (1988) provides an interesting description of wartime conditions]. It hardly seems credible that such an approach would prove acceptable in peace time.

The justification for regulatory intervention usually rests on one of three supports:

(i)   Natural monopoly
(ii) Income redistribution
(iii) Asymmetric information

Asymmetric information refers to the situation where consumers have much less information about what they are buying than the sellers – as in the case of misselling of pensions. This problem does not seem to have any relevance to football.

Regulation for the purposes of income redistribution has been advocated by many fans. One justification for providing a national health service and a free education system is that if consumers had to pay out of their own pockets, the poor might not be able to afford a reasonable standard of either service. Public provision through taxation is thus seen as an acceptable method of income redistribution. Many people argue that football should be treated in the same way, keeping ticket prices down so the poor can afford to attend matches. There are dangers in extending what may be a reasonable principle too far. Football is a form of entertainment rather than an essential service like health or education. It would seem ludicrous if the government tried to regulate the prices of the many forms of entertainment available, on income redistribution grounds. If the government believes that income redistribution is desirable it can achieve its aims more easily through the tax system. In the cases of health and education there is a concern that redistribution through the tax system might still lead to a situation where not enough is spent on the "merit" services. It is hard to see how this argument extends to football.

Natural monopoly is a situation where competition is not feasible since only one firm can reasonably supply the market. In most cases this is on the grounds of cost (e.g. water, electricity). Economic regulation prevents the firm from exploiting consumers, by restricting the prices that can be charged. Some have tried to apply the natural monopoly argument to football but there are several problems with this approach. A football club such as Manchester United is not a monopoly on the grounds of cost, but because to a true United fan no other team is an acceptable substitute. Yet there is unquestionably competition among football clubs, and while committed fans may have unswerving loyalty, every club has to compete at the margin to attract floating voters and new fans entering the market. It makes no more sense to treat Manchester United as a monopoly than it does to treat the soft drink Coca-Cola as a monopoly. The Coca-Cola Corporation has only faced competition policy attention as it has acquired rival soft drinks such as Dr. Peppers, just as Manchester United would not be allowed to buy up all the other teams in the Premier League.

All those who support the natural-monopoly argument should also be concerned about the broadcasting arrangements since this amounts to a collection of monopolies acting in concert. However, this point does not appear to have been appreciated by any of those opposing the OFT on behalf of the fans. In any case, as long as the clubs are viewed as competitors, what is required is to ensure that competition is effective.

4. Conclusions

The direct cause of the OFT's defeat in Restrictive Practices Court was a technicality involving the way in which the court evaluated the benefits derived under the current regime. The court held that the only yardstick of comparison was a world in which no restrictions whatever existed on the broadcasting of matches. Had the OFT known before the case began that the court would apply this standard it would, in all likelihood, have dropped the case. What the OFT envisaged was an alternative, less restrictive, set of arrangements that would preserve some collective selling while permitting the individual sale of club matches not selected for the collective package. The consequence of a ruling in favour of such an arrangement would have been to increase the number of matches available for broadcast and therefore to increase consumer choice.

Some commentators have argued that this outcome is likely in any case because of the development of broadcasting technologies such as digital TV which will enlarge broadcasting capacity so as to make services such as dedicated club channels more attractive. While this may be true, it is already clear that the technology has developed more slowly in the UK than in other countries such as France, Italy and Spain, and that in the absence of competition the incentives to innovate are likely to be dulled.

The broadcasting arrangements may become more liberal in future because of the desire of the clubs to stave off further intervention from the competition authorities. Under the new Competition Act the OFT may choose to challenge the restrictions again, particularly since the standard of comparison required would be more likely to produce the result the OFT wanted. Furthermore, there have already been some indications that the competition authorities in Brussels are concerned about the anti-competitive structure of football broadcasting and could challenge the Premier League on its arrangements. These threats may provoke the clubs to widen access to broadcast matches.

If that were to happen, it should be welcomed by supporter groups. More generally, supporter might be better served if their representatives recognised the contribution of competition policy. Once it is accepted that football is not going to become a nationalised industry, or a closely regulated utility like water or electricity, it becomes clear that the supporters' main allies are the competition authorities. The aim of competition policy is to prevent the exploitation of consumers either through the abuse of market power and a dominant position or through restrictive agreements among competitors. Although the competition authorities need to recognise the peculiar economics of sport that can make activities such as income sharing prorather than anti-competitive, their role is ultimately to ensure full and fair competition. Competition is the best defence for the fan from increasing prices and restricted access to the game they love.

This defence cannot operate without the support of the fans. Part of the reason why the OFT lost in court is that is was not perceived to have any supporters among the fans, many of whom were prepared to testify in favour of the Premier League. In the long term, competition authorities can have little effect if they are not perceived to command public support. Of course, it may be that the OFT was wrong and that fans are better served by cosy deals entered into by the commercial directors of the clubs and the broadcasting executives. However, this does not sound like the typical opinion voiced by representatives of the fans. In the Manchester United/BSkyB takeover and the subsequent MMC inquiry, the fans took the opposite view from that of the clubs (the Premier League took no view and Arsenal, Leeds, Newcastle, Southampton and Tottenham all supported the deal; no Premier League club publicly opposed the deal). When the next Premier League broadcasting deal is announced everyone will be able to take a clearer view of the impact of the current selling arrangements. If the OFT is right, the deal will signal yet further increases in the price of watching football and continued limitations on the access to broadcast matches.

References

Brown, A. (1999) Thinking the unthinkable or playing the game? in S. Hamil, J. Michie & C. Oughton (eds), *The Business of Football*, Mainstream Publishing, Edinburgh, UK.

Cave, M. (2000) Football rights and competition in broad casting, in S. Hamil, J. Michie, C. Oughton & S. Warby (eds), *Football in the Digital Age*, Mainstream Publishing, Edinburgh, UK.

Ferris, J. (1999) Restrictive Practices Court Judgement, 28 July.

Inglis, S. (1988) *League Football and the Men Who Made It*, Collins Willow, London.

5

Broadcasting, Attendance and the Inefficiency of Cartels

David Forrest[a], Rob Simmons[b] and Stefan Szymanski[c]

[a]*School of Accounting, Economics and Management Science, University of Salford, UK*
[b]*Department of Economics, The Management School, Lancaster University, UK*
[c]*Tanaka Business School, Imperial College London*

Abstract

The English Premier League is a cartel of soccer teams that collectively sells the rights to broadcast its matches. Despite considerable demand for their product from broadcasters, the clubs agreed to sell only a small fraction of the broadcast rights (60 out of 380 matches played each season between 1992 and 2001). The clubs have explained this reluctance by claiming that increased broadcasting would reduce attendance at matches and therefore reduce cartel income. However, this chapter produces detailed econometric evidence to show that broadcasting has a negligible effect on attendance and that additional broadcast fees would be likely to exceed any plausible opportunity cost. The chapter concludes that a more likely explanation for the reluctance to market their rights is the failure of the cartel to reach agreement on compensation for individual teams.

Keywords: Attendance, broadcasting, cartels, football, inefficiency

I. Introduction

'it is desirable to limit the number of matches which are televised live because excessive live broadcasting of football would be likely to reduce attendances'

> FA Premier League, Statement of Case, Restrictive Practices Court, 1999.

We are grateful to Bob Rothschild and two anonymous referees for helpful comments on an earlier draft. We also acknowledge comments from Participants at the International Association of Sports Economists, Neuchâtel, 2003.

A typical cartel sets out to maximise the joint profits of its members. Most industrial countries have adopted antitrust laws prohibiting cartel-like behaviour because of the adverse consequences for social welfare of monopolistic behaviour. However, a cartel is more complex than a monopoly. To achieve joint profit maximisation members of a cartel must reach agreement among themselves, and if they fail to reach an agreement consistent with joint profit maximisation the consequences of this may be even more adverse for social welfare than a simple monopoly.[1] This chapter illustrates that argument using the case of the English Premier League, a collection of soccer (henceforth football) teams that agree, *inter alia*, to jointly market their television broadcast rights.

In 1995 the Office of Fair Trading (OFT) challenged the collective selling arrangements of the Premier League. One important reason for the challenge was the excessive restriction on output imposed by the agreement: between 1993 and 2001 an average of only 60 of the 380 Premier League matches played each season were broadcast. The Premier League claimed that if clubs were free to sell their broadcast rights individually they would attempt to sell them for all or nearly all of the matches played, and that this would lead to a significant reduction in attendance at matches themselves. Expert witnesses for both sides debated at great length the econometric evidence on this point, but in the end the court accepted the position of the OFT, and indeed previous research on the impact of broadcasting on match attendance, that this effect would not be such as to have a significantly adverse effect on the clubs (see Restrictive Practices Court (1999), paras 222–229). In this chapter we produce detailed econometric evidence to demonstrate that broadcasting of Premier League matches has had a negligible effect on attendance.

However, this leaves a puzzle. The Premier League itself could have sold more matches, collectively, and the broadcaster, Sky, would have paid more had it been able to acquire this additional programming material. So why, if the robust statistical evidence shows that there will be little cost in terms of attendance, has the Premier League not chosen to sell more matches?

We consider a model of cartel decision making in which it can be rational for clubs to restrict the number of broadcasts below the revenue maximising level. If the opportunity cost to each team of a live broadcast is private information then it is straightforward to show that a contract to broadcast all league matches may violate incentive compatibility constraints. As a result the incentive-compatible equilibrium may involve showing only the matches of the low-cost team. This situation seems to approximate the Premier League contracts agreed in 1992 and 1997, which allowed for the broadcasting of fewer than 20% of all matches, the majority of which involved the larger clubs whose matches have typically been played at or close to capacity. The latest Premier League contract, implemented from the 2004/05 season, provides for 138 matches to be broadcast (see Harbord and Szymanski, 2004).

The chapter is set out as follows: Section 2 reviews English Premier League broadcasting arrangements, Section 3 details our econometric evidence and Section 4 introduces a model that could account for the relatively small number of matches broadcast in England. Section 5 concludes the chapter.

II.   Football on TV in England

1.   BskyB's broadcasting contract

Prior to the formation of the Premier League in 1992, the main competition in England was the Football League which comprised 92 clubs in four divisions, with promotion and relegation to facilitate team mobility. In 1991, with big clubs increasingly frustrated by the small size of receipts from sale of broadcasting rights to terrestrial channels, the Football Association (the FA, the governing body of football in England) proposed the creation of an autonomous "Premier League" as the top tier of English football. This was able to negotiate its own TV contract and retain all of the proceeds (Football Association, 1991). Although autonomous, the Premier League retained promotion from and relegation to the Football League, which reverted to three divisions, also linked by promotion and relegation, with Division One as its top tier.

Having obtained the approval of the FA, the Premier League proceeded to negotiate a £170m four-year contract with pay TV satellite broadcaster BSkyB (Sky) to show 60 live matches per season (out of 462 played in the first three seasons and 380 thereafter) – amounting to less than 15% of all matches played. Under the terms of the agreement each club was to be broadcast at least three times in each season. This part of the agreement seems to have been at the insistence of the smaller clubs which, having formerly opposed all live TV broadcasting, now felt that at least some exposure was desirable. Within these limits Sky could choose which games to show, and not surprisingly tended to weight its selections towards the more popular and successful clubs, notably Manchester United, during this period. The Premier League also introduced a novel distribution formula – allocating 50% of the TV income as an equal share to all member clubs, 25% as a performance bonus and 25% as facility fees paid out to the teams actually broadcast.[2] Some of the broadcasting rules (revenue sharing, 'parachute' payments to compensate relegated clubs) were designed to facilitate agreement between clubs on terms of collective selling. Restrictions on timing of broadcast matches were imposed to eliminate potentially adverse impacts on gate attendance from simultaneous scheduling of televised and non-televised fixtures.

In 1997 a second contract was agreed with Sky for the greatly increased sum of £670m over four years but on essentially the same conditions. About this time the UK competition authorities began to question these arrangements, in particular Rule D.7.3 of the Premier League rulebook that required any club wishing to broadcast a match to obtain permission from the Premier League board. In practice such permission has never been granted, even though only a small fraction of all matches are shown. When this came to court the Premier League based its defence on a number of factors, but one on which they placed great emphasis was the need to protect live gate attendance both of those matches that are being broadcast and of other matches that might be played at the same time. Section 3 deals with our estimates of these two effects for Premier League and Football League clubs over the first six seasons of the Premier League's existence.

2. Previous economic studies

The impact of live broadcasting on match attendance is part of a wider question, namely, the determinants of the demand for sporting events. Demand studies in association football have tended to focus on impacts of playing success of home team, market size, income and uncertainty of outcome (Dobson and Goddard, 2001; Garcia and Rodriguez, 2002).[3] The impact of outcome uncertainty is a significant issue in the present context because collective selling has also been justified on the grounds of this promoting competitive balance.

Studies of the impact of broadcasting on attendance in the UK have exploited the fact that only a fraction of games have been shown live. The first published studies coincided with the creation of the Premier League. Kuypers (1995) and Baimbridge *et al.* (1996) both estimated the effect of broadcasting on Premier League match attendance for the season 1993/94. Kuypers found no significant impact of live TV broadcast on attendance.[4]

Kuypers' preferred model was a Tobit regression to take account of the number of sell-out games, which were about 10% of the total in 1993/94. Collection of this data required particular care since many grounds were under reconstruction during the early 1990s and therefore capacity could vary from match to match.

Baimbridge *et al.* distinguished between matches played on a Sunday and on a Monday night. In the former case, they found no statistically significant effect, while Monday night games were found to have 15% lower attendance. However, they did not estimate a separate coefficient for weekday matches not broadcast. If all mid-week matches had lower attendance, then broadcasting itself would not be the cause of lower attendance, although to the extent that broadcasting causes matches to be rescheduled to weekdays it would still be the indirect cause.[5]

A recent paper by Garcia and Rodriguez (2002) examines the effect of broadcasting on attendance in the top division of Spanish football between 1992 and 1996, during which period about 20% of matches were broadcast. They find that broadcasting had a very large and statistically significant negative effect on attendance by non–season ticket holders.

III.   Estimated effects

3.1.   Data

For our study we have gathered data on all league matches played in the six seasons from 1992/93 to 1997/98 in the Premier League and the Football League First Division. For each match the data provide information on the league position of the home team and the away team (an indicator of the attractiveness and competitive balance of the teams), the day and the date the match was played (to account for day-of-week, holiday and time-of-season effects), the distance of the away team ground from the home team ground (as an indicator of the cost of travelling for away fans) and whether or not the match was broadcast live. In addition, for First Division matches another variable was included to allow for the impact of broadcasting "European" matches[6] involving top English teams at the same time as the First Division match was played. Matches in the European competitions are invariably midweek and attract a large national TV audience. They seldom clash with Premier League matches, but the greater number of teams in the First Division dictates that more games have to be scheduled for midweek.

Thus, using the Football League sample, we are able to investigate not only the effect of own broadcasting of a match on attendance but also the effect of broadcasting of other attractive matches on attendance at a game.

2. Empirical model

The empirical model broadly follows the specification of match day attendances in the literature (see *inter alia* Forrest and Simmons, 2002; Garcia and Rodriguez, 2002) and seeks to identify and quantify the impact of broadcasting on gate attendance in a robust, parsimonious form. (Log) home attendance in game *i* is a function of home and away team quality, last season's average league attendance for home and away teams, distance between locations of home and away teams and various dummies to capture scheduling on days of week, months of year and, of course, broadcasting of games. Team quality is proxied by league position and its square, to allow for non-linearity. The role of last season's average attendance is to control for persistent, core support from loyal fans who are relatively impervious to variations in team quality.[7] Greater distance between locations of home and away teams is likely to deter attendance due both to increased travel costs and to reduced intensity of fan rivalry. Although parsimonious, our model specification is still rich in detail and is more sophisticated than most previous attendance–demand studies. Definition of variables are shown in Table 5.1.[8]

Table 5.1   Definition of variables

Continuous variables	Definition
LOG ATTEND	Log home team attendance
LOG ATTEND LAST	Log average home attendance of home team in previous season
LOG ATTEND LAST AWAY	Log average home attendance of away team in previous season
HOME POS, HOME POS SQ	League position (immediately prior to the match) of home team, and its square
AWAY POS, AWAY POS SQ	League position (immediately prior to the match) of away team, and its square
DISTANCE, DISTANCE SQ	Distance between teams' grounds (miles) and its square
PROM ATT	Log average home attendance of home team in previous season, if promoted
PROM ATT AWAY	Log average home attendance of away team in previous season, if promoted

Table 5.1   (Continued)

Continuous variables	Definition
Dummy variables used in Premiership and Division 1 regressions	
BANK HOL	Bank holiday
Dummy variables used in Premiership regression	
PROM	Home team promoted from Division 1
PROM AWAY	Away team promoted from Division 1
WEEKDAY	Game played on any day excluding Saturday or Sunday, not televised
APRILMAY	Game played in April or May
SKYSUN 1992/93 to 1997/98	Game played on Sunday, televised by BSkyB in the particular season identified (1992/93, 1993/94 to 1997/98)
SKYMON 1992/93 to 1997/98	Game played on Monday, televised by BSkyB in the particular season identified
MIDWEEK	Game, not televised, not a bank holiday, played on Tuesday, Wednesday or Thursday
Dummy variables used in Division 1 regression	
DERBY 1992/93, DERBY 1993/94, DERBY 1994/95, DERBY 1995/96, DERBY 1996/97, DERBY 1997/98	Game between two locally proximate sides, regarded by fans as of intense local interest, not televised in 1992/93 to 1997/98
ITVDERBY 1992/93, ITVDERBY 1993/94, ITVDERBY 1994/95, ITVDERBY 1995/96, ITVDERBY 1996/97	Local derby match televised by ITV
SKYDERBY 1996/97, SKYDERBY 1997/98	Local derby match televised by BskyB
ITV 1992/93, ITV 1993/94, ITV 1994/95, ITV 1995/96, ITV 1996/97	Game televised by ITV in 1992/93, 1993/94, 1994/95, 1995/96, 1996/97
SKYFRI 1996/97, SKYFRI 1997/98	Game televised by BSkyB on Friday in 1996/97, 1997/98
SKYSUN 1996/97, SKYSUN 1997/98	Game televised by BSkyB on Sunday in 1996/97, 1997/98
EUROTV 1992/93, EUROTV 1993/94, EUROTV 1994/95, EUROTV 1995/96, EUROTV 1996/97, EUROTV 1997/98	Game played at same time as a European club tournament match which was televised on Tuesday, Wednesday or Thursday

MONTUES	Game played on Monday or Tuesday, not bank holiday, no competing European televised match
WEDTHUR	Game played on Wednesday or Thursday, not bank holiday, no competing European televised match

3. Premier league attendance estimates 1992/93 to 1997/98

The impacts of broadcasting on football attendance are derived using dummy variables to capture particular matches that are televised. In the case of the Premier League, over the sample period, one broadcaster (BSkyB) was the sole provider; its live games were usually scheduled for Sunday afternoons and Monday evenings. In Division 1, terrestrial regional ITV companies showed live games from 1992/93 to 1996/97, mainly on a Sunday afternoon, but BSkyB bought rights for coverage in 1996/97 and 1997/98. BSkyB Division 1 games were typically televised on Friday evenings. The empirical estimates distinguish between day of transmission and identity of broadcaster.

Table 5.2 reports results of a Tobit regression for Premier League games from 1992/93 to 1997/98, with log attendance as the dependent variable, while Table 5.3 reports results of a fixed-effects OLS regression for First Division games over the same period. Tobit estimation for Premiership games is necessary since many games have attendances at or close to capacity. Retaining these observations for OLS estimation would result in biased coefficients, whereas deleting the censored observations involves loss of information.

Table 5.2 Tobit regression of Premiership attendance

Variable	Marginal effect	*p*-value
HOME POS	−0.0204	0.000
HOME POS SQ	0.00059	0.000
AWAY POS	−0.0168	0.000
AWAY POS SQ	0.00049	0.000
LOG ATTEND LAST	1.725	0.000
LOG ATTEND LAST AWAY	0.582	0.000
PROM ATT	−0.150	0.008
PROM ATT AWAY	−0.0098	0.808
PROM	2.130	0.000
PROM AWAY	0.501	0.174
DIST	−0.0012	0.000
DIST SQ	4.02E−06	0.000
BANK HOL	0.0219	0.111

120

Table 5.2 (Continued)

Variable	Marginal effect	*p*-value
SKYSUN 1992/93	−0.0328	0.152
SKYSUN 1993/94	−0.0378	0.178
SKYSUN 1994/95	−0.0911	0.016
SKYSUN 1995/96	−0.0926	0.004
SKYSUN 1996/97	−0.0063	0.814
SKYSUN 1997/98	−0.0910	0.001
SKYMON 1992/93	0.0698	0.018
SKYMON 1993/94	−0.0122	0.713
SKYMON 1994/95	−0.0389	0.146
SKYMON 1995/96	−0.0550	0.195
SKYMON 1996/97	−0.129	0.003
SKYMON 1997/98	−0.0196	0.635
WEEKDAY	−0.0600	0.000
APRILMAY	0.0576	0.000
Season effects	Yes (significant)	
Log likelihood	33.42	
Sigma	73.56	0.018

Dependent variable is log attendance, $n = 2526$, 688 right-censored observations.

Table 5.3 OLS regression of Division 1 attendance with fixed home team effects

Variable	Coefficient	*p*-value
HOME POS	−0.0272	0.000
HOME POS SQ	0.00067	0.000
AWAY POS	−0.0210	0.000
AWAY POS SQ	0.00067	0.000
LOG ATTEND LAST	0.414	0.000
LOG ATTEND LAST AWAY	0.204	0.000
PROM ATTEND	−0.078	0.049
PROM ATTEND AWAY	−0.127	0.000
PROM	0.837	0.022
PROM AWAY	1.192	0.000
DISTANCE	−0.00178	0.000
DISTANCE SQ	3.85E−06	0.000
DERBY 1992/93	0.127	0.050
DERBY 1993/94	0.199	0.000
DERBY 1994/95	0.182	0.013
DERBY 1995/96	0.152	0.010
DERBY 1996/97	0.147	0.061
DERBY 1997/98	0.054	0.379
ITVDERBY 1992/93	0.033	0.673

ITVDERBY 1993/94	−0.052	0.536
ITVDERBY 1994/95	0.079	0.423
ITVDERBY 1995/96	0.138	0.062
ITVDERBY 1996/97	0.058	0.667
SKYDERBY 1996/97	0.223	0.015
SKYDERBY 1997/98	0.088	0.301
ITV 1992/93	−0.164	0.000
ITV 1993/94	−0.173	0.000
ITV 1994/95	−0.103	0.001
ITV 1995/96	−0.152	0.000
ITV 1996/97	0.213	0.006
SKYFRI 1996/97	−0.125	0.008
SKYSUN 1996/97	−0.157	0.002
SKYFRI 1997/98	−0.079	0.114
SKYSUN 1997/98	−0.095	0.019
EUROTV 1992/93	−0.154	0.000
EUROTV 1993/94	−0.154	0.000
EUROTV 1994/95	−0.082	0.018
EUROTV 1995/96	−0.084	0.017
EUROTV 1996/97	−0.117	0.000
EUROTV 1997/98	−0.129	0.000
MONTUES	−0.025	0.015
WEDTHUR	−0.075	0.000
BANK HOL	0.142	0.000
MARCH	0.027	0.007
APRIL	0.082	0.000
MAY	0.254	0.000
Season dummies	Yes (significant)	
Fraction of variance due to fixed effects	0.669	
R^2 (within)	0.452	

Dependent variable is log attendance, $n = 3312$

In the Tobit estimation of attendance demand, the upper limit of attendance should not be published stadium capacity. Capacity figures are notoriously unreliable since they are not regularly updated to allow for increases in attendance brought about by introduction of flexible seating accommodation or decreases in attendance occasioned by police controls on crowd segregation (where sections of stands may be left vacant on police advice) and "no-shows". In our sample, only 38 out of 2526 matches were strictly capacity constrained, based on official capacity figures, but casual observation suggests a much greater number of "sell-out" games. We decided to adopt an arbitrary capacity limit of 95% of "official" ground capacity to allow for the frequently observed reduction in capacity due to crowd segregation imposed by police. This gives 688 censored observations, representing 27% of the full sample. Our results are robust to stricter censoring at 90% of capacity. Second, we face the econometric problem, noted above, that non-normality of residuals will lead to inconsistent estimates. Tests for normality of residuals from the regression in Table 5.2 could not reject non-normality.

The reported estimates are corrected for identifiable multiplicative hetero-scedasticity in previous season average attendances for home and away teams.

The control variables in the Tobit estimates perform much as expected. Home teams with higher average home attendance in the previous season generate higher match day attendances this season. Likewise, but to a smaller extent, away teams which had higher average home attendance last season draw bigger crowds for the home teams this season. Positions are ranked from 1 (top) to 20 or 22. In 1995/96 the Premiership was reduced in size from 22 to 20 clubs. An improvement in either home or away team position raises attendance at a decreasing rate, with the turning point occurring outside the sample range. Longer distances between team locations deter attendance demand, again in a non-linear manner. It appears that fixtures scheduled in April or May, as the season reaches its climax, attract higher crowds, as do games played on bank holidays. Fixtures played on weekdays, but not televised, attract lower crowds, *ceteris paribus*. The season dummies do not reveal a rising time trend although the 1995/96 and 1997/98 seasons stand out as featuring generally high attendances. Overall, the inconsistent pattern of coefficients on the broadcasting dummies suggests that there is no clear evidence that broadcasting mattered for attendances in the Premier League over our sample period.

In estimating the impact of broadcasting on attendance, it is difficult to separate the impact of scheduling on, say, Monday nights from the impact of broadcasting *per se*. Over our sample period, the vast majority of games were played on Saturday afternoons. It would appear reasonable, therefore, to base our estimate of loss of gate attendance from broadcasting upon the assumption that the alternative scheduling of a televised fixture would be on Saturday. We would expect that *either* a Sunday afternoon *or* a Monday night televised match would have been scheduled for Saturday afternoon in the absence of broadcasting. Our estimates show that the impacts of Sunday broadcasting of Premiership matches on attendances are significantly negative, *compared to regular Saturday games*, in the 1994/95, 1995/96 and 1997/98 seasons only, with marginal effects of 9.11%, 9.26% and 9.10%, respectively. The impact of Monday night broadcasting is significantly negative in the 1996/97 season only with a marginal effect of 12.91%.

As part of the Premier League's contract with the sole broadcaster of live games (BSkyB), clubs taking part in televised matches received a "facility fee" as compensation for potential loss of gate revenue through lower attendance and related inconveniences such as reduced sponsorship, advertising income and catering and merchandise sales.

Our model fails to deliver any significant adverse impact of broadcasting on gate attendance, from either Sunday afternoon or Monday night television scheduling, in the 1993/94 season. In this season, and also for the 1992/93 season, clubs hosting televised matches actually generated a pure financial gain since their attendances were not harmed and they still received the match facility fee. Table 5.4 reports revenue losses from broadcasting for a typical Premier League club, based upon average admission prices reported by Dobson and Goddard (2001) and average Saturday attendances from our own sample. Losses of gate revenue are estimated as £25,648, £32,784 and £39,646 for games scheduled for Sunday broadcasting in seasons 1994/95, 1995/96 and 1997/98, and £54,523 for games scheduled for Monday broadcasting in the 1996/97 season. Even this last figure is well below the level of facility fee. It should be borne in mind that most teams would expect to have games scheduled both on Sunday and on Monday, and the net gain in revenue increases since there is no season for which our model reveals adverse impacts on attendance from broadcasting on both days.

A newly negotiated broadcasting contract between the Premier League and BSkyB was implemented for the 1997/98 season. This provided for a much larger facility fee (£269,551 per game for each participant) and the gains in revenue from broadcasting a particular game were consequently much larger (£229,905) according to our estimates.

Of course, the comparison of revenues with and without broadcasting ought to address some wider issues. For example, advertising (such as boards around the pitch) and sponsorship income will rise when games

Table 5.4 Estimated losses of gate revenue for Premier League clubs from BSkyB broadcasts

	Average ticket price	Average attendance	Loss in revenue
1994/95 Sundays	£11.58	24,339	£25,648
1995/96 Sundays	£12.74	27,670	£32,784
1996/97 Mondays	£14.59	28.969	£54,523
1997/98 Sundays	£14.99	29,064	£39,646

are televised. On the other hand, TV scheduling is not fully known before the season starts and the uncertainty attached to visits from the broadcasters, and associated rescheduling of matches, will adversely affect both season ticket prices and the number of season tickets sold. Should attendances fall at televised games, advertising income may be adversely affected if cameras show sections of empty seats.

Despite these qualifications, the conclusion from our analysis must be that the opportunity cost of broadcasting of Premiership games is small or even zero. In all seasons our results show that the facility fee more than outweighs any loss of gate revenue from broadcasting.[9]

4.   Football league Division 1 estimates

In Division 1, regional ITV companies showed live games from 1992/93 to 1996/97, mainly on Sunday afternoons, but BSkyB bought rights for coverage in 1996/97 and 1997/98. BSkyB Division 1 games were typically televised on Friday evenings. The empirical estimates reported in Table 5.3 distinguish between day of transmission and identity of broadcaster.

For Division 1, empirical analysis is simplified by the much lower frequency of sell-out games. On the other hand, greater complexity is introduced by the co-existence of satellite and terrestrial (ITV) broadcasters in the live coverage of these games. We proceed to show OLS estimates in Table 5.3, with fixed effects for home teams. The same controls for home and away positions and for distance are used as for the Premier League analysis. For Division 1 games we add further controls for local 'derby' matches (games between local rivals), both televised and not televised.[10] Coverage of Division 1 games by ITV was undertaken by regional TV companies within the ITV network, always on Sunday afternoon, and tended to involve a disproportionate number of local derby matches in order to generate viewer interest at the local level. We also adopt controls for appearances of European tournament matches on television in mid week.

The impacts of the control variables have the expected signs with coefficients of similar order of magnitude to the marginal effects obtained from the Tobit estimates shown for the Premier League. Home and away teams with higher league positions draw bigger crowds; home and away teams with larger average support last season generate higher attendances and longer distance between teams deters attendance. Games played on Monday or Tuesday evening suffer a 2.5% reduction in attendance compared to non-televised weekend games while those played on Wednesday and Thursday evenings suffer a 7.5% loss in attendance. Games played in the latter part of the season (March, April and May) add to the attendance, as the season's denouement approaches, with a particularly large boost to attendance (25.4%) from games played at the very end of the season in May.

With 24 teams in Division 1, as opposed to 20 in the Premiership, the fixture schedule is more crowded and there is a greater incidence of mid-week evening matches. Clubs find it impossible to avoid scheduling Division 1 games in mid week when Premier League teams are competing in televised European matches. Our model shows the impact of scheduling alongside televised European fixtures to be between 8% and 16%. The loss of revenue from such games is not compensated for in any way, as Premier League teams receiving broadcast income from, say, the European Champions' League are under no obligation to share revenues from this source to indirectly affected clubs in lower divisions.

Matches televised on the terrestrial ITV channels are associated with substantial (more than 10%) percentage reductions in attendance, given control variables, in every season. Significant reductions are also obtained for broadcasting of Division 1 matches by BSkyB in the 1996/97 and 1997/98 seasons, except for Friday evening broadcasts in 1997/98. However, although the coefficients are somewhat larger than the comparable marginal effects for the Premier League Tobit model, attendances and ticket prices are typically lower in Division 1. Hence, as Table 5.5 shows, the estimated revenue losses for an average Division 1 club are between £7,000 and £14,000 with a notable outlier of £21,341 for ITV transmission in 1996/97.

Matches between locally proximate teams tend to generate more intense rivalry and fan interest than do other matches. The impact of televising these local derby matches can be assessed against non-televised local derby matches using a set of Wald tests. These revealed

Table 5.5 Estimated losses of gate revenue for First Division clubs from ITV and BSkyB broadcasts

	Average ticket price	Average attendance	Loss in revenue
1992/93 ITV	£6.21	10,677	£10,874
1993/94 ITV	£6.64	11,761	£13,510
1994/95 ITV	£6.46	10,820	£ 7,199
1995/96 ITV	£7.62	11,944	£13,833
1996/97 ITV	£7.96	12,587	£21,341
1996/97 BSkyB Friday	£7.96	12,587	£12,524
1996/97 BSkyB Sunday	£7.96	12,587	£15,730
1997/98 BSkyB Friday	£9.30	15,137	£11,121
1997/98 BSkyB Sunday	£9.30	15,137	£13,374

no significant difference in attendance as between non-televised and televised matches, with the single exception of ITV coverage in 1993/94.

Table V reports revenue losses from televising games which are not designated as local derby matches. Unfortunately, facility fees for televised Division 1 games are not published. We conjecture that (a) facility fees for Division 1 games were considerably less than those for Premier League games and (b) facility fees for Division 1 games broadcast by ITV were considerably less than facility fees for BSkyB broadcasts. If Football League clubs were alarmed by losses of revenue when ITV broadcast Division 1 matches, such fears would have been alleviated by the new BSkyB arrangements from the 1996/97 season and the eventual demise of ITV broadcasting of matches at this level. A useful benchmark for assessing losses from broadcasting of Division 1 games by BSkyB can be discerned from its rugby league contract in operation at the same time. A typical rugby league match commanded a facility fee of £20,000 in the 1994/95 season according to Carmichael *et al.* (1999). We would expect the facility fee for Division 1 soccer matches to be greater than this, reflecting larger audience ratings, but £20,000 is a useful benchmark with which to compare estimates of gate revenue losses. We can see from Table V that revenue losses from BSkyB broadcasts of Division 1 games, for an average club, are estimated from our model to be less than the conservative £20,000 figure assessed as compensation.

IV. A model of collective selling with unobservable costs

On the basis of our regression results for Premier League and Football League Division 1 attendances, and subsequent computations of revenue losses, the opportunity cost of broadcasting games is small or even zero relative to the value of broadcast contracts, particularly in the case of the Premier League. If the opportunity cost of broadcasting additional matches is less than the expected gain in broadcast income, but the clubs choose not to make the matches available to broadcasters, we need to find some explanation for this apparent inefficiency.

We now develop a simple model of collective selling where the opportunity cost to each club (in terms of foregone attendance revenues) is unobservable to show how it might be impossible to ensure that the optimal number of matches are broadcast under the type of contract adopted by the Premier League.[11] In particular, we consider a sharing rule that captures the three main elements of the Premier League broadcast contracts (25% allocated to facility fees, 50% divided on an equal share basis and 25% allocated according to league performance).[12]

The basic insight we are highlighting is that this kind of sharing agreement may not be incentive compatible under some circumstances and therefore can result in fewer than the joint profit maximising number of matches being broadcast.

Of course, the nature of the Premier League rules governing collective selling may prevent joint profit maximisation for reasons other than restrictions on the number of games broadcast. Our focus is on the welfare impacts of restrictions on the number of games shown, as a quantity restriction. We show that imposition of such restrictions will lower joint revenues, compared to the outcome without such restrictions. The requirement for the cartel to satisfy incentive compatibility for its membership will lead to a departure from the (constrained) joint profit maximising outcome. In the context of established cartel theory, this is a logical and unsurprising result.

We suppose there are only two clubs and two matches played, one at the ground of each club. Suppose that each match is equally valuable when broadcast, and that the value of each match (V) is independent of whether the other is broadcast. This value is taken as pre-determined as part of the terms of the broadcasting agreement. The opportunity cost may take one of two values c^h and c^l ($c^h > c^l$) both of which are private information (or too costly to verify). The terms of the collective broadcasting contract are assumed to specify that if a match is broadcast the home team will receive $(2 + p)V/4 - c^l$ where the facility fee and equal share are each $V/4$ and p is the probability that the home team whose match is broadcast wins the prize. The probability of the visiting team winning the prize is $1 - p$, and it will receive $(2 - p)V/4$.

The game involves several stages:

Stage 1: Teams decide whether or not to enter into a collective deal
Stage 2: Teams observe their private signal (c^h or c^l)
Stage 3: Given a collective deal, a contract is signed contingent on the announcement of opportunity cost types
Stage 4: Each team announces its cost type
Stage 5: Broadcasts are scheduled and teams receive compensation contingent on their announcement

If individual contracts could be signed, stages 3–5 would be irrelevant. We assume that competition would induce each team to sell its rights at its opportunity cost if there is no collective deal – although, rather extreme, this enables us to normalise the outside opportunity to zero. The value of collective selling may lie in the exclusivity that the broadcaster achieves by buying the championship (as was argued by the broadcaster Sky during the Premier League case). There is no reason to suppose that under individual selling, teams will fail to realise profitable opportunities where they exist.

We need to consider three cases:

Case (a) If $V - c^h > 0$ – Broadcasting all matches is always optimal
Case (b) If $V - c^l > 0 > V - c^h$ – Broadcasting of the c^l match only is optimal
Case (c) If $V - c^l < 0$ – Broadcasting of any match is never optimal

We assume that the values of c^h and c^l are common knowledge, and therefore we can dispose of case (c) immediately since neither team has any interest in offering matches for broadcast. Case (a) is straightforward.

i.   Case (a)

A contract must be both individually rational and incentive compatible. Incentive compatibility requires that there is no gain to misrepresenting your type:

$$t^{ll} - c^l \geq t^{hl} - c^l \tag{1a}$$

$$t^{lh} - c^l \geq t^{hh} - c^l \tag{2a}$$

$$t^{hl} - c^h \geq t^{ll} - c^h \tag{3a}$$

$$t^{hh} - c^h \geq t^{lh} - c^h \tag{4a}$$

where t is payment to each team contingent on its report and the report of the other team, and the first superscript term refers to a team's own report and the second to the report of the other team. Thus equation (1a) says that when both teams have a low opportunity cost it must be more profitable for a team to report its low opportunity cost than report untruthfully that it is high.

Individual rationality requires that the expected gain from reporting your type (truthfully) is positive:

$$t^{ll} - c^l \geq 0 \tag{5a}$$

$$t^{lh} - c^l \geq 0 \tag{6a}$$

$$t^{hl} - c^h \geq 0 \tag{7a}$$

$$t^{hh} - c^h \geq 0 \tag{8a}$$

PROPOSITION 1. When all matches are to be broadcast there is no incentive to misreport the cost parameter. However, the expected return may be less than opportunity cost of broadcasting, so that the Premier League allocation rule may not be individually rational and may therefore fail to implement the first best.

Proof. Since both matches are shown the broadcast revenue is $2V$. Since both matches are always broadcast regardless of a team's report, the payments under the Premier League contract are each $(3 + 2p)V/4$ for the home team and $(5 - 2p)V/4$ for the visiting team, regardless of either team's report. The incentive compatibility constraints are reduced to strict equalities and are therefore satisfied. The individual rationality constraints (5a)–(8a) may all be violated. For example, if we consider the home team, whose probability of winning is p, even though by assumption $V > c^h$, this does not guarantee that $(3 + 2p)V/4 > c^h$. If $p = 0$ the constraint may not be met for the visiting team whose probability of winning is $1 - p$. Hence, only if the league is perfectly balanced ($p = 1/2$) will constraints be met for both teams. $\square$

   This suggests that teams with low expectations of receiving a share of the performance-related element may prefer not to participate in the collective broadcast agreement. However, in practice, the Premier League teams *did* agree to a contract formula in 1992 and have stuck to it ever since.

ii. Case (b)

In case (a) it was always optimal to broadcast all matches. Under case (b) it is only optimal to broadcast the matches of teams with a low opportunity cost. This means that teams announcing c^h should not be scheduled, and the total revenue from broadcasting depends on the announcements of the two teams. If both announce c^l then both matches should be shown and revenue is the same as in case (a). If both announce c^h neither match should be shown and broadcasting revenue is zero. If one announces c^h and the other c^l, then only the match of the latter team will be shown.

This alters the incentive compatibility constraints, which are now as follows:

$$t^{ll} - c^l \geq t^{hl} \tag{1b}$$

$$t^{lh} - c^l \geq t^{hh} \tag{2b}$$

$$t^{hl} \geq t^{ll} - c^h \tag{3b}$$

$$t^{hh} \geq t^{lh} - c^h \tag{4b}$$

Of the individual rationality constraints (5a) and (6a) are unchanged, but the remaining two are altered due to the fact that an announcement c^h means no broadcasting. Thus in sum we have

$$t^{ll} - c^l \geq 0 \tag{5b}$$

$$t^{lh} - c^l \geq 0 \tag{6b}$$

$$t^{hl} \geq 0 \tag{7b}$$

$$t^{hh} \geq 0 \tag{8b}$$

PROPOSITION 2.   In case (b) The Premier League contract cannot guarantee to implement the first best broadcasting schedule.

Proof. Consider again the home team whose probability of winning is $1/2$. Constraints (1a) and (1b) each require that the payoff to a team if it reports that its opportunity cost is low is greater than the payoff to announcing a high opportunity cost. In both cases this reduces to the condition that $(2+p) V/4 - c^l \geq 0$, which cannot be guaranteed. Suppose for example that $p = 0$, then V, the value of the broadcast right, must equal at least twice the opportunity cost of broadcasting. In other words, a team with a low opportunity cost may refuse to enter a collective broadcast contract because the private gain for the team does not exceed the opportunity cost, even though it would be efficient from the cartel's perspective that the match be shown. Once again, only if the probability of winning is $1/2$ will the incentive compatibility constraints be met for both teams.   □

This result is reminiscent of the cartel literature where firms can collude over output but the marginal cost of each firm is private information. In such situations side payments are necessary from low-marginal-cost firms to persuade high-marginal-cost firms to reveal their cost truthfully (see Vives, 1999, pp. 264–273). Cramton and Palfrey (1990) show that, where firms do not know rivals' costs initially, incentives for truthful cost revelation tend to break down in cartels bigger than five in number.

Clearly, if facility fees could be differentiated according to the type of match, an efficient broadcasting arrangement would be possible – but this would require agreement on the opportunity cost of matches. Reaching this kind of agreement would be extremely difficult. In general, the bigger teams might be thought to have a higher opportunity cost, since they have bigger crowds and might lose more gate revenue. On the other hand, the bigger clubs also tend to be sold out more often, and may therefore have a lower opportunity cost. There are no simple indicators of opportunity cost.

In the example above no match is broadcast even though it would be profitable to broadcast one or both matches. In a more general setting with several teams it might be the case that it would not be profitable to broadcast some matches, that some matches would be profitable to broadcast but would not be made available and that some matches would have a value large enough relative to their private opportunity cost that they would be broadcast.

Our model offers a particular coordination cost explanation for the fact that only 60 Premier League games were broadcast by BSkyB under the terms of its agreement with the Premier League. A rival explanation for the low number of games broadcast is simply that the marginal value of an extra game to the media provider was too small.[13] If marginal broadcaster valuation of an extra game is less than the value of lost gate attendance then it is jointly rational for both broadcaster and clubs for this extra game to be excluded from broadcast.

We can estimate the broadcast value of matches as follows. Between 1997/98 and 2000/01 BSkyB paid £670m for the rights to broadcast an average of 60 games per season, out of a total of 380, over the contract period. This was equivalent to £167.5m per season. In the 1997/98 season, the last in our data set, total TV audience was 87.5m for 61 games (Monopolies and Mergers Commission, 1999). This converts to a valuation of £1.91 per viewer. Assuming that the matches selected by BSkyB in 1997/98 were the games with highest audience potential, we can estimate an audience equation determined by rank of audience (1 as top to 61 as bottom):

$$Log(audience) = 14.058 - 0.017\ Rank\ (audience) \qquad R^2 = 0.95$$

$$(0.19)\ (0.0005)\ (standard\ errors\ in\ parentheses)$$

This equation reveals that each successively less popular match broadcast attracts an audience 1.7% smaller than the next highest game in the rankings. We can use the estimated equation to predict the audience, and estimated audience value, of each game in the full set of 380 games played in the 1997/98 season (Table 5.6).

Based on our figures, 260 out of 380 Premier League games had an audience valuation greater than our maximum estimate of the value of lost gate equal to £54,523. Our estimates of audience value in Table 5.6 are lower bound figures since many of the games not shown may have been more popular than some of the games broadcast. Hence, we conclude that the marginal valuation of an extra game to the broadcaster was sufficient for it to be worthwhile from the point of view of Premier League clubs collectively to permit broadcasting, beyond the 60 scheduled games in 1997/98, since this extra provision would have been revenue-augmenting for the clubs concerned and the broadcaster.

Table 5.6 Estimated audience and audience value from Premier League games 1997/98

Game number	Estimated audience £000	Estimated value £000
62	808	1546
70	705	1349
80	594	1138
90	501	960
100	423	809
125	276	529
150	180	345
175	118	226
200	77	147
225	50	96
250	33	63
275	21	41
300	14	27
325	9	18
350	6	11
380	4	7

V.   Policy implications and conclusions

This chapter has focused on a cartel decision-making problem: how to market and share the income from the broadcast rights to matches played in a professional sports league. It was motivated by the observation that broadcasters have been willing to pay to broadcast many more English Premier League matches than they have in fact been allowed to broadcast over the last decade. The chapter examined the econometric evidence behind the cartel's claim that broadcasting would not in fact increase profits because of the opportunity cost implied when fans stay at home to watch the match on TV rather than pay to attend at the stadium. We found that this argument had no statistical basis, and that any small loss of attendance implied by our estimates would have been more than compensated by the large facility fees paid by broadcasters to the home team for every match.

We have advanced one explanation for this puzzle, namely that cartels are seldom able to negotiate efficient joint profit maximising decisions. We have provided an example where a revenue sharing agreement of the type used by the English Premier League might result in some matches failing to be broadcast even though efficiency would require them to be broadcast. A more complex contract could ensure that an efficient number of matches are broadcast, but the cartel may not be able to reach agreement on this. It is striking that the Premier League was unable to reach an agreement to broadcast any significantly greater number of matches from its foundation in 1992 until 2001. Following a series of exchanges with the European football leagues, the European Commission launched an investigation into collective selling of football broadcast rights in England and Germany in December 2002 (Harbord and Szymanski, 2004). This pressure may be partly responsible for the increase in number of games broadcast to 106 games under the 2001 contract and then to 138 games per season under the contract implemented from 2004/05. This still leaves two-thirds of games unavailable for broadcast. Even though BSkyB has agreed to sub-contract eight games to free-to-air broadcasters from 2004/05 it still retains a monopoly position as England's provider of live football broadcasting.

Notes

1. There is a substantial literature on the possibility of implementing efficient cartel agreements (see, e.g. Roberts, 1985; Cramton and Palfrey, 1990). It is also possible that an inefficient cartel agreement works in the interests of consumers, but that is not the case in the example advanced in this chapter.

2. The precise formula for the performance element is $V_R = \frac{n+1-R}{\sum\limits_{i=1}^{n} R_i}$ where V_R is the prize awarded to the Rth ranked team and n is the number of teams in the League. There is also a 'parachute' payment made to teams relegated from the Premier League in the previous season, that is deducted from the equal-share portion.

3. There is a substantial literature in the US on the effect of broadcasting on attendance at major league sports (e.g. Putsis and Sen, 2000; Siegfried and Hinshaw, 1979).

4. One weakness in Kuypers' specification is that it did not differentiate broadcast matches by day of the week. About half the games in that season were shown on a Sunday afternoon, while most of the remainder were broadcast on Monday nights (an innovation borrowed from the US). One might reasonably expect the effect on attendance *via* displacement from live TV to be greater for a Monday night game, since fans may find it difficult to get to the game after work, compared to a Sunday.

5. The econometric modelling of Baimbridge *et al.* was less sophisticated than that of Kuypers. They only estimated an OLS equation, implicitly ignoring capacity restraints, and reported few diagnostic tests.

6. The Champions' League, UEFA Cup and Cup Winners' Cup competitions.

7. This core support will depend, *inter alia*, on income and population; inclusion of last season's attendance allows for the influence of these omitted variables.

8. We experimented with, but dropped, a set of variables to capture weather, such as temperature and dummy variables to denote freezing conditions, rainfall and sunshine. Coefficients on weather variables were not statistically significant, at 5%, either directly or through interaction with TV coverage.

9. Our econometric analysis of Premier League attendances relates to the first two contracts with BSkyB under which the average number of broadcast games per season was 60. The 2001–04 contract provided for 106 games per season, with 46 on BSkyB's pay-per-view channel, while the 2004–07 contract provides for 138 games per season, with 8 sub-contracted to free-to-air broadcasters (Harbord and Szymanski, 2004). The impact of increased broadcasting of Premier League matches on gate attendance merits further research.

10. The list of local derby matches inevitably contains an element of subjectivity. Such matches cannot simply be defined by distance, which is already controlled for. In East Anglia, for example, Ipswich against Norwich counts as a local derby because these are the only two clubs in a sparsely populated region and notwithstanding that the two grounds are over 40 miles apart. But Bury against Stockport in Greater Manchester is not deemed to be a local derby even though the distance between them is only 15 miles; there are many clubs within the Manchester conurbation and these two are on opposite sides of the conurbation with no tradition of rivalry.

11. This idea was first explored informally in Ross and Szymanski (2000).

12. In fact the contract also allocates some of the money for administrative expenses, some for payments outside the League and some to teams that were relegated over the previous two seasons. We abstract from these complications.
13. We are grateful to an anonymous referee for highlighting this point.

References

Baimbridge, M., Cameron, S., & Dawson, P. (1996) Satellite television and the demand for football: A whole new ball game, *Scottish Journal of Political Economy*, 43, pp. 317–333.

Carmichael, F., Millington, J., & Simmons, R. (1999) Elasticity of demand for rugby league attendances and the impact of BSkyB, *Applied Economics Letters*, 6, pp. 797–800.

Cramton, P. & Palfrey, T. (1990) Cartel enforcement with uncertainty about costs, *International Economic Review*, 31, pp. 17–47.

Dobson, S. & Goddard, J. (2001) *The Economics of Football*, Cambridge University Press, Cambridge, UK.

Football Association (1991) *The Blueprint for the Future of Football*, Football Association, London.

Forrest, D. & Simmons, R. (2002) Outcome uncertainty and attendance demand in sport: The case of English Soccer, *Journal of the Royal Statistical Society, Series D (The Statistician)*, 51, pp. 229–241.

Garcia, J. & Rodriguez, P. (2002) The determinants of football match attendance revisited: Empirical evidence from the Spanish football league, *Journal of Sports Economics*, 3, pp. 18–38.

Harbord, D. & Szymanski, S. (2004) Football trials, forthcoming, *European Competition Law Review*, February 2004, 2, pp. 114–119.

Kuypers, T. J., (1995) The beautiful game? An econometric study of why people watch english football. Discussion Papers in Economics, University College London, pp. 96–101.

Monopolies and Mergers Commission (1999) *British Sky Broadcasting Group plc and Manchester United plc: A Report on the Proposed Merger*. Cmnd 4305. The Stationery Office, London.

Putsis, W. & Sen, S. (2000) Should NFL blackouts be banned? *Applied Economics*, 32, pp. 1495–1507.

Restrictive Practices Court (1999) Premier League Judgement, 28 July, 1999, E&W No. 1.

Roberts, K. (1985) Cartel behaviour and adverse selection, *Journal of Industrial Economics*, 33, pp. 401–413.

Ross, S. & Szymanski, S. (2000) Necessary restraints and inefficient monopoly sports leagues, *International Sports Law Review*, 1, pp. 27–28.

Siegfried, J. & Hinshaw, C. (1979) The effect of lifting television blackouts on professional football no-shows', *Journal of Economics and Business*, 32, pp. 1–13.

Vives, X. (1999) *Oligopoly Pricing*, MIT Press, Cambridge, MA.

6
A Market Test for Discrimination in the English Professional Soccer Leagues

Stefan Szymanski
Imperial College, London

Abstract

This chapter proposes a market test for racial discrimination in salary setting in English league soccer over the period 1978–93 using a balanced panel of 39 clubs. If there is a competitive market for the services of players, the wage bill of the club will reflect their productivity and hence the performance of the club in the league. Discrimination can be said to exist if clubs fielding an above-average proportion of black players systematically outperform clubs with a below-average proportion of black players, after one controls for the wage bill. Statistically significant evidence of discrimination in this sense is found.

I. Introduction

Statistical testing for the presence of racial discrimination remains one of the most controversial fields in economics. Discrimination in the sense of unequal pay for equal work is conventionally identified through the construction of an earnings function. This relates personal characteristics that influence productivity to earnings so that any residual

I am indebted to Michael Crick, Izzet Agoren, Lamin Sabally, Tim Kuypers, and Andrew Craven for their help in compiling the data set used in this chapter. I have benefited considerably from the advice of Ron Smith, Steve Machin and Ian Preston. I would like to thank seminar participants at Imperial College and University College London and an anonymous referee for helpful comments.

differences in the earnings of two groups can be attributed to discrimination. A fundamental criticism of this test is that omitted-variable bias may have created a mistaken impression of discrimination. If unobserved characteristics that affect productivity are correlated with group membership, it will appear that one group suffers discrimination when in fact it has systematically lower productivity (see, e.g., Heckman 1998). This chapter proposes an alternative, a "market test". There is evidence of discrimination in the market when some firms can earn systematically higher monetary profits by hiring an above-average proportion of one group of workers. An employer with a "taste for discrimination" will have a lower demand for otherwise identical workers who possess the relevant attribute [the approach here is essentially that of Becker (1957)]. If there are enough employers with a taste for discrimination, workers with this attribute will attract a lower market wage rate. Employers with a greater taste for discrimination will earn lower monetary profits than their less discriminating rivals. Lower monetary profits are compensated by higher "psychic" profits. Arrow (1973, 1998) argued that this kind of discrimination would be competed away by the market since profit maximizers will compete to obtain the services of the underpriced factor and will drive the discriminators out of the market. This is a testable hypothesis.

This chapter implements a test in the market for professional soccer players in England.[1] Soccer (association football) is the "national game" in England, and spectator interest focuses on annual league competition between established clubs. Clubs are businesses owned by shareholders and file annual accounts open to public inspection. Clubs generate income primarily from ticket sales and incur costs primarily associated with the player payroll. There is a highly competitive market for players, who are traded openly for cash. Since the early 1970s there has been a significant influx of black players into English soccer. Racial discrimination and harassment are well-documented problems in English soccer (see, e.g., Williams 1994). It has been suggested that certain clubs have at different times operated a color bar, and prejudice is believed to be widespread.[2] Nevertheless, black players now account for a significant minority (around 10%) of all players in the professional leagues.

Using a database of 39 clubs over the years 1978–93, I examine the performance of clubs on the basis of payroll costs and the proportion of all black players in league soccer employed at each club. The econometric results show that teams with a below-average proportion of black players have tended to achieve inferior playing performance compared to other teams, suggesting that discrimination both exists among club owners and has not been competed away by the market.

Section II outlines the structure of English soccer and the market for players. Section III presents a simple model of discrimination, and Section IV analyzes the presence of black players in English soccer. Section V describes the data, testing and results. Section VI discusses some robustness issues and draws some conclusions.

II. Professional English soccer and the market for players

The economics of English league soccer bear some resemblance to the economics of team sports in the United States, a subject on which there is an extensive literature [see, e.g., the review of Fort and Quirk (1995)]. From the point of view of this chapter, there are three salient features of professional league soccer in England.[3]

  i) League competition is hierarchical, with four divisions each containing around 20 teams. At the end of each season the highest-ranked teams from a lower division swap places with the worst-performing teams from the immediately senior division. There are no play-offs, and hence competition is focused simply on league ranking.[4] Redistribution of income is limited, and other measures to maintain competitive balance (e.g., draft picks or salary caps) are not used.[5]
 ii) There is a free market for players. Players are frequently traded between clubs, with more than 10% of professionals changing clubs each season. Effective freedom of contract dates from 1978.[6] There is no collective bargaining over player salaries, and there are no salary cap restrictions.
iii) The density of clubs in the United Kingdom is high, leading to greater competition among clubs for spectators and sponsorship than in the United States. For example, within 100 miles of Manchester United, currently the most popular club in the country, there are around 50 other professional soccer clubs participating in league competition.

If both player and fan markets are competitive, players will earn wages that reflect their talents, and club expenditure on players will be a fairly reliable indicator of talent. The data suggest that the English market is quite competitive. A simple regression of league rank on the club wage bill produces an R^2 of about 0.9. This relationship is

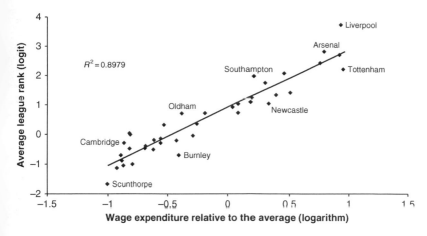

Figure 6.1 Performance and club wage bill, 1978–93

illustrated in Fig. 6.1 for my sample of 39 clubs averaged over the years 1978–93.

III.   A model of discrimination in sports leagues

Suppose that team owners maximize a utility function[7] that is a weighted average of profits (π) and the share of white players (s) in the team (reflecting a taste for discrimination). Thus the objective function for team i is given by

$$\Omega_i = \alpha s_i + (1 - \alpha)\, \pi_i. \tag{1}$$

The most important feature of equation (1) is that the owners are assumed to have a taste for discrimination represented by the proportion of "white" playing talent (t_w) in the team (discrimination is assumed to be based on the perception that a player is either black or white):

$$S_i = \frac{t_{iw}}{t_{iw} + t_{ib}}. \tag{2}$$

The taste for discrimination is defined in terms of talent rather than simply the numbers of players. Since the credit for winning is usually ascribed in proportion to the talent of the players, it is assumed that the discriminator aims to ascribe success to white playing talent.[8]

Profit depends on revenues, which are a function of playing success, and costs, which depend on the cost of playing talent:

$$\pi_i = R_i\,[w_i\,(T_i)] - c\,(s_i)\,T_i. \tag{3}$$

Sporting success (w) could be measured by the percentage of wins, championship success, or, as is usually the case in league soccer, league position. Sporting success in turn depends on the quantity of sporting talent hired by the club: $T_i \equiv t_{iw} + t_{ib}$. In line with much of the earlier literature (see, e.g., El-Hodiri and Quirk 1971; Atkinson et al. 1988), it is assumed that while talent differs according to the functions of the players, it can be aggregated across specialisations and treated as a homogeneous input. Talent is not differentiated by race or color, and no assumption is made about the actual distribution of talent between blacks and whites. I assume that revenue as a function of winning and winning as a function of talent are both strictly concave functions.

Costs are affected by a discriminatory policy. The cost of hiring a given quantity of talent will generally be greater if the owner requires that the talent hired possesses an additional characteristic. For a given intensity of discrimination (α), talent is assumed to be supplied at a constant marginal cost. The marginal cost of talent to a club depends on its owners' taste for discrimination:

$$c_i(s_i) = \begin{cases} c_{i0}[1 + (s_i - s^*)^2] & \text{if } s_i > s^* \\ c_{i0} & \text{if } \leq s^*, \end{cases} \tag{4}$$

where s^* represents the proportion of white players employed in the team beyond which the club begins to pay a premium for white talent. The value of s^* will be determined endogenously by the supply of and demand for black and white talent in the market. Owners who discriminate by hiring exclusively or predominantly white playing talent pay a premium because they are restricting themselves to a subset of the market. Discriminators also drive down the cost of playing talent to non-discriminators, who acquire a degree of monopsony power. If there is discrimination, s^* will be at least as great as the proportion of white players in the market. Owners may be able to discriminate to a limited degree without paying a premium. For example, if there are only a small number of professional black players, discriminating owners face virtually the same supply of talent as non-discriminators. However, once the supply of black talent forms a significant part of the market, discriminators will pay a premium for restricting their choice.[9] Using equations (1) – (4), we can derive first-order conditions for firm i:

$$t_{iw}: \ \alpha \frac{\partial s_i}{\partial t_{iw}} + (1-\alpha)\left(\frac{\partial R_i}{\partial w_i}\frac{\partial w_i}{\partial t_{iw}} - c_i'\frac{\partial s_i}{\partial t_{iw}}T_i - c_i\frac{\partial T_i}{\partial t_{iw}} \right) = 0 \tag{5}$$

and

$$t_{ib}: \alpha \frac{\partial s_i}{\partial t_{ib}} + (1-\alpha)\left(\frac{\partial R_i}{\partial w_i}\frac{\partial w_i}{\partial t_{ib}} - c_i'\frac{\partial s_i}{\partial t_{ib}}T_i - c_i\frac{\partial T_i}{\partial t_{ib}}\right) = 0 \qquad (6)$$

When we subtract equation (6) from equation (5), noting that

$$\frac{\partial s_i}{\partial t_{iw}} - \frac{\partial s_i}{\partial t_{ib}} = \frac{1}{T}$$

the solution for a discriminating owner ($\alpha > 0$) implies

$$t_{iw} = s^*T + \frac{\alpha}{2(1-\alpha)c_{i0}} \qquad (7)$$

In the absence of a taste for discrimination ($\alpha = 0$), the share of white playing talent in the team is indeterminate but will be no more than s^* (roughly the share of white players in the total talent represented in the league). When an owner discriminates, the share of white playing talent in the team will become significantly greater than its share in the population as a whole. But this also implies that a discriminating owner will pay a higher price per unit of talent hired.

The implication of the model is that a taste for discrimination acts like a tax on the success of the team.[10] Thus the expected performance (measured by league position) for a given level of expenditure will be worse for teams owned by discriminators than for teams owned by non-discriminators. This difference in expected performance should be detectable in a regression of performance on wage expenditure. If discrimination is the reason that some clubs hire a relatively low proportion of black players, then these clubs will have a significantly higher cost per unit of playing success than the norm. If the distribution of black players were purely random, then the expected performance of a club, after one controls for wage expenditure, would be unaffected by the color composition of the team.

IV. Black players in English soccer

The first black people to come to England were probably soldiers in the army of Julius Caesar, long before the "indigenous" Anglo-Saxon population arrived. However, the black population in England did not become a significant proportion of the total population until the 1950s. Around that time, immigrants were invited into the country by successive governments because of chronic labor shortages. Immigrants came mostly from South Asia (India, Pakistan, Bangladesh and Sri Lanka) and the Caribbean, with lesser numbers of Chinese and black Africans. According to the 1991 official census, around 900,000 people living in the United Kingdom describe themselves as black, about 1.6% of the total population.

By the 1970s there was a significant number of black professional soccer players in England. Data on black players appearing for the 39 league clubs in my sample (from a population of 92) were constructed by a painstaking analysis of player records for the period 1974–93. In 1974 there were only four black players appearing a total of 77 times for the sample clubs, whereas by 1993 there were 98 players appearing 2,033 times. Given an average squad size of around 30 players, by 1993 about 8% of all players were black. The distribution of appearances indicates marked differences between individual clubs. The lowest number of appearances (i.e., matches played by black players) for any club in the data over the entire sample period is two. Two clubs in the sample had fewer than 10 appearances by black players, and four had fewer than 100. Four clubs registered more than 1,000 appearances by black players.

To analyze player characteristics, a matching stratified sample of non-black players was assembled in which each stratum contained the same number of players with a given birth year as the black players (salary data are not available). Table 6.1 reports the mean values for selected

Table 6.1 Playing careers

	Players born 1957–74		Players born 1957–74 and having 20 or more league appearances	
	Black (1)	Non-black (2)	Black (3)	Non-black (4)
Sample size	193	193	166	115
Year born	1964.7	1964.7	1964.0	1964.3
Percentage born:				
Overseas	0.114	0.047	0.108	0.026
In the North	0.223	0.539	0.222	0.609
In the Midlands	0.207	0.150	0.204	0.130
In the South	0.464	0.264	0.476	0.235
Year playing career started	1983.7	1983.8	1983.0	1983.3
Last year of playing career	1990.0	1987.7	1990.2	1989.1

Career length (years)	6.3	3.9	7.1	5.8
Number of clubs represented	3.0	2.1	3.3	2.7
League appearances	147.6	95.4	170.6	154.8
Goals scored during playing career	25.1	11.8	29.0	19.4
Percentage who represented their country	0.358	0.228	0.386	0.293
Percentage playing in defense	0.265	0.321	0.271	0.362
Percentage playing in midfield	0.150	0.264	0.133	0.241
Percentage playing in attack	0.585	0.332	0.596	0.328
Percentage goalkeepers	0.000	0.078	0.000	0.069

Source: Hugman (1992).

characteristics. Columns 1 and 2 show the means for the entire sample, and columns 3 and 4 give the mean values for the players who made at least 20 league appearances in their career.[11] Black players enjoy greater playing longevity than non-black players: they play for more years and have more league appearances. The differences are all statistically significant at the 5% level. Black players are more likely to play in attack and less likely to play in defense than non-black players. Perhaps as a consequence they score more goals. There were no black goalkeepers in the sample.[12] Black players are more likely to represent their country (be it England or another country), an achievement that is generally associated with a higher level of playing ability. It is tempting to surmise from the table that black players possess higher ability and greater "staying power" than the average player.

V. A market test of discrimination

Given a competitive market for players, it will be possible to detect any systematic discrimination against sub-groups of professional players. Discrimination will imply that players in the sub-group command a lower market wage for their talents, and therefore teams containing an above- (below-) average proportion of such players will over- (under-) perform relative to the average. Performance is measured here by position achieved in the league, which is usually taken to be the ultimate yardstick of quality.[13] The regression model takes the following form:

$$
\begin{aligned}
p_{it} = \alpha_i + \sum_{j=1}^{3} \beta_j \mathrm{div}_{jit} + \beta_4 \left(w_{it} - \overline{w}_t \right) \\
+ \beta_5 \left(\mathrm{play}_{it} - \overline{\mathrm{play}}_t \right) + \beta_6 \left(\mathrm{black}_{it} - \overline{\mathrm{black}}_t \right)
\end{aligned}
\tag{8}
$$

This specification follows the earlier work of Szymanski and Smith (1997). The term p is position transformed into the log odds of position,[14] which gives a higher weight to progress further up the league. Aggregate wages are measured as the log difference of club wage spend to the annual average ($w_{it} - \overline{w}_t$), taken from published club accounts. The aggregate number of players used in a season relative to the average ($\mathrm{play}_{it} - \overline{\mathrm{play}}_t$) is also included since a rapid turnover of players is unsettling for team performance. Turnover usually reflects a high level of injuries sustained ("bad luck", in other words). Finally, the presence of black players in each club is measured by the percentage of total appearances by black players each season (for the sample clubs) accounted for by each club ($\mathrm{black}_{it} - \overline{\mathrm{black}}_t$).[15]

Club-specific attributes that may affect performance (e.g., culture, geography and demographics) are accounted for by fixed effects (α_i). They are eliminated in the regression by first-differencing.[16] Divisional dummies (div_{it}) control for the fact that clubs are constrained by their divisional status within each season even though they can move divisions across seasons.[17] The main results are reported in Table 6.2. Column 1 pertains to the full sample of 39 clubs over the 16 years since the establishment of free agency. Column 2 uses a sub-sample from the first eight years, and column 3, for the last eight years. Column 4 is based on a sub-sample of the 19 largest clubs in terms of average ground capacity over the sample period, and column 5 reports the estimates for the 20 smallest clubs.

Wages and the number of players used both have the right sign and are highly significant.[18] Wu–Hausman tests (using lagged wages and performance as instruments) indicated that weak exogeneity of the wage variable cannot be rejected (for column 1, $t = -1.21$). Szymanski and Smith (1997) reported a similar finding using a data set of 48 clubs over the period 1974–89. Thus we find no evidence that causation flows in the opposite direction, from position to wages rather than from wages to position. Time dummies were included in some versions but were not significant.

Table 6.2 Regression estimates: First differences with instrumental variables

	39 Clubs			19 Largest clubs,	20 Smallest clubs,
	1978–93 (1)	1978–85 (2)	1986–93 (3)	1978–93 (4)	1978–93 (5)
Observations	624	312	312	304	320
Relative wage	−0.535	−0.691	−0.557	−0.632	−0.368
bill	(0.169)	(−0.201)	(0.236)	(0.336)	(0.172)
Number of	2.067	1.704	2.323	2.257	1.885
players used	(0.190)	(0.213)	(0.331)	(0.306)	(0.205)
Share of black	−0.026	−0.014	−0.136	−0.101	−0.008
players employed	(0.011)	(0.010)	(0.049)	(0.052)	(0.007)
p-value for black player coefficient	0.021	0.166	0.005	0.049	0.247

Notes: [1] Dependent variable: Log-odds of position
[2] Robust one-step standard errors are in parentheses. The two-step procedure was inappropriate since the number of groups is relatively small. The reset test for non-linearity is insignificant in all cases. Some evidence of non-normality was found as a result of excessive kurtosis, probably caused by outliers in the data. Wu–Hausman tests indicated that all variables were pre-determined. Note that the entire data set runs from 1974 to 1903, but only the years from 1978 onward are of interest since this is the date at which free agency was introduced. This means that when one is constructing first differences, no degrees of freedom are lost. since the pre-1978 data can be used.

The variable measuring the percentage of annual appearances by black players accounted for by each club is negative and significant for the full sample. This means that a club with a higher-than-average proportion of black players would expect to achieve a systematically higher league position than the wage bill would appear to justify. This gain would be achieved at no extra financial expense. The fact that this opportunity is implied by the data suggests that a black player receives a lower return on his talents than a white player of equal ability. Columns 2 and 3 indicate that this discrimination effect is much more pronounced in the 1986–93 period than in the 1978–85 period. The small coefficient in the earlier period is probably a consequence of the small number of black players in professional soccer up to that date (about 3% of all appearances in the first period compared to around 7.5% in the second). Columns 4 and 5 indicate that the effect of appearances of black players is more pronounced in the clubs with larger ground capacities (generally the more successful clubs) than in the smaller clubs.

The cost penalty associated with a taste for discrimination depends on the overall standard of the team aimed at by the club. Discrimination is more expensive at the top end of the league than at the bottom end since the total player spend is proportionately higher. The cost also varies from year to year because of the high rate of player wage inflation. The estimates imply that a club hiring no black players would have paid a 5% premium in terms of its total wage bill to maintain any given position in the league compared to a non-discriminating team (i.e., one that hired an average number of black players). Given that a top club in 1993 had a total wage bill of around £5 million, this implies a cost penalty of around £250,000 (by 1993 the average team fielded two to three black players).[19]

VI.   Robustness and conclusions

This paper has shown that soccer clubs in England hiring a below-average proportion of black players have tended to perform worse than would have been predicted in the market. From this it can be inferred that those owners hiring a below-average proportion of black players have been discriminating, and for this they have paid a premium in the player market. This inference does not rely on the heroic assumption that all the factors that determine player productivity have been captured in the regression (as in the earnings function approach). Instead, the critical assumption is that there is an efficient market for talent.

The hypothesis of player market efficiency is supported by the evidence that such a large proportion of the variation in league performance can be attributed to wage expenditure alone. However, if other variables that might affect productivity also turned out to be significant in the regression, then the hypothesis is undermined. Experiments were carried out including variables accounting for managerial performance,[20] the proportion of players developed entirely within the club (as opposed to bought on the market) and the total number of professionals in the squad. These variables turned out to be insignificant. For example, the proportion of homegrown players in a squad was positively correlated with league performance (correlation coefficient 0.38), but once the effect of the wage bill was allowed for, clubs with a greater proportion of homegrown players did not fare significantly better than their rivals. Thus the evidence from other productivity-related variables supports the hypothesis of market efficiency.

While the evidence presented in this chapter is consistent with discrimination by owners, an alternative hypothesis is that the fans discriminate and owners are only responding to the tastes of the fans (see, e.g., Gwartney and Haworth 1974; Nardinelli and Simon 1989). This was tested by running regressions for both attendance and revenues on league performance, the proportion of black players and other relevant variables (e.g., ticket prices and success in other competitions). The proportion of black players did not significantly affect revenues or attendance, and so no evidence was found to support the hypothesis of fan discrimination [see Szymanski (1998) for further details].

The findings in this chapter are consistent with the notion that some soccer club owners indulge in what Becker described as a "taste for discrimination". As Arrow (1973) pointed out, in a competitive market, this kind of discrimination would be competed away since non-discriminatory firms would hire the black players (because they were cheaper). Such firms would be more successful than discriminating firms, and so the latter would be driven from the market; the wages of black players would be bid up and the returns to talent would be equalized. Historically there has been a very limited market for corporate control, and clubs have tended to be "hobby" businesses for wealthy businessmen. However, in recent years a market has begun to emerge. The first major club to float on the stock market was Tottenham Hotspur in 1983, followed by Manchester United in 1991. Then in 1996/97 (outside of the sample period) a further 18 clubs raised capital on the stock market in one form or another. The introduction of professional investors might lead to the elimination of discrimination in the sense used here.

The market test of discrimination is in many ways preferable to the usual earnings function approach. Its main advantage is that it is not subject to the usual omitted-variable bias problem. It is also informationally less demanding, in the sense that once wages and team (or firm) productivity are known, no other data are required. Indeed, while a detailed analysis of the characteristics of black players was performed for this chapter and contrasted with non-black players, the differences identified are not relevant to the finding of discrimination. All that is required to infer discrimination is that a team with an above-average proportion of black players would have performed better, *ceteris paribus*, than its wage bill warranted.

Notes

1. Ayres and Waldfogel (1994) applied a version of the market test to the case of bail setting in Connecticut.
2. The owner of one leading team notoriously commented that "the problem with black players is they've great pace, great athletes, love to play with the ball in front of them . . , when it's behind them it's chaos. I don't think too many of them can read the game. When you're getting into the midwinter you need a few of the hard white men to carry the athletic black players through" (quoted in the *Sunday Times*, September 15, 1991).
3. Szymanski and Kuypers (1999) provide a historical overview, and Hoehn and Szymanski (1999) survey the main differences between the organization of soccer in Europe and that of American team sports.
4. The top division seceded from the Football League in 1993 and renamed itself the Premier League but retained the promotion/relegation relationship with the Football League. Clubs also compete in knockout cup competitions, which are organized independently, including European-wide cups; however, clubs play most of their games in domestic league competition.
5. Until 1982, up to 20% of gate receipts were shared with the visiting team. Television revenue has traditionally been shared, but the sums involved did not become significant until 1993.
6. A settlement was agreed between the players' union and the League representing the clubs. As part of the settlement, a buying club was still obliged to pay a fee to the selling club proportional to the perceived market value of the player (settled by a tribunal in the case of disputes). In 1995, transfer fees for players out of contract were abolished following the Bosman judgment of the European Court of Justice (see Szymanski 1999).
7. There has been much discussion of the appropriate objective function for sports clubs in the literature. See, e.g., Fort and Quirk (1995) and Vrooman (1997) for the US view and Sloane (1971) and Cairns *et al.* (1986) for UK views.
8. I ignore the possibility' that some owners might have a taste for discrimination in favor of black players.
9. The specification of equation (4) does not allow for the possibility that there would be a cost to discriminating against white players, since such behavior is not modeled here. If two-way discrimination did occur (i.e., some owners discriminating in favor of white players and some owners discriminating against), then there would be a tendency toward segregation and the wage differential created by one-way discrimination would be reduced.
10. It has sometimes been argued that club owners maximize playing success subject to a budget constraint. It should be clear that while this formulation might yield different levels of success and profit, the implication of an increased taste for discrimination would be qualitatively the same.
11. This adjustment is made to ensure that the results do not simply reflect missing observations for black players who appeared on only a small number of occasions.
12. A number of studies, summarized by Kahn (1991), have found significant positional bias for black players in American baseball and football.

13. In English soccer, at least. League position depends on the outcome of over 40 matches over an eight-month period and therefore is likely to be a much better indicator of performance than success in cup competitions, which is significantly affected by chance events such as the luck of the draw.
14. This is $\ln[p/(93-p)]$ since there are a total of 92 professional teams in the four interlocking divisions.
15. Other variables considered for inclusion in the regression are discussed in Section VI.
16. The regressions were estimated using the DPD98 program of Arellano and Bond (1998).
17. These dummies are not reported here. The full regression results are available from the author on request.
18. Recall that better league performance leads to a smaller value of the position variable.
19. Given that by 1998 club wage bills in the top division had reached £15 million, the cost of discrimination is rising.
20. Other studies of the effect of management and coaching on team performance in English soccer have found no evidence of strong managerial effects (e.g., Audas *et al.*, 1997). Evidence of managerial effects is much stronger in the US literature (see, e.g., Scully 1994), perhaps because of the rookie draft and the more limited nature of player trading in the United States. In soccer the players themselves are able to appropriate almost all the rents that accrue to the improvement of their talent, regardless of how the improvement was achieved. Most managers see themselves simply as selectors. In the words of Johan Cruyff, one of the greatest players of all time and a manager of many years' experience, the job of the manager "is to look for good players and put together the best possible squad. If your players are better than your opponents, 90 per cent of the time you will win" (King and Kelly 1997).

References

Arellano, M. & Bond, S. (1998). "Dynamic Panel Data Estimation Using DPD98 for Gauss: A Guide for Users." Working paper, London: Inst. Fiscal Studies, 1998.

Arrow, K. J. (1973) The theory of discrimination, in O. Ashenfelter & A. Rees. (eds), *Discrimination in Labor Markets*, Princeton University Press, Princeton, NJ.

——. "What Has Economics to Say about Racial Discrimination?" *Econ. Perspectives* 12 (Spring 1998): 91–100.

Atkinson, Scott E., Stanley, Linda R., and Tschirhart, John. "Revenue Sharing as an Incentive in an Agency Problem: An Example from the National Football League." *Rand J. Econ.* 19 (Spring 1988): 27–43.

Audas, Richard, Goddard, John, and Dobson, Stephen. "Team Performance and Managerial Change in the English Football League." *Econ. Affairs* 17 (September 1997): 30–36.

Ayres, Ian, and Waldfogel, Joel. "A Market Test for Race Discrimination in Bail Setting." *Stanford Law Rev.* 46 (May 1994): 987–1047.

Becker, Gary S. *The Economics of Discrimination.* Chicago: Univ. Chicago Press, 1957.

Cairns, John, Jennett, Nicholas, and Sloane, Peter J. "The Economics of Professional Team Sports: A Survey of Theory and Evidence." *J. Econ. Studies* 13, no. 1 (1986): 1–80.

El-Hodiri, Mohamed, and Quirk, James. "An Economic Model of a Professional Sports League." *J.P.E.* 79 (November/December 1971): 1302–19.

Fort, Rodney, and Quirk, James. "Cross Subsidization, Incentives, and Outcomes in Professional Team Sports Leagues." *J. Econ. Literature* 33 (September 1995): 1265–99.

Gwartney, James, and Haworth, Charles. "Employer Costs and Discrimination: The Case of Baseball." *J.P.E.* 82 (July/August 1974): 873–81.

Heckman, James J. "Detecting Discrimination." *J. Econ. Perspectives* 12 (Spring 1998): 101–16.

Hoehn, Thomas, and Szymanski, Stefan. "The Americanization of European Football." *Econ. Policy,* no. 28 (April 1999), pp. 203–40.

Hugman, Barry J. *Football League Players Records, 1946–92.* Taunton, U.K.: Tony Williams Publications, 1992.

Kahn, Lawrence M. "Discrimination in Professional Sports: A Survey of the Literature." *Indus, and Labor Relations Rev.* 44 (April 1991): 395–418.

King, Jeff, and Kelly, John. *The Cult of the Manager.* London: Virgin Books, 1997.

Nardinelli, Clark, and Simon, Curtis. "A Direct Test of Customer Racial Discrimination." Manuscript. Clemson, S.C.: Clemson Univ., 1989.

Scully, Gerald W. "Managerial Efficiency and Survivability in Professional Team Sports." *Managerial and Decision Econ.* 15 (September–October 1994): 403–11.

Sloane, Peter J. "The Economics of Professional Football: The Football Club as a Utility Maximiser." *Scottish J. Polit. Econ.* 18 (June 1971): 121–46.

Szymanski, Stefan. "A Market Test for Discrimination in the English Professional Soccer Leagues." Discussion paper. London: Imperial Coll., Management School, 1998.

———. "The Market for Soccer Players in England after Bosnian: Winners and Losers." In *Player Market Regulation in Professional Team Sports,* edited by Stefan Késenne and Claude Jeanrenaud. Antwerp: Standaard Uitgeverij, 1999.

Szymanski, Stefan, and Kuypers, Tim. *Winners and Losers: The Business Strategy of Football.* London: Penguin Books, 1999.

Szymanski, Stefan, and Smith, Ron. "The English Football Industry: Profit, Performance and Industrial Structure." *Internat. Rev, Appl. Econ.* 11 (January 1997): 135–53.

Vrooman, John. "A Unified Theory of Capital and Labor Markets in Major League Baseball." *Southern Econ. J.* 63 (January 1997): 594–619.

Williams, John. "Lick My Boots: Racism in English Football." Manuscript. Leicester: Leicester Univ., Sir Norman Chester Centre Football Res., 1994.

7

The Financial Crisis in European Football: An Introduction

Umberto Lago[a], *Rob Simmons*[b] *and Stefan Szymanski*[c]

[a]*University of Bologna*
[b]*Lancaster University*
[c]*Imperial College London*

Abstract

Is there currently a crisis in European professional football? Surely there exists a common set of problems afflicting clubs, with negative financial implications for all. Moreover, a crisis in one large club or group of clubs threatens to damage the financial stability of other clubs. This introduction reviews the financial crises in football in several European countries, searches for common explanations of these crises, and proposes a few solutions, ranging from tighter financial regulation to the restructuring of competition, with the aim of easing the financial burden for smaller clubs in particular.

On March 12, 2004, a group of economists representing 11 of the national associations of the Union of European Football Associations (UEFA) met under the auspices of the University of Bologna at Rimini, Italy, to discuss the present financial state of football clubs in Europe. This introduction summarizes the conclusions of the group and sets the scene for the articles on specific European football leagues that follow. Our conclusions can be grouped under three distinct headings: (a) Is there currently a crisis? (b) What are the causes of the current financial problems of football clubs? and (c) What are the solutions?

Is there currently a crisis?

There is currently much talk about a crisis in European football, but there is a need for caution before the word crisis is used. Individual football clubs across Europe have experienced financial crises on many occasions in the past. Such cases, however, cannot be considered examples of a general crisis in football. A general crisis implies that some deep-seated problems have produced a state of affairs in which a fundamental restructuring of the game itself is the only long-term solution. When individual clubs have fallen into difficulty in the past, such problems may have arisen as a result of particular local conditions, particular forms of conduct and simply bad luck. In some cases a football club may have been restructured, whereas in others it may have disappeared altogether, but in either case the crises have been narrowly located, and their implications for the competitive structure of football as a whole have been limited. Today, there is talk of a systemic crisis. The notion of a systemic crisis has two features:

1. There exists a common set of problems afflicting all clubs, with negative financial implications for all; and
2. The crisis in one club or group of clubs threatens to damage the financial stability of other clubs (this idea of contagion is similar to the notion of a banking crisis).

The possibility of contagion is a special problem for a system of sporting competition, not shared by many other types of commercial activity. In most industries, the financial failure of one company is likely to benefit its rivals, because the disappearance of one competitor will increase the demand for the products of the others and will tend to increase their profitability and hence their financial stability. Banking is an exception to this rule, because banks tend to depend indirectly on one another through the credit system: The liabilities of one bank are often the assets of another, and hence the failure of a bank because of an inability to meet its liabilities also implies a reduction in the assets of other banks. In sports, the interdependence arises through the process of sporting competition: One team cannot play without the cooperation of another. If clubs fail, they may be unable to complete their fixture lists, undermining the value of the competition as a whole. If clubs with limited followings fail and are replaced by clubs with stronger followings, it can still be the case that the remaining clubs gain, but if popular clubs fail, the quality of the competition and the finances of all clubs may deteriorate.

Talk of a financial crisis is set against a period in which the income of football as a whole has risen dramatically. Figure 7.1 shows how income has risen dramatically in the top divisions in large European leagues.

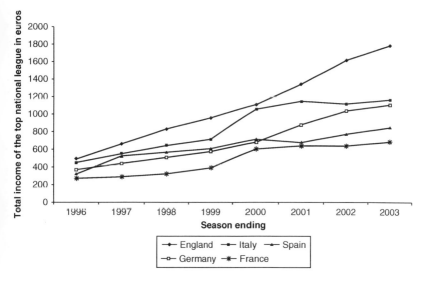

Figure 7.1   The growth of income in European football
Source: Annual review of football finance 2004.

Although growth has not always been as spectacular, smaller leagues have also enjoyed rapid income growth.

Thus, if there is a crisis, it is not a crisis of income. Even if we allow that there has been a downturn in income in the past two or three years, income still remains significantly higher than it was a decade ago. Moreover, there is no reason to believe that income will ever fall back to earlier levels. In general, economists think of football as a "normal good", meaning the kind of product for which demand increases as income rises. It is not usual to think of a period of rising income coinciding with financial crisis, although in the next section we discuss how this could happen.

Two kinds of evidence can be presented to demonstrate the possibility of crisis. First, there is the imbalance between income and expenditures, and second, there is evidence of rising debt.

The reliability of operating-losses as an indicator of the financial health of sporting businesses has long been challenged in the United States. Many studies have shown that club owners frequently disguise the profitability of their franchises to manage their tax liabilities and to put pressure on municipal authorities to subsidize new facilities-such as stadiums (see, e.g., Fort, 2006; Noll & Zimbalist, 1997; Quirk & Fort, 1992; Siegfried & Zimbalist, 2000). American commentators, however, also broadly agree that the owners of sporting franchises are driven primarily by commercial objectives (e.g., Zimbalist, 2003). In Europe, by contrast, there is a broad consensus that profit motives have been more restrained, although cases vary according to country. Thus, in France, Spain and Germany, for example, the ability of clubs to operate as profit-maximising businesses has been limited either by regulation or voluntarily, whereas in Italy and England, the scope for adopting commercial objectives has been greater. Yet even when profits may have been pursued by owners, the opportunities to disguise profits or to exploit accounting loopholes have been more limited in Europe than in the United States. This reflects in part the fact that in Europe, sporting clubs have generally not fallen under the control of larger business empires (although Italy is a significant exception) and in part a different culture and tradition.

Operating losses in themselves do not imply a crisis, as long as they can be funded. There is a great deal of evidence from the past that football was able to sustain such losses over a long period of time without financial failure, except in one or two exceptional cases. Funding historically might originate from a number of different sources: wealthy patrons, banks, municipal authorities, and tax and social security systems. The fact that many clubs have found it increasingly difficult to meet funding gaps reflects the increasing difficulty clubs have faced in locating these traditional sources of finance. By and large, however, our discussions illustrated that the crisis in most of Europe, where it exists at all, is primarily to be found among the small clubs. Table 7.1 illustrates the situation in each country.

Table 7.1   Football clubs' financial crises in European countries

Country	Large clubs in crisis?	Small clubs in crisis?
Italy	Yes	Yes
England	No	Yes
Scotland	No	Yes
Belgium	No	Yes
Portugal	No	Yes
France	No	No
Germany	No	No
Spain	No	No
The Netherlands	No	No
Greece	No	No
Switzerland	No	No

Only in Italy was it clear that both large and small clubs are facing a financial crisis. The extent of this crisis is revealed by Baroncelli and Lago in their article in this issue. Total operating losses in Serie A increased from €144 million in 1996–97 (€8 million per club) to €982 million in 2001–02 (€54 million per club). The current losses appear unsustainable when set against the total revenues of only €1.148 billion (excluding extraordinary items such as player trading). As a result, total indebtedness in Serie A increased to €1.742 billion in 2002. Although AC Milan and Juventus can be reasonably confident that these losses will be absorbed by the conglomerate enterprises that support them (the Silvio Berlusconi empire and Fiat, respectively), few other clubs have reason to be optimistic that their debts can be serviced in the longer term. Moreover, there must be a genuine risk that more than one Serie A club will fail at the same time, and hence a general financial crisis seems quite likely.

In England, Scotland, Belgium and Portugal, there is evidence of a financial crisis among the smaller clubs but not among the larger clubs. That is to say, even if some larger clubs have run into financial difficulties (e.g., Leeds United in England) or have registered large losses in recent years (e.g., Benfica and FC Porto in Portugal), these losses are either exceptional (Leeds United) or likely to be financed (by public subsidies in the Portuguese cases). Buraimo *et al.* (2006) show how the financial crisis is apparent among the smaller English clubs. Twenty-two of the 72 professional clubs in the Football League (i.e., outside the Football Association Premier League) have entered administration in the past 6 years, a process that requires complete financial restructuring to avoid bankruptcy. Morrow's article (2006) on Scotland reveals that the two major clubs, Celtic and particularly Rangers, are facing difficult financial circumstances. However, to an extent, their financial positions are eased by very large and loyal supporter bases that provide substantial recurring income and as in the case of Rangers, through the financial support provided by its majority shareholder. Elsewhere in the Scottish Premier League, the situation is much worse: Three of the 12 Scottish Premier League clubs are currently in administration, another has only narrowly avoided this fate thanks to cuts in player wages, and the directors of a further club are attempting to sell the club's stadium to meet its debts. For Belgium, Dejohnge and Vanderweghe (2006) report in their article that five professional clubs have disappeared from the top division in the past five years because of financial difficulties. Some play at lower levels, one has merged, and the others have disappeared altogether. In Portugal, Barros (2006) found that smaller teams, such as Santa Clara and Setubal, have incurred significant losses, without much evidence that they have the means to cover them.

In a majority of countries represented in our analysis, there is no evidence of a generalized crisis at the level of either small or large clubs. In some countries, there may be some clubs that have fallen into financial difficulties, but as explained above, this has been part of the pattern of football since its earliest days. But there is little evidence of any general crisis, for small or large clubs, either in the larger footballing nations (Germany, France and Spain) or in the smaller nations (The Netherlands,[1] Greece and Switzerland).

What are the causes of the current financial problems of football clubs?

Paradoxically, the root cause of the financial crises in some European countries has been the increasing amount of income entering the game, from TV and other sources. This massive increase triggered an even greater increase in spending on players. Thus, whereas clubs entered the 1990s more or less in financial balance, by the new millennium, clubs in countries experiencing crises had seen spending outstrip income and hence significant accumulations in debt, which in many cases can no longer be financed.

Why should increasing incomes cause such overspending? One reason is simply speculative: If incomes are expected to rise on average, then average expenditures will tend to rise in line. But if the increases on average incorporate a good deal of variation, teams that underachieve may face significant financial deficits. A related reason may be the expectation of growing inequality. If the income of every club increases in percentage terms by the same amount, the gap in absolute terms between the biggest and the smallest grows (e.g., suppose that one team has an income of €1 million and another an income of €2 million and that each enjoys an increase of 100% in its income, in which case the gap between the big club and the small club has also grown from €1 million to €2 million). If small clubs have ambitions to rival the large clubs, they will also anticipate that the absolute cost of bridging that gap will grow over time and may rationally calculate that "now" is the last opportunity to attempt to bridge that gap. But in doing so, they may also place themselves under increased financial risk.

But if increasing income alone can cause a financial crisis, why has it affected some countries but not others? To answer this question, it is easiest to consider why there is apparently no general crisis in the six countries discussed at the end of the previous section. There are three broad reasons.

First, in countries such as France, there is relatively tight regulation of football clubs by the national authorities. This regulation is analyzed in the article by Goughet and Primault. They show that French clubs' finances can be closely monitored by the national association. As a result, it is relatively difficult for clubs to spend beyond their present means without facing external sanctions. It is notable that France experienced a financial crisis in football at the beginning of the 1990s and as a result imposed draconian rules to regulate club finances. For example, if a player purchase is deemed to be beyond the financial capacity of a club, the league can legally invalidate that transfer. Such regulation seems to have been highly effective in ensuring that clubs have not fallen into financial crisis.

Second, the ownership structure may have helped avoid crisis. For example, in Germany, as shown in the article by Frick and Prinz, most clubs have a limited capacity to borrow money, and in general, loans must be personally guaranteed by the club officials. An ownership structure of this kind provides a significant disincentive to engage in financial speculation, and therefore, there has been limited opportunity for the clubs to jeopardize their futures.

Third, in some countries, local government stands ready to bail out failing clubs. The contribution by Ascari and Gagne pain in this issue makes clear that there is no chance that Real Madrid or Barcelona would ever be allowed to go bankrupt, whatever be the financial problems of these big-spending clubs. Thus, although there may exist a crisis for lenders, the clubs themselves are immune to all threat. Such cases are common in Spain but also in other countries, such as Greece.

These explanations can help us understand why crises have occurred in other countries. The third explanation can also account for the problems in Belgium and Portugal, where traditionally, local governments have been willing to support failing football clubs but much more reluctant to do so in recent years. Other sources of finance, such as wealthy local businessmen, may also have been in relatively short supply (the absolute cost of bailing out a typical club has increased dramatically, and therefore, there is now a smaller pool of people with enough wealth to perform this task, making it more likely that no one will be found in the end).

The second explanation may also help explain some of the problems. In Italy, England and Scotland, the directors of small clubs have been willing to gamble everything on success by borrowing large sums from banks while facing only limited personal risk. If shareholders exercised proper restraint on the activities of directors, there would be some disincentive to engage in such behavior, but, in common with many other businesses in the Anglo-Saxon culture, shareholder influence has been relatively limited. In most industries, shareholders leave directors to make choices, comfortable that a broad spread of investments will produce winners as well as losers. In football, however, the threat of systemic risk raises the question as to whether this investment strategy will be effective in the long term.

The first explanation also plays a significant role. Regulation has been much lighter in Italy, England and Scotland than it has been in France, and as a result, clubs have had more opportunities to make mistakes (but equally to have successes). This is perhaps the ultimate paradox relating to the regulation and management of sports leagues. By and large, those leagues with lighter regulations have sustained higher levels of spending on players and hence have enjoyed higher levels of success in competition. Examples include English, Italian and Spanish clubs in the Champions League. On the other hand, leagues with heavier regulation (e.g., in France) have, by and large, spent less on players and have as a result had less success (e.g., in the Champions League).

What are the solutions?

We have suggested that the greatest problems lie with the financial situations of small clubs in a subset of European countries. These problems have been triggered by the substantial growth of football clubs' incomes during the 1990s, primarily from TV rights. Competition for the greatest share of this expanding income has driven owners and managers of clubs, where they are able to do so, to in effect gamble the assets of the businesses on future success. Although this has led to spectacular collapses, such behavior is not necessarily irrational, any more than any other kind of gambling is irrational. However, it is often the case that actions that seem privately rational are collectively disastrous.[2] To the extent that selfish actions bring on one's own ruin, it can be argued that such disciplines are necessary in a responsible society. Football clubs are not run by children, and if we treat them as children, absolving them of responsibility for their decisions, the risk must be that they will become even more irresponsible. However, irresponsibility has consequences for other clubs in a league, and hence there is a case for implementing measures that ensure that club directors cannot take actions that destabilize the league as a whole (or the European system as a whole).

UEFA has already taken steps in this direction through the introduction of the club-licensing plan. UEFA has stipulated that all
clubs expecting to participate in its competitions (Champions League,
UEFA Cup) must meet the specified criteria. Beginning in 2004–05,
these are

- annual audited financial statements,
- proof that a club has no overdue payments for transfer activities, and
- proof that a club has no payments owed to employees (including
  taxes and national insurance contributions).

Additional criteria to be imposed beginning in 2006–07 are

- a liquidity plan demonstrating a club's ability to meet liquidity needs
  for the license period;
- a declaration of liquidity shortfalls "as they appear" and regular
  monitoring by UEFA, together with action plans; and
- notification of negative deviations from the pre-announced budgeted
  profit-and-loss account.

Eventually, at a date to be decided, UEFA will move to a general
requirement of proof of positive equity.

These steps are a move in the direction of tighter regulation of the
kind already imposed in France. The sanction of exclusion from the
Champions League and UEFA Cup will clearly impose significant dis-
cipline on many of the larger clubs, but as we have already seen, it is
not in general the larger clubs that are in crisis. Moreover, even for the
larger clubs, these rules will require strict enforcement, and in many
cases, they may not be credible. What would happen, for example, if
Real Madrid or Manchester United were in breach of the rules? Would
UEFA be willing to exclude either team from the competition, given the
value of broadcasting rights generated by these clubs? Given the current
difficulties of so many of the large Italian clubs, UEFA's resolve may be
fully tested in the coming seasons.

UEFA's plan is unlikely to have much impact on the behavior
of smaller clubs that are unlikely to qualify for UEFA competitions.
Although national associations may seek to introduce licensing systems
that harmonize with UEFA's system, once again, the issue of credibility
arises.

Because credibility is such a problem, it is worth pausing to ask how it
can be achieved. In France, this was achieved in the early 1990s by the

establishment of an independent commission to monitor the finances of football clubs and with powers, supported by law, to enforce their rulings. Moreover, the commissioners themselves held appointments of sufficiently long duration that the fear of dismissal was not likely to play a role in their decision making. The legal power of the commission was established through a number of test cases.

Could the French scheme be easily translated into a European context? This seems quite unlikely. It is very unlikely that national or European legislation would ever confer the necessary powers to the federations so that they would be able to establish these kinds of commissions. Any voluntary scheme is likely to face severe political pressures. Thus, despite the apparent success of the French plan in establishing financial stability, it is unlikely to be adopted more widely. As suggested above, French fans have paid a significant price (not for their own system but for the excesses of the systems in other countries), because despite producing an exceptional generation of footballing talent and success at the national level, success at the club level in Europe has been limited. It is tempting to speculate that only if French teams started to achieve success at the European level would other associations see the benefits of adopting, to the extent that it is legally possible, a similar style of regulation.

There is an alternative to tighter regulation: the adoption of American practices. Even though this is anathema to many in Europe, it must be observed that the American major leagues (baseball, American football and basketball) are much more financially stable than European football. The major leagues have in place a number of mechanisms that have the effect of maintaining both competitive balance and financial stability. These include salary caps, draft rules, roster limits, revenue sharing and other redistributive measures, many of which have been advocated in Europe. One of the key reasons that clubs in the United States agree to these measures whereas European football clubs seem unwilling to do so is precisely the openness of competition in the European context, exemplified by the system of promotion and relegation. In the United States, clubs that are successful today are willing to share with the less successful because they know that in the future, the positions are likely to be reversed, and they will one day benefit from the system. In Europe, however, large clubs fear the idea of sharing with weaker clubs in case the latter do become strong and cause the relegation of the former at some later date. There can be little doubt that many of the larger clubs have been looking at a European super league that would be either closed or have restricted access, not only to develop more attractive competition (to TV at least) but also to bring about a basis for a more secure financial system.

In other words, we conclude that there are two broad approaches to dealing with financial instability in European football. The first is to impose tighter financial regulation from above, as exemplified by UEFA's club-licensing plan. Within the current system, we doubt whether such mechanisms can be credible without strong legal backing such as is provided in the French system, as outlined by Gouget and Primault. The alternative to tighter regulation is are structuring of football competition in Europe to create a more sustainable basis for smaller clubs in particular. This would involve adopting greater restrictions on the mobility of the clubs up and down the leagues.

Notes

1. In The Netherlands, a new team (AGOVV in Apeldoorn) was given a license for professional football in 2003, expanding the number of professional football teams to 37. A number of smaller teams have had financial problems recently, but they have all been bailed out by local government or local businesses.
2. Other examples include the overfishing of the oceans or the emission of greenhouse gases, which lead to global warming.

References

Annual review of football finance 2004. (2004). Deloitte and Touche, Manchester, UK.

Barros, C.P. (2006) Portugues football. *Journal of Sports Economics*, 7, pp. 96–104.

Dejonghe, T. & Vandeweghe, H. (2006) Belgian Football, *Journal of Sports Economics*, 7, pp. 105–113.

Fort, R. (2006) The value of Major League Baseball ownership, *International Journal of Sport Finance*, 1, pp. 1–27.

Morrow, S. (2006) Scottish Football: It's a funny old business, *Journal of Sports Economics*, 7, pp. 90–95.

Noll, R. & Zimbalist, A. (1997) *Sports, Jobs and Taxes*, Brookings Institution, Washington, DC.

Quirk, J. & Fort, R. (1992) *Pay Dirt*, Princeton University Press, Princeton, NJ.

Siegfried, J. & Zimbalist, A. (2000). The economics of sports facilities and their communities, *Journal of Economic Perspectives*, 14, pp. 95–114.

Zimbalist, A. (2003) Sport as business, *Oxford Review of Economic Policy*, 19, pp. 503–511.

8
English Football

Babatunde Buraimo[a], *Rob Simmons*[b] *and Stefan Szymanski*[c]

[a]*University of Central Lancashire, UK*
[b]*Lancaster University, UK*
[c]*Imperial College, London*

Abstract

Financial distress is not an uncommon occurrence in English football. The number of clubs falling into financial difficulties has escalated, yet this coincides with an era when the revenues accrued to English football have reached unprecedented levels. This chapter examines the finances of the Premier League and the Football League and assesses the sources of financial distress experienced by many clubs. We find that as clubs in the lower divisions engage in the seasonal race for promotion to higher divisions where financial rewards are greater, excessive wage expenditure and the collapse of a major broadcaster have combined to threaten the already fragile existence of many clubs. We assess some policy proposals designed to deal with the financial precariousness of English football.

The institutional structure

The governing body of English football, the Football Association (FA), was founded in 1863. In those early years, football was played mainly on an amateur basis, but the competitive nature of the FA Cup, inaugurated in 1871, and the potential to generate income from selling tickets to matches sharpened the competition to the point that players were being offered financial inducements to play. Initially, the FA was opposed to professionalism, but by the mid-1880s, this position was no longer tenable, and it was legalized in 1885. This reform led to the creation of a new format for competition (the Football League, founded in 1888) and the increased commercialization of football clubs. Until this

162

period, football clubs were also clubs in a legal sense, being managed by an elected committee.

Under English law, financial transactions entered into by a club committee, such as borrowing money to fund the construction of a building, are the personal liability of the committee members. This means that if the investment fails to yield enough money to pay the interest on the debt, the committee members must pay the debt out of their personal finances or face the possibility that their own assets will be seized to repay the debt. Once football clubs started to build large stands to accommodate paying fans and to spend heavily on transfer fees, the potential financial burden was too great for most committee members, and thus an alternative financial structure needed to be found. The joint stock structure, whereby the ownership of a company is vested in its shareholders, who have the right to elect the board of directors and to receive dividends out of company profits but whose liability for company losses is limited to the extent of their initial investments, was becoming popular in England in the 1880s. Until 1856, any new joint stock company required the approval of the British Parliament, so that only after this law was repealed did its widespread adoption become feasible. The Football League expanded rapidly, and by 1923 it had 88 members divided into four divisions, all employing professional players and almost all organized as joint stock companies. This has remained the dominant legal structure to this day. Although the clubs were not obliged by the league or the FA to restrict their activities to football, and there is no restriction regarding the takeover of clubs by larger businesses, it is rare for any football club to be involved in or connected with any other business activity.[1]

From the foundation of the Football League, there existed tension with the FA, the latter controlled largely by 'gentleman amateurs' who disapproved of commercialism in sport. This had two consequences: First, the clubs were restricted in the financial returns that they could offer to shareholders, with a maximum dividend of 5% of paid-up share capital being imposed in 1896. Although this ceiling was subsequently raised, it represented a significant disincentive to open commercialization. Second, the FA tended to support the players against the league in matters relating to transfers. It viewed the 'retain and transfer' system, which the league clubs introduced from their earliest days, as an unjust restriction on the mobility of players. What the FA objected to was economic competition between the clubs, and its sanctioning of a maximum wage in 1904 should also be seen in that light. The league clubs were successful in extending control through the transfer system, and the maximum wage helped them control costs. Neither the league nor the FA exerted control over the financial conduct of individual clubs, although clubs were required to file their annual accounts and provide other financial information such as transfer fees. For clubs that did fall into financial difficulty, the only solution was restructuring or resignation from the league.

The history of financial instability in English soccer

One of the principal reasons advanced by the founders of the Football League for its formation was the need for financial stability. By providing a settled fixture list, the clubs could ensure that they generated enough income to pay the salaries of the teams. As football grew in popularity in the period leading up to 1914, income also increased rapidly, but, nonetheless, some clubs fell into financial difficulty.

A pattern of financial crisis followed by rescue at the hands of wealthy patrons has been typical of English football, with most clubs being able to point to at least one such episode in their histories. Patriarchal figures have frequently emerged to save clubs from financial collapse, partly as a result of civic pride and partly because of the favorable publicity. Moreover, the financial cost of such intervention has traditionally been small. Local businessmen with relatively small fortunes have always been capable of financing the rescues of small teams out of their own pockets. Without rescuers of this kind, clubs that are unable to pay their debts typically follow the same procedures as any other business. Under English law, a club that is unable to pay its creditors can choose or be forced into "administration". It is not an attractive option for creditors, because an administrator is entitled to pay himself or herself for his or her work, and the charges are often high. An administrator tries to sell assets of the business to make it viable, meaning that potential buyers know that they have a strong bargaining position. Entering administration was rare in English football before the end of the 1990s. In most cases, clubs in financial difficulty would sell players, reduce their ambitions and often suffer relegation to lower divisions as a consequence. Teams that reached the bottom of the lowest division of the Football League were required, until the mid-1980s, to seek re-election to the league by the other clubs. In practice, even if a club had been in financial difficulties, it would be re-elected. However, in extreme cases, teams might fail to be re-elected, in which case they could join junior leagues. Thus, very few teams would disappear altogether, typically only in cases of gross financial mismanagement.

An example of a team resigning during a season is Wigan Borough, a team elected to the league in 1920. It struggled to attract support, faced with strong competition from two Rugby League teams also located in the town. The club appears to have spent heavily to achieve some success (see Sutcliffe and Hargreaves, 1928/1992, pp. 223–224), and in September 1931, it revealed to the League Management Committee that it was £20,000 in debt (at a time when the English transfer fee record stood at £10,890) and appealed for a subsidy. The league demanded that the club produce a rescue plan within four days or face expulsion from the league. In the event, the club resigned, and the games it had played up to that point in the season were declared null and void. Wigan was the most extreme example of financial failure during the depression of the 1930s.

After World War II, football enjoyed a boom in the 1950s as attendances reached an all-time high. By the 1960s, however, football was coming under pressure from alternative leisure activities, and weaker teams in particular began to face falling attendances. Moreover, the decline of traditional British industries such as textiles affected northern and particularly Lancashire-based clubs, which were disproportionately represented in the league. Accrington Stanley, a team that was elected to the league in 1921 but had struggled financially for many years, offered to resign in March 1962, faced with debts of £62,000. At the time, this event provoked great shock, because football was generally seen to be in a healthy state. The club continued to play in the Lancashire Combination League until 1966, but then folded.

Another wave of financial crises hit the Football League in the early 1980s, triggered by a combination of declining attendance and increasing player wages.[2] Clubs said to be in financial trouble included Bradford City, Bristol City, Charlton, Derby, Halifax, Hartlepool, Hereford, Hull, Middlesbrough, Newport, Rotherham, Southend, Swansea, Tranmere, and Wolverhampton. These were "smaller" clubs, the ones that had traditionally struggled to make ends meet, but now questions were raised about the indebtedness of "big" clubs such as Aston Villa, Chelsea, Leeds, Manchester City, and Nottingham Forest. A report published in 1982 found that the match receipts for that season for all 92 league clubs totaled £35 million, generating a £6 million operating loss. During this period, clubs in distress started to approach the players' union to negotiate wage cuts and in many cases direct subsidies. Other clubs, such as Preston, Leeds, and Wolverhampton, solved the crisis by selling their grounds to local authorities. Clubs with attractive locations were able to sell land for redevelopment (Brentford, Bolton, Bournemouth, Crystal

Palace, Hull, and Tranmere). Several clubs that did not own their own grounds were forced to relocate because of an inability to pay the rent (e.g., Bristol Rovers and Charlton). Despite this, no club failed during this period.

By the mid-1980s, the league had started to generate increased income through sponsorship and TV deals, so that by the end of the decade, league football was in a much healthier state. Indeed, the separation of the FA Premier League (FAPL) from the Football League was prompted by the desire of the top clubs to retain control of the new TV income coming into the game. Up until the 1991–1992 season, clubs in divisions 1, 2, 3, and 4 were allocated 50%, 25%, 12.5% and 12.5% of the TV revenue, respectively. Although gate revenue sharing had been abolished in 1985, save for the FA Cup, big clubs were still dissatisfied with the extent of cross-subsidy to smaller clubs.

Governance, revenue, and ownership in the 1990s

Dissatisfied with this income redistribution, the major clubs of the time (Arsenal, Manchester United, Tottenham, Everton, and Liverpool) led a breakaway of the top-division clubs to form the FAPL for the 1992–1993 season. For the first time, the rights were sold to a pay-TV broadcaster, leading to an explosion of income over the following decade. For the 1993–1994 season, total revenue was about £380 million. By the 2002–2003 season, this had increased to £1.6 billion. Figure 8.1 shows the seasonal increase in revenue, adjusted for inflation. Table 8.1 indicates the growth of value of broadcast rights for FAPL clubs.

As income has grown, so has the FAPL's share of total income of the four professional divisions. From 1993–1994 to 2002–2003, the FAPL's share of revenue was 74%, compared with 18%, 6% and 3% in Divisions 1, 2, and 3 of the Football League, respectively. Over this period, revenue, adjusted for inflation, in each division increased by 311%, 77%, 158%, and 140% (respectively, FAPL, Division 1, Division 2, and Division 3). Given the total revenues in 2002–2003 of £1.25 billion and £206 million in the FAPL and Division 1 of the Football League, respectively, the respective standard deviations were £35 million and £5 million. Under a promotion and relegation system, increasing income differences between divisions create incentives to take greater risks to avoid relegation or gain promotion.

Profit maximization and financial return on investments are not widely held to be strong motives in English football. However, by the end of the 1980s, traditional restraints on profit seeking were

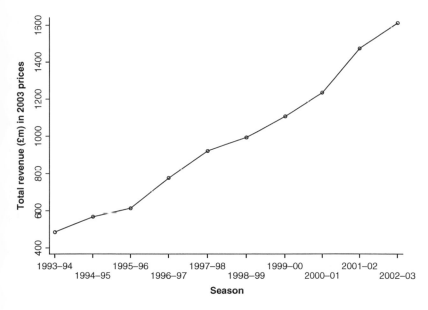

Figure 8.1   English football's revenue by season from 1993–1994 to 2002–2003
Source: Deloitte and Touche (various years).

Table 8.1   Rights values for live and highlights packages for the Football
Association Premier League (FAPL)

Year	Length of contract	Live match broadcaster	Live matches per season	Annual rights fee for live football (£m)	Highlights Broadcaster	Annual rights fee for highlights package (£m)
1992	5 years	BSkyB	60	38.3	BBC	4.6
1997	4 years	BSkyB	60	167.0	BBC	18.3
2001	3 years	BSkyB	66	343.0	ITV	56.7
2004	3 years	BSkyB	138	341.3	BBC	35.0

Source: FAPL Limited.

being relaxed. In 1981, payments to full-time directors were permitted, and rules restricting dividend payments were first relaxed and then
abolished in 1998. Given the need to invest in new stadiums following the *Hillsborough Report*, the FA argued that football clubs should
become investor friendly. During this period, a number of football clubs
floated on the stock market. In 1983, Tottenham Hotspur listed on the
London Stock Exchange, followed by Millwall in 1989 and Manchester

United in 1991. Between October 1995 and October 1997, another 16 clubs floated some or all of their equity on the market.

Flotation was an opportunity for clubs to generate more revenue, which could be used for stadium development and investment in player assets, but balancing the demands of city investors and on-the-field performances has proved difficult. Many clubs have failed to achieve the right balance between football and financial performance; apart from Manchester United, shareholder returns have been poor, and since 1997, several clubs have delisted. The bankrolling of clubs by wealthy individuals has been much more successful (for the clubs). In the early 1990s, Jack Walker's considerable wealth bankrolled a small-market team, Blackburn Rovers, to promotion to the FAPL and the FAPL title in 1993–1994. The Walker estate continues to support the team today. Most recently, Russian billionaire Roman Abramovich has spent in excess of £200 million in the transfer market and on player wages to generate an FAPL championship–winning team for Chelsea.

In the Football League, mutualization and trust status, allowing all profits to be retained for football purposes, have been recently suggested as an alternative financial model (Hope, 2003; Michie & Walsh, 1999). Although trusts have emerged as a reaction to the financial crisis facing some clubs, they are not widespread. As of August 2005, there were just three fan-owned Football League clubs: Stockport, Rushden, and Chesterfield.

Another novel approach to financing has been 'securitization', whereby lending is provided by investors against anticipated cash flows, such as season ticket sales or total gate receipts including corporate hospitality income (Morrow, 2003). Examples of English clubs entering into such arrangements are Leeds United, Manchester City, and Newcastle United.

Securitization is a means of insuring against risk. But in some cases, that risk can actually be increased if the finances drawn from securitization are poorly spent. In 2001, Leeds United entered into a 25-year, £60 million securitization drawn against ticket and corporate hospitality income and used the funds to finance the purchases of player registrations. Some of these purchases were at above-market transfer prices, and other valuations fell once Leeds United entered into financial crisis and was forced into a 'quick fire sale' of players. Also in 2001, Leicester City obtained a £28 million securitization deal drawn against future media revenues. These media revenues were severely reduced on relegation to Division 1 at the end of 2001–2002 and further reduced by the collapse of ITV Digital. According to Morrow (2003), 'the revenue flows on which football club securitisation rely are simply too uncertain and too risky to make this a credible financing strategy' (p. 159). But the problems surrounding securitization have as much to do with a lack of proper monitoring of club directors' securitization strategy as with the method itself. Hence, the Independent Football Commission's 2003 annual report called for the FA to establish a code of corporate governance for all clubs over and above a 'fit-and-proper-person test' for club directorships.[3]

Profitability and clubs falling into financial difficulties

According to the accounting data, English football has sustained losses in eight of the ten seasons since 1993–1994. Between 1995–1996 and 2001–2002, the reported net loss was £957 million. When profitability is examined by division, the losses are somewhat varied. In the FAPL, there have been erratic moves between pre-tax profit and losses, but the overriding effect is a net loss. In the other three divisions, no profits were declared, and Deloitte and Touche report that the total operating loss for the Football League was £52 million at the end of the 2003–2004 season. The profitability of each division is shown in Fig. 8.2.

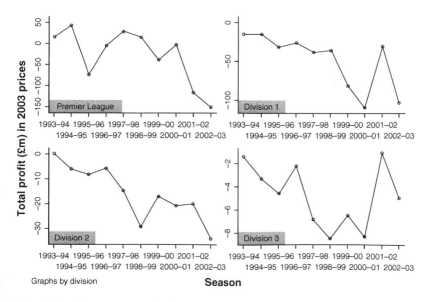

Figure 8.2 Net pre-tax profit (loss) in English football by division and season from 1993–1994 to 2002–2003

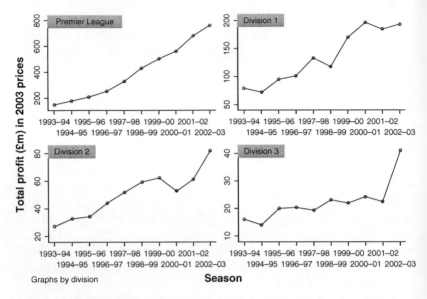

Figure 8.3   Seasonal wage bills for the FAPL and Divisions 1, 2 and 3, From 1993–1994 to 2002–2003
Source: Deloitte and Touche (various years).

Given the massive increase in income in the 1990s, financial losses can be explained only by excessive wage spending (if we discount the various tricks used by major franchises in the United States). Figure 8.3 shows the increases in wage bills by division. The FAPL has each year increased its wage expenditures. One reason behind this is the risk attached to relegation. It can be shown that for the FAPL, the probability of relegation is inversely related to relative expenditures on wage bills (Simmons & Forrest, 2004). Given the increased differences in revenue between the FAPL and Division 1, much of the increase in wage expenditures is motivated by the retention of FAPL status. Likewise, the extra revenue that can be generated from European competition is an incentive to increase investment in player talent. Conversely, qualification to European competition is positively correlated with relative wage bill (Simmons & Forrest, 2004).

The wage bill/revenue ratio also provides a perspective on clubs' performances. In the FAPL, the ratio has been rising but has consistently remained below or around 0.6. In Division 1, however, the wage/revenue ratio has been in excess of 0.6 and in 2000–2001 exceeded 1 (see Fig. 8.4). Given the problems with the broadcasting agreement between

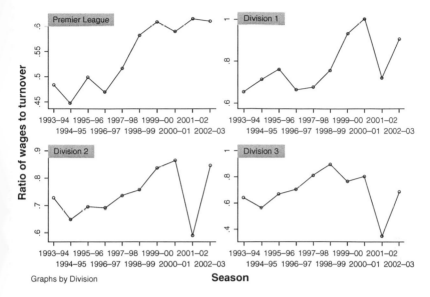

Figure 8.4   Wage/revenue ratio for the FAPL and Divisions 1, 2 and 3 by season from 1993–1994 to 2002–2003
Source: Deloitte and Touche (various years).

ITV Digital and the Football League, clubs have been forced to adjust their wage bill/revenue ratios, and this is evident in subsequent seasons.

In the past five years, several clubs have taken the step of going into administration.[4] As noted above, this is essentially a court order that places a football club, as with any other business, under the control of an insolvency expert and offers legal protection.

Over the period from 1999 to 2004, 22 Football League clubs, just under a quarter of the total, experienced administration, and three clubs (Bradford, Luton, and Swindon) experienced two spells. Of these 22 clubs, 14 had experienced relegation within the previous five seasons, although only five (Barnsley, Bradford, Ipswich, Leicester and Wimbledon) had enjoyed FAPL status. Overall, these clubs had accumulated large debt burdens and had failed to adjust club balance sheets to match their new lower status. The debts of clubs entering administration were largest for clubs relegated from the FAPL to Division 1. Large debts, of the order of £30 million to £40 million, were accumulated by clubs in administration at Bradford (May 2002 to August 2002 and February 2004 to December 2004), Ipswich (February to May 2003), and Leicester (October 2001 to February 2003). But even relatively small debts, on the order of £1 million, were enough to force clubs such as Barnsley and Chesterfield into administration. Table 8.2 reports some details of the 20 periods of administration endured by Football League clubs since 2001 (Deloitte and Touche, 2003).

One notable feature is the low attendance/capacity ratio of several clubs entering administration, symptomatic of weak drawing markets and, in the case of Darlington, excessive stadium size. Although no FAPL club has yet experienced administration, growing levels of debt

Table 8.2   Administration spells 2001 to 2005

Club	Period	Division on Entry	Division on Exit	Average Attendance	Estimated Debt (£m)
Barnsley	10/02 to 3/03	2 (relegated)	2	13,323	0.9
Bradford	5/02 to 8/02	1 (relegated)	1	15,489	36
Bradford	2/04 to 12/04	1	2	12,501	
Bury	3/02 to 5/02	2	3 (relegated)	3,923	
Carlisle	6/02 to 10/02	3	3	3,204	
Chesterfield	4/01 to 1/02	3 (relegated)	3	4,846	1.3
Darlington	12/03 to 9/04	3	3	3,312	20
Huddersfield	3/03 to 8/03	2 (relegated)	3	9,506	22
Ipswich	2/03 to 5/03	1	1	25,455	35
Leicester	10/02 to 2/03	1	1	29,231	30
Lincoln	5/02 to 7/02	3	3	3,223	
Luton	7/03 to 3/04	2 (promoted)	2	6,747	
Notts County	6/02 to 12/03	2	2	5,956	
Oldham	8/03 to 1/04	2	2	6,699	
Port Vale	12/02 to 4/03	2	2	5,210	2.4
Queens Park Rangers	4/01 to 5/02	1 (relegated)	2	12,013	11
Swindon	3/02 to 8/02	2	2	6,354	
Wimbledon (Milton Keynes Dons)	6/03 to 6/04	1 (relegated)	2	2,787	25
Wrexham	11/04 to present	2 (relegated)	3	4,751	2.6
York	12/02 to 3/03	3	3	3,147	

Sources: BBC Sport, Hope (2003), Deloitte and Touche (various years).
Note: Division 1 is now Championship, Division 2 is now League One, and Division 3 is now League Two.

have been reported at some clubs. The most notable case is that of Leeds United, a public limited company quoted on the London Stock Exchange, whose debt was unofficially estimated at about £120 million and whose shares were suspended from trading while new owners were sought. The case of Leeds is all the more remarkable in that the team reached the semifinals of the European Champions League in the 2000–2001 season and had a pool of valuable playing talent.

Causes of financial crisis

The proximate cause of entry into administration is usually a claim made by a creditor. This could be a lender, such as bank or sponsor.[5] Often, the claim is made by the tax authorities (Inland Revenue, Customs and Excise) for unpaid taxes. The usual reasons cited to explain why clubs enter into large levels of debt are an inability to sell players as assets through the transfer market, a loss of revenues consequent on relegation and an inability to align costs and revenues on the loss of divisional status, an inability to maintain loan payments on capital expenditure such as a new stadium, and a failure to realize expected revenues from TV broadcasting deals.

In Division 1 especially, the rewards for promotion to the FAPL have been growing, and this in turn created extra incentives and pressure to acquire more expensive talent, both players and coaching staff members, to realize the ambition (or dream) of FAPL status. Even if a promoted club acquires elite status for one season, the potential benefits from promotion are considerable. On the other hand, several of the clubs in financial difficulty were relegated to lower divisions with expensive player contracts that were expected to be settled. Clubs such as Barnsley, Bradford, and Ipswich have found relegation costly as players acquired with high transfer fees had low sell-on values and had been awarded lucrative long-term contracts for which the clubs were liable.

Overall, the fundamental causes of financial crisis appear to be

- Insufficient revenue-generating capability, as shown by the large amounts of unused stadium capacity for several of the clubs placed in administration;
- a loss of revenues from relegation, through the loss of TV broadcasting revenue[6] and the loss of gate receipts as attendances fall;
- excessive wage costs, partly reflecting overoptimistic aspirations for the club by owners, management and fans; and
- an inability to adapt player wage contracts to demotion to lower divisions.

How a crisis is dealt with

An English club's financial crisis is dealt with by various measures. In the short term, a crisis requires immediate action, and this will typically include

- wage deferrals or wage cuts agreed to by players;
- sales of player registrations (transfer fees, with valuations often reduced for a quick sale);
- the involuntary redundancy of staff members, including players and commercial staff members; and
- loans from the Professional Footballers' Association (PFA).

The involvement of the players' union is intriguing, because it is the only example in which a trade union lends money to employers to maintain the employment and earnings of trade union members.[7] It is understandable in this context as a quid pro quo for the privileged position players occupy as preferred creditors under Football League rules. If that preferred position were to be revoked, it is doubtful whether PFA support would be forthcoming. At present, the British government is reviewing the 'super creditor' rule, because it clearly contravenes the British legal convention of equal creditor status.[8] The consensus among administration practitioners is that the obligation to fulfill players' and coaches' contracts impedes their ability to help clubs restructure debt and find new owners. This view receives large support from club financial directors (PKF Football Services Group, 2005).

When a football club emerges from administration, it is usually with new ownership. In several cases, supporters' trusts are part owners (e.g., Bury, Chesterfield, Huddersfield, Lincoln, and York; Hope, 2003). Most often, a new set of businesspeople take over the club. There are very few examples, such as Ipswich, in which the same set of club owners retain their position on exit from administration.

In the medium term, further adjustments need to be made to a club's financial position:

- debt rescheduling;
- the write-off of loans; and
- sales of land, including the stadium or training ground, to third parties.

One problem with the methods involved in solving a financial crisis listed above is that several are very short term. Cutbacks on playing staff members are likely to lead, along with voluntary player exits, to a weaker playing squad and a higher probability of relegation. Reduced commercial staff will threaten a club's ability to achieve potential revenues through effective marketing. The experience of clubs after leaving administration is mixed, with six clubs showing improved league positions and four (Bradford, Bury, Chesterfield, and York) exhibiting worsening performance. Within administration, five clubs actually improved position or status (Barnsley, Chesterfield, Ipswich, Leicester, Luton, and York), whereas four clubs experienced declines in divisional status.

A financial crisis with a period of administration does not necessarily result in worse post-administration performance. Several clubs currently playing in the FAPL endured serious financial crises in the 1980s and 1990s but were able to recover through investment by new owners. Examples include Bolton, Charlton, Chelsea, Fulham, Middlesbrough, Portsmouth, and Wolverhampton. However, these examples of successful recovery occurred when the gap in revenues between top division and the next tier were not as great as they are now.

Effect of financial crisis on other clubs

It could be argued that a financial crisis for one group of clubs makes the league as a whole weaker. In the extreme case, which has only occurred twice in the entire history of English football, clubs could liquidate within a season, leaving fixtures unfulfilled. This would be a regrettable outcome for the leagues, and measures would be taken to avoid such a situation. It undermines the credibility and integrity of the competition, because anomalies would occur and fans would probably react adversely.

English football clubs have managed to sustain persistent losses that in other industries would have invited creditor reaction. The patience of banks, Inland Revenue, and other creditors is partly due to a reluctance to call in overdrafts and unpaid bills in recognition of community disapproval that would follow. But ultimately these creditors have to be paid, and confidence is required in the ability of clubs to settle debt eventually.

Moreover, the current English practices relating to insolvency leave scope for free-riding behavior. One case of this type was that of Leicester City. This club was in administration for a long period, October 2002 until February 2003, during which it continued to sustain a respectable pool of playing staff members. Top players were retained, yet large bills to some creditors were not paid. In particular, one contractor involved in the construction of the new Walker Stadium was forced to write off

£7 million owing. The team secured promotion to the FAPL in May 2003, and rival clubs complained both that the process of administration, while a consortium established a successful takeover bid, was unduly long and that during this period Leicester had not paid creditors. Largely as a response to these complaints from rival clubs, the Football League reviewed its procedures relating to clubs in administration.

Impact of changes at the European level

The financial stability of clubs is threatened by the growth of the European Champions League. First, the extra tier of competition further widens the gap between excluded FAPL clubs and Football League clubs, and those clubs that qualify. This gap would already be considerable because of greater revenue potential in the top places in the FAPL. Second, the extra effort needed to compete effectively in the European Champions League raises wage costs. Essentially, clubs face a steeper trade-off between higher risk and higher returns. The need for effective commercial and team management becomes much greater. Third, the European Champions League and the less appealing Union of European Football Associations (UEFA) Cup are televised, and this could lower TV audiences for lower-level football, reducing their value of broadcast rights. Fourth, European Champions League and UEFA Cup matches are played mid week, and it is inevitable that Football League games will clash. Forrest and Simmons (2006) offer evidence showing that gate attendances at mid-week Football League matches are reduced if rival European football is shown on the same evening, thus damaging revenues. In contrast to arrangements within domestic leagues, there is no mechanism for the cross-subsidization of revenues between clubs participating in European competition and clubs excluded from these competitions.

It is important to stress that the prize for earning large revenues and success in European competition does serve as a powerful incentive for teams to invest in playing talent. As such, the domestic competition could become more attractive both to fans at the stadium and to TV audiences.

One particularly difficult problem that English football will need to confront is pressure to reduce the size of the FAPL from 20 clubs at present (with only Spain's La Liga of comparable size within Europe) to 18 or even 16. This would further raise the revenue gap between Division 1 and the FAPL and in turn increase the costs of relegation and the risk for insolvency. If the FAPL were to respond by cutting the number of promotion places from three to two, it would impair mobility through the league structure, thus creating disincentives for investment in playing talent. This pressure to reduce the size of top-level football raises issues about the optimal design of the FAPL that should be carefully analyzed in a pan-European context.[9]

Remedies

The football authorities in England and in Europe in general recognize now the reality of financial crises and the growing threat to the integrity of their competitions that results. Accordingly, there are three types of remedies for financial crisis currently being proposed to apply to English football:

- the Football League's proposals for sanctions to apply to clubs entering administration, together with limits on wage bill/turnover ratios;
- UEFA's licensing system, which could be extended to domestic leagues;
- a promotion test (Szymanski, 2002), which specifies that clubs that exceed a stipulated wage bill/turnover ratio should be denied promotion.

Football league proposals 2004–2005

As a response to the financial crisis, the Football League now has a policy that all clubs must submit annual budgets. Further proposals in force for the 2004–2005 season are

- clubs in Divisions 2 and 3 to spend just 60% of their turnover on wages,
- a ten-point 'sporting sanction' incurred by clubs entering administration from the end of 2003–2004, as a deterrent against excessive spending,
- player contracts to indicate pay levels for different divisions played in during the term of the contract, and
- promoted Division 1 and 2 clubs to contribute to a parachute payment fund for clubs relegated to Divisions 2 and 3.

Inspection of Deloitte and Touche's (various years) *Annual Review of Football Finance* suggests that the majority of Division 2 and 3 clubs had wage bill/turnover ratios in excess of 0.6 in the 2001–2002 and 2002–2003 seasons (see Fig. 8.4). Hence, the Football League's proposals would probably be binding on several clubs. In the 2004–2005 season, Wrexham entered administration and quickly received a ten-point penalty that eventually led to its demotion from Division 2. This early application of the sanction was meant to enforce the credibility of the Football League's proposals.

Of course, these proposals are specific to the Football League. The FAPL announced a proposal of a nine-point penalty for any club entering administration from the start of the 2004–2005 season.[10]

UEFA licensing

UEFA has stipulated that all clubs expecting to participate in its competitions (European Champions League, UEFA Cup) must obtain a licence. For 2004–2005, the UEFA requirements for a license to be granted are

- annual audited financial statements,
- proof that a club has no overdue payments for transfer activities, and
- proof that a club has no payments owing to employees (including taxes and national insurance contributions).

Additional criteria are to be imposed beginning in 2006–2007, and the extra requirements are

- a liquidity plan demonstrating a club's ability to meet liquidity needs for the license period,
- a declaration of liquidity shortfalls 'as they appear' and regular monitoring by the FA together with action plans,
- notification of negative deviations from the pre-announced budgeted profit-and-loss account.

Eventually, at a date to be decided, UEFA will move to a general requirement of proof of positive equity. A system of club licensing is already in place in France and Germany and is about to be installed in Scotland.

A promotion test

This contains just one proposal, first suggested by Szymanski (2002), that may be combined with others drawn from the Football League's or UEFA's list. It requires that all promoted teams, regardless of which division or league they emanate from, do not exceed a particular wage bill/turnover ratio in the season they are promoted. Szymanski nominates 70% as a feasible ratio that clubs could adhere to without unduly sacrificing the quality of playing staff members.

Discussion

Problems with the Football League's proposals are, first, that the ten-point deduction is both arbitrary (why not 6 or 16?) and, second, that it may be non-binding. Chesterfield was handed a nine-point penalty in 2001 for breach of league rules yet overcame this handicap to gain promotion to Division 2. On the other hand, the ten-point penalty applied to Wrexham in 2004–2005 was clearly instrumental in its relegation. The wage bill/turnover ratio is meant to apply to all clubs in Divisions 2 and 3 and would require monitoring the spending of all clubs. This would be intrusive and difficult to perform given the disorganised accounts at some clubs. Furthermore, why should a poorly performing club not spend more than the stipulated wage/turnover ratio to rise from the lower reaches of the division?

The difficulty of applying the UEFA's licensing criteria to the domestic leagues is simply that the criteria are not exact, being more in the nature of general guidelines. As such, they do not specify credible incentives for appropriate behavior; it is the lack of such incentives that lies at the root of the English financial crisis. There is also the risk that the UEFA's guidelines will not be binding, so no club is ever excluded from UEFA competitions, analogous to the rare application of licensing rules to recalcitrant clubs in France and Germany. Alternatively, if the guidelines are not met and some clubs are excluded from competition, it might be done in an unfair and arbitrary fashion.

The advantages of the promotion test proposal are that

- It minimizes interference in competition in that it confines attention to excessive spending aimed at promotion and restricts the scope of regulation to one particular aspect of club finances;
- It specifies a simple rule that is not open to judgmental considerations, as a general licensing procedure would be; and
- It specifies a clear target for clubs and as such reduces the costs of monitoring and compliance.

The promotion test deserves further consideration by league governing bodies. In the absence of a promotion test, restrictions on wage/turnover ratios with clear sanctions imposed for violation appear to be the only credible mechanism for alleviating England's football crisis.

Notes

1. This is in sharp contrast to the United States, where most clubs have become part of larger business empires (e.g., the *Chicago Tribune* and the Chicago Cubs or News Corporation and the Los Angeles Dodgers in baseball). In 1999, the UK Monopolies and Mergers Commission blocked the takeover of Manchester United by BSkyB, implicitly prohibiting broadcasters from owning football clubs, but this was on the grounds that the broadcaster would be likely to abuse its bargaining power with the league and would restrict competition in broadcasting markets.

2. This latter effect is a common theme in the story of football's financial distress. However, although declining attendance may be beyond the control of a club, payroll is not, raising the question as to why clubs so persistently spend themselves into financial trouble.

3. Birkbeck College's Football Governance Research Unit's annual report for 2002 undertook a survey of 47 clubs, that found that less than 25% of the clubs had internal audit committees, 32% had no regular board reviews of risk assessment, and several stated that they would not provide information on the share register to shareholders, apparently unaware that this would be contrary to company law. Birkbeck's 2003 report cites a lack of understanding of corporate responsibility and a core failure to monitor and ensure the quality of corporate management. Morrow makes a strong appeal for greater transparency in the corporate governance of football clubs.

4. Alternatively, clubs can arrange with creditors to enter creditor voluntary agreements.

5. In the case of Huddersfield, the appeal for entry into administration was made by the players.

6. What is also evident from the losses is the pattern of expenditure. In the late 1990s, ITV and its subsidiary company ITV Digital made an aggressive entry into the football rights market and, along with its portfolio of Champions League football, secured the 2001–2002 to 2003–2004 rights to the FAPL's highlights package and the live and pay-per-view rights to the Football League. ITV Digital was only able to provide a fraction of the agreed £315 million, but Football League clubs, particularly those in Division 1, had already made large expenditures in anticipation of revenues that were not realized.

7. Toward the end of the 2004–2005 season, Cardiff City received a short-term loan from the PFA to cover players' wages. This was objected to by other Division 1 clubs, because Cardiff was involved in a struggle against relegation and the loan was perceived as giving Cardiff an unfair advantage against other relegation-threatened clubs.

8. The abolition of the super creditor rule was recommended by the All Party Parliamentary Football Group in 2004.

9. See Szymanski (2003) for a theoretical discussion of the optimal size of a sports league.
10. The start is deemed to be the date of the annual general meeting in June, which ratifies league membership.

References

Annual review of football finance. (various years). Manchester, UK: Deloitte and Touche.

Forrest, D. & Simmons, R. (2006) New issues in attendance demand: The case of English league football. *Journal of Sports Economics, 7*, 3, pp. 247–266.

Hope, S. (2003) *The Ownership Structure of Nationwide League Football Clubs 2002–03*, Football Governance Research Centre, Birkbeck College, London.

Michie, J. & Walsh, A. (1999) Ownership and governance options for football clubs, in S. Hamil & J. Michie (eds.), *The Business of Football: A Game of Two Halves?* (pp. 209–224), Mainstream, London.

Morrow, S. (2003) *The People's Game? Football, Finance and Society*, Palgrave Macmillan, Basingstoke, UK.

PKF Football Services Group. (2005) *Controlling Club Performance—The Annual Survey of Football Club Finance Directors*, Author, London.

Simmons, R. & Forrest, D. (2004) Buying success: Team salaries and performance in North American and European sports leagues, in R. Fort & J. Fizel (eds.), *International Sports Economics Comparisons* (pp. 123–140), Praeger, New York.

Sutcliffe, C. E. & Hargreaves, F. (1992) *The History of the Lancashire Football Association*, Yore Publications, Harefield, UK (Original work published 1928).

Szymanski, S. (2002) The promotion test, *World Economics, 3*, pp. 171–183.

Szymanski, S. (2003) The economic design of sporting contests, *Journal of Economic Literature, 41*, pp. 1137–1187.

9

Income Inequality, Competitive Balance and the Attractiveness of Team Sports: Some Evidence and a Natural Experiment from English Soccer

Stefan Szymanski
Imperial College, London

Abstract

This chapter examines the relationship between financial inequality, competitive balance and attendance at English professional league soccer. It shows that while financial inequality among the clubs has increased, competitive balance has remained relatively stable and match attendance appears unrelated to competitive balance. A clearer test of the relationship is suggested by comparison with FA Cup matches. Because income inequality is primarily driven by inter- rather than intra-divisional inequality, the FA Cup has been a much more unbalanced competition than the divisional championships. Attendance at FA Cup matches relative to the corresponding league matches has fallen over the last 20 years.

1. Introduction

It is widely accepted that a degree of competitive balance is an essential feature of attractive team sports.[1] Sporting competition is a process that

I would like to thank Syariza Kamsan for valuable research assistance. I also thank Steve Ross, Chris Walters, seminar participants at Edinburgh University, Salford University, London Economics and two anonymous referees for valuable comments.

establishes a hierarchy among the participants – winners and losers. Competitive balance refers to the rational expectations of fans about who will be the winners. In a perfectly balanced contest, each participant starts with an equal chance of winning, so that the outcome will be completely uncertain. If there is no competitive balance, then the exact outcome can be predicted with probability one. Without at least a degree of competitive balance, fans will lose interest in a competition. However, it is less clear that every decline in competitive balance will lead to a falling off of fan interest.

This is not merely a matter of academic concern. In the recent Premier League Broadcasting case, heard in the UK Restrictive Practices Court, the court decided that selling broadcast rights collectively (and preventing clubs from selling any broadcast rights individually) was in the public interest, in part because the collective sale promoted financial equality, which in turn promoted competitive balance/uncertainty of outcome. Similar views underlie the US Sports Broadcasting Act of 1961 (which exempts the collective sale of broadcast rights on national TV from antitrust prosecution), and the comments of the Advocate General of the European Court of Justice in the Bosman case.

Thus the received opinion contains two logical steps: (i) increasing income inequality tends to reduce competitive balance and (ii) competitive imbalance tends to reduce fan interest.[2]

This chapter does two things: First, it develops a simple theoretical model of league competition to show that increasing competitive balance is not always desirable. Fan interest depends on several factors, and while competitive balance is one, an equally important consideration is the success of each of the teams that fans support. If fan support is unequally distributed between teams (e.g. for demographic reasons), then a utilitarian welfare function is likely to suggest that imbalance in favour of more strongly supported teams is optimal. For example, it is currently said that 50% of committed football fans in England support Manchester United; if this is so, it is difficult to argue that aggregate welfare is not enhanced by the relative success of this team.

The second contribution of this chapter is to suggest a natural experiment to test for the relationship between income inequality, competitive balance and fan interest. Testing for the existence of the hypothesised relationships is fraught with difficulties because of the many factors that affect fan interest from season to season. While it may be possible to test whether or not the competitive balance of a match affects interest (e.g. attendance), it is more difficult to test for the competitive balance of an entire competition. Yet in terms of the theory, it is presumably the competitive balance of a competition which is most important in the long run.

English soccer provides a natural experiment that overcomes these problems. Because teams compete simultaneously in both league (Football League and Premier League) competition and cup (FA Cup) competition, we can compare the trend in support for each of these competitions. In the league competitions teams are segregated into divisions, while in the Cup competition teams from different divisions can be drawn against each other. Over recent years income inequality has grown, most noticeably between rather than within the divisions. This implies that the FA Cup has become a much more unbalanced competition relative to the league division championships. We can thus ask whether attendance at FA Cup matches has declined relative to league matches. We do this by creating a matched sample of same-division matches played in the league and the Cup (these constitute around half of all matches in most seasons). The matching controls for many of the possible differences between matches (e.g. team strength, local interest, demographic and economic factors). What remains can be attributed to the intrinsic imbalance of the FA Cup relative to league championships.

The results do indeed show a relative decline in attendance at same-division matches. The rest of this chapter is set out as follows. The next section develops a simple theoretical analysis of league structure and competitive balance. The following section develops the natural experiment and discusses some robustness issues. The final section draws some conclusions.

2.   Competitive balance in theory

The relationship between income distribution, competitive balance and the attractiveness of sporting competition has received a limited amount of attention in the theoretical literature. This literature has been primarily been concerned with the proposition that income redistribution will lead to greater equality of outcomes. Fort and Quirk (1995) and Vrooman (1995) analysed this question and concluded that competitive balance would be unaffected by redistributive mechanisms such as gate sharing. Under gate sharing, the visiting team receives a fixed percentage of the home team gate (e.g. in the US NFL 40% of gate income is allocated to the visitors). The basis of their argument is as follows: If teams earn more from home matches when they are expected to win (i.e. winning teams attract more support) and the visiting team shares the gate revenue, then the visiting team would prefer to be less successful compared to the case where they do not share in the gate receipts. This will lead both teams to invest less in winning (i.e. to invest less in playing talent) compared to the case where there is no gate sharing, but in their models this effect impacts equally on both teams so that competitive balance is unaffected.

Szymanski (1998) argues that gate sharing may even have the perverse effect of reducing competitive balance. In a model where there is constant marginal cost of talent but revenue is a strictly convex function of playing success (measured by win percentage), gate sharing will diminish the investment incentives of small-market teams by more than that of large-market teams. Intuitively, small teams stand to gain more from the success of the big teams than the big teams stand to gain from the success of the small teams. Hence small teams reduce investment in talent by more than the big teams. However, that paper also shows that the impact of redistribution on competitive balance depends critically on the objectives of the teams and on the type of redistribution scheme. The standard models of team sports in the United States assume clubs are profit maximisers, while researchers in Europe (e.g. Sloane, 1971) have presented evidence that, at least traditionally, clubs have been 'win maximisers' (or some variant of this). Win maximisation implies all surplus income is reinvested in talent. Under these circumstances, income redistribution from large to small clubs will tend to improve competitive balance.

Even if clubs are profit maximisers, schemes that raise income independently of playing success (e.g. collective selling of TV income), and then redistribute that income on the basis of playing success, will tend to improve competitive balance. This is because what matters for competitive balance is the investment decision of the teams, which in turn depends on the access of teams to the income pool *ex ante*, rather than the *ex post* share-out. Income raised through lump sum taxes will not distort incentives, while redistribution on the basis of performance will give equal incentives to all. Teams with a small drawing power are no longer deterred from investing in talent because of the limits imposed by their local market.

TV income is an interesting case, not least because of the interest expressed by competition authorities in the desirability of centralised collective selling. In theory, collective selling and the distribution of TV income purely on merit (e.g. on the basis of league ranking) will enhance competitive balance by giving small-market teams equal access to the TV market. A club with a small local market can finance a successful team if TV income is the dominant source of finance. In practice collective TV revenues tend to be distributed equally (as in the US NFL) or only partly on the basis of merit. In the English Premier League only 25% is distributed on the basis of league ranking, while 50% is allocated as an equal share and the remaining 25% is awarded on the basis of the number of TV appearances.

However, researchers have also questioned the value of competitive balance. If some teams draw on larger (or more devoted) fan bases, then the success of these teams will yield greater total utility than the success of teams with small fan bases will. The important theoretical issue is whether unfettered competition or a regulated market will deliver the socially optimal outcome. A simple model may help to illustrate this point. Suppose that there is a sports competition consisting of two teams, one of which enjoys a larger domestic market than the other, in the sense that it will generate a higher level of fan utility for a given level of playing success. Fan utility depends on playing success, which in turn depends on the proportion of playing talent hired by each team. Hence the fan utility for each team can be written as follows:

$$U_1 = \mu_1 \omega_1 = \frac{\mu_1 t_1}{t_1 + t_2}, \qquad U_2 = \mu_2 \omega_2 = \frac{\mu_2 t_2}{t_1 + t_2} \qquad (1)$$

where $\mu_1 > \mu_2$ reflects the intensity of support, ω is the win percentage of each team and t is the quantity of playing talent hired by each team. Total utility will depend not only on the utility of committed team fans, but also on spectators with no particular loyalty to a team. These supporters might be labelled 'uncommitted', or, more pejoratively, 'couch potatoes', watching matches on TV and motivated only by an attractive spectacle. The utility of these spectators is thus dependent on competitive balance.[3] We adopt here a simple cardinal representation of total utility:

$$U = U_1 + U_2 + \theta \omega_1 \omega_2 \qquad (2)$$

where θ represents the weight of couch potatoes relative to committed team fans in total utility. Maximising total utility with respect to the win percentage yields the following social optimum:

$$\omega_1^* = \frac{1}{2} + \frac{\mu_1 - \mu_2}{2\theta} \qquad (3)$$

As θ becomes very large, only competitive balance matters. However, depending on the difference between the intensity of support for each team, as θ diminishes, the social optimum implies higher degrees of inequality. Unless the two teams are equally well supported, there will exist a critical value of θ which implies that total utility would be maximised even if the more popular team never lost. The model implies a trade-off between the interests of the committed and uncommitted fans. The optimal balance depends on the relative weights placed on each of these populations.

It is clear from this that if redistribution of income led to an equal distribution of resources, the outcome would be an equally balanced contest. This would be socially optimal only if either the intensity of support for each team were equal or the weight attached to utility of the uncommitted fans dominated completely. Perfect balance is not generally desirable.

To model the outcome of a competitive market some assumptions are required about the objectives of clubs and the form of their objective functions. Here it will be assumed that clubs are profit maximisers, in line with the US literature, and an increasingly plausible assumption in English soccer now that the largest clubs are quoted on the stock market. It is assumed that the clubs are able to appropriate a fraction of the utility of fans through the sale of tickets and related products, while they can hire playing talent in the market at a constant marginal cost. Thus

$$\pi_i = \phi_i \mu_i \omega_i - c t_i \tag{4}$$

where ϕ is the fraction of winning utility that the clubs can appropriate. It is also assumed that clubs are unable to appropriate any of the utility derived by the uncommitted fans. This may be somewhat extreme, but in general one might expect that it is relatively difficult to generate income from this group. It is easy to show that profit maximisation implies the ratio of talent at each club will equal the ratio of intensity of support (μ_1/μ_2). Comparing this with the socially optimal level of talent at each club implied by equation (3), it is clear that the socially optimal level of competitive balance would arise only by chance. If $\mu_1 = \mu_2$, the market outcome is socially optimal. However if $\mu_1 > \mu_2$, then the social optimum would only be achieved for a particular value of θ. This critical value is increasing in μ_1. In other words, the greater the weight attached to the utility of uncommitted fans the stronger the intensity of support for team 1 would have to be to achieve the social optimum. If intensity of support for team 1 is too large, the contest will be less balanced than the social optimum; if it is too small, the contest will be more balanced than is socially optimal.

A simple model such as this captures some basic ideas about the relationship between inequality in the distribution of resources, competitive balance and social optimality. The basic insight is that while perfect competitive balance is not desirable, the market equilibrium is unlikely to achieve the social optimum. In particular, intensely supported teams are likely to create excessively unbalanced competitions. This might be taken as the grounds for limited redistribution. Whether members of a league or the league authorities themselves will be able to impose such redistribution depends largely on their ability to appropriate the surplus of uncommitted fans – otherwise they have no incentive to act and no basis for an agreement. In such cases, intervention by an independent regulator committed to the best interest of the sport will be desirable, at least in theory.

3.   Competitive balance: A natural experiment

3.1.   The trend in English league soccer

Before developing the natural experiment it is useful to review the data from the league alone to indicate the difficulty in analysing competitive balance. This chapter deals with competitive balance in a sense which has not generally been examined in the earlier literature. Kuypers (1997)[4] defines competitive balance in three senses: the balance of attractiveness of a match, the closeness of a championship race and the absence of long-run domination. Most previous studies have concentrated on competitive balance in the first two senses. Thus Jennett (1984), Peel and Thomas (1988), Cairns (1988), Jones and Ferguson (1988) and Kuypers (1997) concentrate on the match uncertainty. They hypothesise that uncertain matches will attract greater support and focus on finding suitable proxies for match uncertainty. Demmert (1973), Noll (1974), Whitney (1988) and Kuypers (1997) concentrate on the closeness of specific championship races and examine whether this increases attendance at matches. In the present study the focus of interest is the balance of the entire championship over a period of time. In league competition this can be measured by the variance of team winning (win percentage) over time or the dominance of high ranks by particular teams. For cup competition, since the teams also participate in hierarchical leagues, competitive balance can be analysed by looking at the success of teams from different divisions.

The growing financial inequality in English League is widely remarked upon. However, most of this growth in inequality is inter- rather than

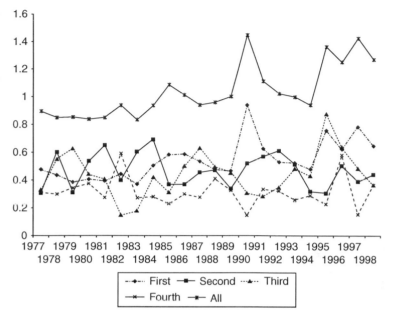

Figure 9.1 Coefficient of variation of sales by division 1977–98

intra-divisional, as is shown in Fig. 9.1. This graph shows the coefficient of variation of income for a sample of 39 clubs over the 22-year period from 1976/77 to 1997/98. This makes it difficult to test for the impact of growing inequality in league soccer, since there are no inter-divisional matches. Moreover, it is not evident that there has been any significant increase in intra-divisional competitive balance either within or between seasons. Table 9.1 illustrates the absence of any significant trend in dominance over time, measured by the number of teams accounting for the top positions over different time periods (three and seven years). While there is some slight evidence of increasing dominance in the Premier League over the last three years in the sample, there is no clear trend.

It is useful to consider the mobility of teams between the divisions. In any one year there are 92 league clubs, and over the seasons 1976/77 to 1997/98 there have been 99 teams participating in the four divisions, given that there have been a small number of demotions to the lower semi-professional divisions. Of these 99 teams, only 5 have never been relegated or promoted over the period, indicating that there is a fairly high degree of mobility between the divisions.[5] Furthermore, over the

Table 9.1 Number of teams in each of the top N Positions by three- and seven-year intervals (1978–98)

(a) Three-year intervals

Period	Number of teams in top 3 division				Period	Number of teams in top 5 division				Period	Number of teams in top 10 division			
	1	2	3	4		1	2	3	4		1	2	3	4
1	6	9	9	6	1	9	12	15	11	1	13	18	18	16
2	6	8	9	9	2	9	11	12	13	2	13	15	19	22
3	6	9	7	8	3	8	13	11	13	3	11	20	16	22
4	6	9	8	8	4	8	14	14	12	4	12	18	18	21
5	8	7	9	7	5	10	11	13	11	5	15	19	20	21
6	6	7	6	8	6	10	11	12	11	6	15	18	19	19
7	4	8	9	8	7	7	13	13	13	7	13	19	18	22

(b) Seven-year intervals

Period	Number of teams in top 3				Period	Number of teams in top 5				Period	Number of teams in top 10			
	1	2	3	4		1	2	3	4		1	2	3	4
1	8	17	15	17	1	10	17	22	23	1	12	19	25	31
2	7	14	17	19	2	9	17	20	28	2	11	21	23	34
3	8	12	16	20	3	11	17	19	27	3	15	17	25	31

period more teams have ranged between three divisions (43) than have moved only between two (32), while 12 teams managed to visit all four divisions over the space of 22 years.

Dominance within seasons is considered in Fig. 9.2. This shows the standard deviation of win percentage over time. This measure is the most widely used indicator of competitive balance in the US literature, and although there is a greater proportion of drawn games in soccer, win percentage is still a reliable indicator of success. It is closely correlated with the more usual measures of success such as league position (correlation coefficient 0.91) and points scored (0.95). Perhaps surprisingly, the charts show that there is no clear trend in win percentage, suggesting that divisional championships have not tended to become more one-sided over time. Figure 9.2 also illustrates the change in attendance at league matches over the 22 seasons, that may be taken as an indicator of fan interest. There have been two very distinct phases – a secular decline in attendance until 1985 and a consistent increase thereafter. This is in itself puzzling given that most pundits have generally dated the recovery of interest in English football at 1990 (when England reached the semi-final of the World Cup) or even 1992 (the foundation of the Premier League). There were still problems in English football in the late 1980s (high levels of crowd violence, poor facilities at stadiums

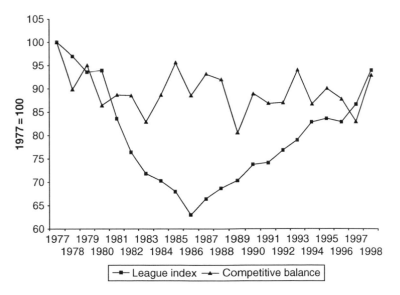

Figure 9.2 Competitive balance and league attendance trends 1977–98

and high levels of policing. Worst of all was the Hillsborough stadium disaster of 1989 in which 95 fans were crushed to death).

One explanation may be derived from the model outlined in Section 2. The trend of growth in financial inequality started from a point in the early post-war period when income was quite evenly distributed and clubs were restricted by a maximum-wage rule that limited team expenditure. Thus until 1961 teams with large potential supporter bases were constrained to hire teams of roughly equal ability to those with small potential supporter bases. In terms of the model, the constrained equilibrium meant that the success of the larger teams was below the optimal level. Once the maximum wage was abolished clubs could utilise their greater resources to achieve a higher rate of success and this may have led both to less competitive balance and to greater interest in the league football.

3.2.   The natural experiment

The idea of a natural experiment is to identify two sets of data in which competitive balance differed significantly but all other relevant factors were the same. In US team sports, where clubs compete only in a single tournament, such natural experiments are not available, but this is not true of soccer. Traditionally teams participate in two main competitions during the season, a league competition and a cup, or knock-out, competition. The oldest such competition in the world is the FA Cup in which all 92 league clubs compete annually. The FA Cup is in fact open to all registered football clubs in England, and amateur teams compete in preliminary rounds. However, the first round of the Cup consists mainly of the teams in the two lowest divisions. The teams in the top two divisions do not enter the competition until the third round, which consists of 64 teams.

In each round of the competition the matches are determined by a random draw. In many cases the opposing teams are from different divisions, but on average one-third of matches from the third round onwards are contests between teams from the same division, and an even greater proportion of matches in rounds 1 and 2 are same-division matches. This is the basis for a natural experiment. Using a sample of about one thousand same-division FA Cup matches over the last 22 years we can compare attendance with attendance at the equivalent league fixture played in the same season (this includes equivalence in the sense that the same team has home advantage). As was pointed out in the previous section, the main source of the growth in inequality between league teams has been the growth of inter-divisional income inequality. If income inequality leads to a less balanced contest, we should expect to see a lower degree of fan interest in a Cup fixture, which forms part of a more unequal championship than the corresponding league fixture. The test is therefore not a test of the attractiveness of a fixture in its own right, say as a function of the quality of the teams or the history of competition between the two teams, rather it is a test of the relative attractiveness of the championships in which the two teams are participating. In fact it is a very low-powered test. It excludes from consideration matches between teams from different divisions, which might be thought to be particularly unbalanced and therefore to attract fewer spectators. These contests are excluded because there are no equivalent league fixtures with which they can be compared.

Of course, the natural experiment cannot control for every possible source of difference between the two fixtures. Match attendance can be affected by the current form of the two teams, the day of the week on which a match is played (weekend matches tend to have higher attendance) and the point of the season at which the match is played (end-of-season matches tend to have higher attendance). These factors can be controlled for through a regression analysis, although one might expect that in a matched sample as large as one thousand, these factors would not exert systematic effect.

While the data make clear that income inequality between the divisions has grown over recent years, it is not so easy to establish that competitive balance has in fact declined. The standard deviation of win percentage or other indicators of success make little sense in this context. One way to compare is to look at the survival of teams from different divisions. There is surprisingly little evidence of a trend toward domination by the larger clubs, perhaps because even in 1977 the large clubs dominated the FA Cup. Thus in that season 78% of all appearances in the FA Cup from the third round on were from teams in the first and second divisions. Given that 64 teams enter the third round of which 44 are from the top two divisions, the theoretical maximum share of the top two divisions is 84% (106 out of 126 appearances) while the theoretical minimum is 44% (56 appearances). Over the period the share of the top two divisions never fell below 72%, within 12% of the theoretical maximum (see Fig. 9.3). The top-division clubs dominate the final rounds of the competition. There were only three cases of a club from outside the top division appearing in the final in the 22 years from 1977 to 1998, and only 15 cases out of a possible 88 of such a team playing in a semi-final. The lowest number of top-division clubs

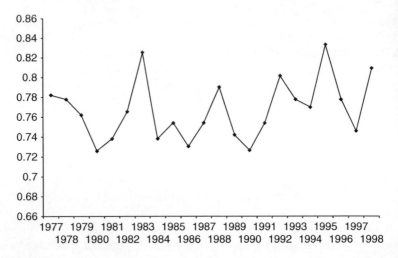

Figure 9.3 Share of division 1 and 2 teams in all FA Cup matches played from the third round onwards

to survive to the fourth round in any year during this period was 10, while on average 14 survived. Since the Premier League was reduced to 20 teams in 1996 at least 15 teams have survived the third round in each year.

There is some evidence of increasing dominance. The proportion of cases where a team from a lower division wins a match has declined. Between 1977 and 1987 on average just over 11 of the 63 matches played per season (from the round third on) resulted in a win for the lower-division team. From 1988 to 1998 the average fell to just under 10. The incidence of 'giantkilling', defined as a team beating an opponent placed at least two divisions higher, has also fallen. Such events are in any case rare, there having been only 67 cases in the 22 seasons covered by the data, an average of three per season. Between 1977 and 1987 there were 42 cases, an average of over four per season, while between 1988 and 1998 there were only 25 cases, an average of only just over two per season. This evidence seems to suggest that an already unbalanced contest has become yet more unbalanced.

The natural experiment suggested here is that if the competitive balance of a championship taken as a whole affects the attractiveness of individual matches, we should see a relative decline in attendance at matches in a championship whose balance is deteriorating fast. Since the inequality of income has grown faster as between participants in the FA Cup competition and participants in divisional championships, we

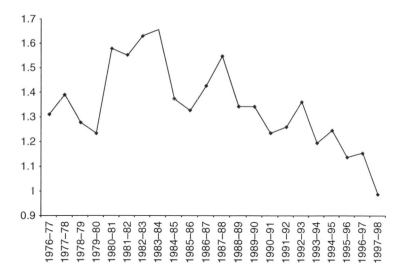

Figure 9.4   FA/league attendance ratio

should expect to see a relative decline in attendance at FA Cup matches. This does indeed appear to be the case, based on the sample of 997 same-division matches played between 1977 and 1998.[6]

Figure 9.4 shows a graph of the ratio of average attendance at FA Cup and league matches over time. FA Cup matches are traditionally better supported than league matches, and between 1977 and 1987 the average FA Cup fixture would attract an audience 43% larger than the equivalent league match. This difference declined to 25% in the second half of the data period, and declined almost continuously until 1998 in which year FA Cup matches attracted a slightly smaller audience on average. Thus, even with this very low-powered test, there appears to have been a significant decline in the relative attractiveness of the FA Cup during a period when inter-divisional income inequality was growing and there appears to have been some deterioration in the competitive balance of the FA Cup.

The database was compiled using matches from the first two rounds of the Cup, involving the lower divisions, as well as the later rounds. This ensures that the sample contains a large number of Cup matches between teams in the lower divisions. It might be suspected that the effect shown here was related primarily to the Premier League, where much of the media interest has been focused. It might also be suspected that the results were due to the fact that many top-division cup matches tended to be played to capacity stadia, and that the falling ratio was an artefact of this constraint during a period when interest in football was growing. To deal with this issue and other potential factors that might influence attendance a regression approach was adopted.

The matched sample for the seasons 1982/83 to 1997/98 was used to analyse any trend in attendance at FA Cup matches relative to league matches. The results are reported in Table 9.2. Column 1 reports an OLS equation for the full data set. Column 2 reports a Tobit equation for the full sample, with upper censoring to account for the fact that about 10% of matches appear to have been played at capacity. The capacity figure was approximated as 95% of the figure reported in the Rothmans

Table 9.2   Attendance regressions 1982/83–1997/98 seasons

	OLS whole sample	Tobit whole sample	OLS excluding first division
Constant	28,323	27,774	12,867
	(23.095)	(38.317)	(13.814)
Second division	−11,442	−11,181	
	(−19.592)	(−18.416)	
Third division	−17,525	−17,012	−6,452.5
	(−35.905)	(−41.573)	(−15.001)
Fourth division	−20,043	−19,373	−8402
	(−40.134)	(−48.418)	(−19.973)
Sum of team league positions	−262.38	−174.58	−138.34
	(−12.73)	(−12.812)	(−7.852)
Match played on Sunday	1,690.8	1,609.4	913.31
	(1.712)	(1.949)	(1.104)
Season month	129.73	−201.89	253.44
	(1.301)	(−3.149)	(3.397)
Replay	−1,145.1	−1,080.2	458.53
	(−1.812)	(−2.536)	(0.758)
FA Cup match 1983–86	3,617.5	3,519.9	1,998.8
	(4.322)	(6.706)	(2.815)
FA Cup match 1987–90	3,456.3	3,283.3	1,989.3
	(4.255)	(7.408)	(3.777)
FA Cup match 1991–94	912.61	926.63	543.19
	(1.410)	(1.803)	(1.302)
FA Cup match 1995–98	−138.29	−179.21	279.83
	(−0.166)	(−0.35)	(0.449)
Observations	1,286	1,286	772
R^2	0.637		0.479
Log L	−13,856	−12,713	−7,766

Heteroscedastic consistent errors in parentheses. Time dummies included but not reported. Tobit coefficients are marginal effects.

Football Yearbook. This Rothmans figure is likely to be an overstatement because capacity is limited for some matches by the requirement to have adequate segregation of fans, leaving many seats deliberately unoccupied.[7] Column 3 reports an OLS equation for the sample omitting top-division teams, which account for 92% of sell-outs in the data. The models were estimated with heteroscedastic consistent errors. In the case of the Tobit estimation a multiplicative model of heteroscedasticity was adopted (see Greene, 1993). In both the OLS and the Tobit models there was evidence of non-normality using Pagan Vella tests. This is known to be a particular problem in the Tobit model since it renders the estimator inconsistent. However, the consonance of the Tobit and OLS results provides a little comfort.

The regressions account for the day of the week the game was played, the sum of league positions, the month and whether the match was an FA Cup replay as well as divisional and time dummies. Sunday matches tended to attract a higher attendance than did Saturday matches, possibly because broadcast matches are usually scheduled for a Sunday and broadcasters select the most attractive games.

Most FA Cup replays are in mid week, and as a result these two variables tended to pick up the same effect. If anything, the replay variable worked better. The sum of league positions variable (positions at the date the game was played) picks up the quality of the teams on show. If competitive balance mattered for attendance at individual matches, one might have expected that the absolute difference in league positions would be significant – but in fact it was not.

The FA Cup effects are represented as dummies for successive four-year periods. The estimates suggest that between 1982/83 and 1989/90 an FA Cup match would attract about 3000 more spectators than a league match. The OLS figure is somewhat higher; the figure for the lower three divisions is somewhat lower. For the seasons 1990/91–1993/94 FA Cup matches still attracted more bodies on average, but the size of this effect (between 500 and 1000 people) is not statistically significant at the conventional 5% level.[8] The dummy variables for the last four-year period (1995–98) are all much smaller (two indicate a negative impact of FA Cup matches on attendance) and are all statistically insignificant. Thus the regression analysis appears to support the evidence of Fig. 9.4 – in the 1980s FA Cup matches would attract significantly higher attendance than equivalent league matches. In the 1990s this effect has disappeared, and FA Cup matches attract attendances that are no higher on average than equivalent League matches. The 'magic of the Cup' seems to be fading.

Before concluding, there are two possible flaws in the natural experiment that should be considered. If other factors had altered the relative attractiveness of attending matches in league and Cup competitions, then the trend in the ratio might be attributed to these factors rather than competitive balance. First, if the price of tickets for Cup matches relative to league matches had risen, this might have caused the relative decline in attendance. Price data are not available for the entire period, but the annual Football Trust Digest of Football Statistics provides an analysis of FA Cup and League gate receipts between 1984/85 and 1994/95. The ratio of prices derived from these data shows no overall trend during a period when the relative decline of FA Cup attendance was pronounced. A more serious question is raised by the increasing tendency to sell season tickets. This means that for an increasing proportion of fans the marginal cost of attendance at league matches is effectively zero. This could account for the relative decline of interest in the FA Cup. However, the fact that clubs can sell an increasing proportion of seats for league matches in advance suggests that the attractiveness of the league competition has increased. If interest in the FA Cup had grown at the same rate, we might observe FA Cup season tickets being sold or simply higher prices for FA Cup matches. The fact that we do not suggests that the relative attractiveness of the Cup has indeed declined.

A second weakness of the experiment might be that the structure of the competitions themselves had changed enhancing the relative attractiveness of the League. Since 1986/87 a system of play-offs for some promotion places was introduced into the lower three divisions. The effect of this was to give more teams at any given time an interest in the possibility of promotion, and to involve every team a longer fraction of the season in contention. This has almost certainly stimulated interest in league competition in the lower divisions. To see if this effect was driving the relative decline of FA Cup attendance, those matched pairs which involved league matches played from March onwards (at which point progressively more teams are ruled out of contention) were omitted from the sample. However, for the remaining matches the relative decline of FA Cup attendance appeared just as pronounced as for the full sample.

4. Conclusions

This chapter has attempted to draw out the relationship between the unequal distribution of resources, competitive balance and the interest of the fans. The resurgence of interest in English league football, in particular the Premier League, has occurred at a time when the distribution of income has become much more unequal. Many commentators have bemoaned this fact, worrying that it will lead to a decline of interest in soccer. So far, there is only weak evidence that the concentration of income has been associated with a decline in competitive balance, and no evidence at all that it has reduced interest in league football. It may be that the polarisation of recent years has been an adjustment away from an excessively egalitarian distribution toward an unequal distribution that more accurately reflects the interest of the fans. It may also be the case that competitive balance is only sensitive to very large changes in the income distribution, and hence growth in inequality may only have caused small changes in competitive balance.

There are many factors that influence attendance, and isolating the effect of competitive balance using only a short time series is unlikely to reveal or capture all the dynamics of the underlying relationship. However, by comparing same-division fixtures that occur in both the FA Cup and the league we can conduct a natural experiment on the effect of growing inequality. The only important difference between the matched pairs is the competition in which they are played. Other sources of difference such as home advantage, the quality of the teams, form over recent seasons and so on are filtered out by the matching. Since inter-divisional inequality has grown much faster than intra-divisional equality, the FA Cup is a competition where the resources of the participants have become more unevenly distributed (compared to the league) over time. The data show, just as one might have predicted, that this relative increase in inequality has led to a relative decline in attendance. In the 1970s it was not unusual for attendance at an FA Cup match to be 50% higher than the attendance at the equivalent league fixture. By 1998 the average attendance at FA Cup matches was lower than that at the matched fixture. Thus the natural experiment appears to confirm the standard hypothesis about the impact of income inequality and competitive balance on the attractiveness of sporting competition.

Notes

1. This may be a peculiarly modern phenomenon reflecting ethical sensitivities – the Romans, for instance, appear to have enjoyed the unbalanced contest between lions and Christians.
2. '...An important element in the maintenance of the quality of the Premier League competition is competitive balance, that is to say the unpredictability of the outcome of a high proportion of the matches played within the competition and thus uncertainty about which club will win the

championship...we accept that an increase in financial inequality will tend to result in a reduction of competitive balance' *RPC Court Judgment, Premier League.*

'[A] professional league can flourish only if there is no too glaring imbalance between the clubs taking part. If the league is clearly dominated by one team, the necessary tension is absent and the interest of the spectators will probably lapse within a foreseeable period...it is of fundamental importance to share income out between the clubs in a reasonable manner...' *Advocate-General Lenz, Bosnian.*

3. Most fans are likely to value the total quality of the playing talent involved in a match as well as competitive balance. The addition of total playing talent as an argument in the social welfare function will not affect the qualitative results.
4. Kuypers (1997) and Szymanski and Kuypers (1999) provide a useful survey; for an earlier survey see Cairns *et al.* (1986).
5. Four of these teams have remained in the top division (Arsenal, Coventry, Everton and Liverpool) while one has remained in the lowest division (Rochdale).
6. The database includes replays of drawn matches. The inclusion of these games might be thought to bias the average FA Cup gate downwards since replays tend to be scheduled at times other than the weekend, making it more difficult for fans to attend. On the other hand, a replay may be a good indicator of an exciting match, since the previous draw already indicates a degree of competitive balance. In any case, a separate analysis of decisive matches only did not indicate any systematic difference in the underlying trend.
7. Capacity data is problematic. The Rothmans figure is also misleading for the 1990s when there was significant stadium rebuilding, often during the season. However, no other capacity figures are available.
8. In the Tobit model the marginal effect is significant at the 10% level.

References

Cairns, J. A. (1988) 'Outcome Uncertainty and the Demand for Football', Discussion paper 88–02, University of Aberdeen Department of Economics.
Cairns, J. A., Jennett, N. & Sloane, P. J. (1986) The economics of professional team sports: A survey of theory and evidence, *Journal of Economic Studies*, 13, pp. 3–80.
Court of Justice of the European Communities (1995) Case C-415/93 (The Bosman Judgment).
Demmert, H. (1973) *The Economics of Professional Team Sports*, Lexington Books, Lexington, MA.
Greene, W. (1993) *Econometric Analysis* 2nd Edn, Macmillan, Basingstoke, UK.
Fort, R. & Quirk, J. (1995) Cross-subsidisation, incentives and outcomes in professional team sports leagues, *Journal of Economic Literature*, 33, 3, pp. 1265–1299.
Jennett, N. (1984) Attendance, uncertainty of outcome and policy in Scottish league football, *Scottish Journal of Political Economy*, 31, pp. 176–198.
Jones, J. C. H. & Ferguson, D. G. (1988) Location and survival in the national hockey league, *The Journal of Industrial Economics*, 36, 4, pp. 443–4557.

Kuypers, T. (1997) Unpublished PhD Thesis, University College London.

Noll, R. (ed.) (1974) *Government and the Sports Business*, Brookings Institution, Washingtan, DC.

Peel, D. & Thomas, D. (1988) Outcome uncertainty and the demand for football, *Scottish Journal of Political Economy*, 35, pp. 242–249.

Restrictive Practices Court (1999). 'In the Matter of an Agreement between the Football Association Premier League Limited and the Football Association Limited and the Football League Limited and their Respective Member Clubs and in the Matter of an Agreement relating to the supply of services facilitating the broadcasting on television of Premier League football matches and the supply of services consisting in the broadcasting on television of such matches.' (28th July).

Sloane, P. J. (1971) The economics of professional football: The football club as a utility maximizer, *Scottish Journal of Political Economy*, 17, 2, pp. 121–146.

Szymanski, S. (1998) 'Hermetic Leagues, Open Leagues and the Impact of Revenue Sharing on Competitive Balance', paper submitted as evidence to the Restrictive Practices Court in the Premier League/Sky/BBC case.

Szymanski, S. & Kuypers, T. (1999) *Winners and Losers: The Business Strategy of Football*, Penguin Books.

Vrooman, J. (1995) A general theory of professional sports leagues, *Southern Economic Journal*, 61, 4, pp. 971–990.

Whitney, J. (1988) Winning games versus winning championships: The economics of fan interest and team performance, *Economic Inquiry*, 26, October, pp. 703–724.

10
The Champions League and the Coase Theorem

Stefan Szymanski

Tanaka Business School, London

Abstract

This chapter considers the relevance of the Coase Theorem to the analysis of sports leagues. It is widely believed that there exists an ideal competitive balance between teams in a sporting contest, and that without competitive restraints to redistribute resources championships will be too unbalanced. The chapter reviews the empirical evidence on this issue to date, and then examines a model where the outcome may be either too little or too much competitive balance. Empirical evidence from English football suggests that the bias is likely to be in favour of too much competitive balance. The implications for European football in general and the Champions League in particular are then discussed.

I Introduction

The Coase Theorem is both one of the simplest and most profound ideas in economics. Coase's insight was first expressed in print as a theorem by George Stigler, following the publication of the famous article 'The Problem of Social Cost' by Nobel Laureate Ronald Coase (1960). Stigler stated it thus: 'with zero transactions costs, private and social costs will be equal'. The significance of this statement is that 'if private cost is equal to social cost, it follows that producers will only

This chapter is based on my inaugural lecture delivered on 11 May 2005. I would like to express my warm gratitude to all those who have helped me develop my research over the years, but above all to Hayley for all her love and support.

engage in an activity if the value of the product of the factors used is greater than the value which they would yield in their best alternative use' (Coase, 1988, p. 158). In other words, bargaining in an unrestricted market will produce full economic efficiency (assuming zero transactions costs), obviating the need to invoke government intervention in the form of Pigouvian taxes and subsidies to correct externalities. The implications for social policy are profound – simply by establishing property rights, all externalities will be internalised and private transactions will be publicly optimal. Most notably, the lesson of Coase Theorem for environmental economics is that we need only to establish property rights over the quantities of greenhouse gases in the atmosphere and toxins in the oceans, and pollution will be controlled at socially optimal, sustainable levels. Many economists would echo the words of Avinash Dixit and Mancur Olson (2000): 'In his article "The Problem of Social Cost", Ronald Coase introduced a very powerful idea of great importance. Coase's article has been arguably the single largest influence on thinking about economic policy for the last three decades. It is one of the most – if not the most – widely cited economics article in recent times.'

Big theorems are notoriously difficult to test. Darwinism remains resolutely untestable, no one is holding out much hope of testing the theories of Freud or Marx and even in physics developments such as the string theory remain testable only in principle. One problem with big theories is that they require big experiments – experimental frameworks that are capable of capturing a substantial degree of the complexity that a big theory addresses. In the world of economics, big theorems such as the fundamental theorems of welfare economics or the law of demand are generally approached through specific examples. In this chapter the Coase Theorem is approached through the medium of a sports league. While Coase's article dates back to 1960, a colleague at Chicago University published a discussion of the market for baseball players in 1956, which almost completely anticipates the more famous paper (Rottenberg, 1956). As in any team sport, the players are the principal asset, and teams have historically traded these assets, frequently for cash. In baseball, a rule enforced by the owners, known as the Reserve Clause, prohibited players from moving teams without the permission of their current employer, effectively endowing the employer a monopsony right over the income stream of the player. As this restraint comes under pressure from the players and their union, the owners sought to defend their rule by arguing that if players were free to move they would quickly migrate to the wealthiest teams, disturbing the essential element of 'competitive balance' allegedly fostered by the Reserve Clause. Rottenberg argued, in the manner of Coase, that ownership rules would make no difference to the distribution of talent in a league. If owners controlled the movement of players, trade between clubs would cause each player to move to the location where his (marginal revenue) product is greatest. If players were free to move, bidding by the clubs to hire players would produce the same distribution (the only difference being that any economic rents would now accrue to the player, not to the owner).

This chapter re-examines the application of the Coase Theorem to the market for players in a sports league. It shows that plausible trading mechanisms will not achieve Coasian efficiency. This result is demonstrated using data from English football. The implications of these results for the development of the UEFA Champions League is then discussed.

II   The Coase theorem and its discontents

The Coase Theorem has been subject to significant scrutiny in the economics literature and has been widely challenged (see, for example, Ellickson, 1991; Samuelson, 1995). Three examples of academic critiques are discussed here:

(i) Practicality (e.g. Canterbery and Marvasti, 1992). Even if it is true that costless bargaining with full property rights produces efficiency, many economists have argued that this is of little practical value, as most market failures, which the Coase Theorem addresses, refer to situations where property rights are very difficult to define precisely or in a way that it is legally enforceable (e.g. rights over the ocean fisheries – even if territorial waters are assigned, the fish often fail to respect the boundaries so that enforcing rights over fish that temporarily stray into another's jurisdiction is likely to be difficult). Additionally, the relevance of the costless bargaining paradigm is questionable as most of the difficult and important problems arise where bargaining costs are very high (e.g., pollution rights).

(ii) Tautology (e.g. Usher, 1998). He argues that in a zero transaction cost world, efficiency must be guaranteed among maximising agents, regardless of whether property rights exist at all – as otherwise there will exist unrealised gains from trade. Hence, while it is strictly true that any allocation of property will produce efficiency in such a world, the existence of property rights is not necessary.

The Coase Theorem, stripped of the necessity of property, merely becomes the statement that in a world where agents are willing and able to bargain until all potential gains from trade are realised, the outcome will be economically efficient, which, as stated, appears tautological, as economic efficiency is defined as the realisation of all potential gains from trade.

(iii) Falsity (e.g. Aivazian and Callen, 2003). These authors relate the Coase Theorem to Edgeworth's notion of the core. The core is defined as the set of efficient equilibrium bargains among parties. The perfectly competitive equilibrium of neoclassical economics belongs to the set of resource allocations that are in the core, but others may exist as well. Clearly the outcome of Coasian bargaining must be in the core as well. Different initial allocations of rights might produce different allocations of resources, but all outcomes should be in the core (e.g. the allocation of resources will be different if the polluter has the absolute right to pollute compared with a situation where citizens have an absolute right to protection from the effects of pollution, but the Coase Theorem says that the amount of pollution should be fixed at the efficient level in both cases). However, if an allocation of property rights exists for which the core is empty – that is, there is no equilibrium bargain that is efficient – then the Coase Theorem fails. Aivazian and Callen provide a simple example of just such a case.

While theoretical objections abound, it is perhaps more important to understand whether the implications of the Coase Theorem are really relevant for economic policy. In other words, we need to understand whether, in a world where property rights are well defined and bargaining is not too costly, the outcomes of bargaining are plausibly close to efficiency. The team sports literature has been widely cited as an example of a situation where the Coase Theorem is put to a practical test.

III The Coase theorem in the sports literature

One common characteristic of team sports as they developed on both sides of the Atlantic has been the desire of the owners of teams belonging to professional leagues to control the market for players, in particular to establish monopsony rights. Thus the Reserve Clause of baseball (see, e.g. Quirk and Fort, 1992, for an explanation) functioned in much the same way as the retain-and-transfer system of English soccer (see, e.g. Sloane, 1969).[1] This inevitably led to challenges in the courts by the players claiming the right to move freely between employers. Simon Rottenberg's celebrated (1956) article examined this issue and presented the team owner's rationale:

> the defense most commonly heard is that the reserve rule is necessary to assure an equal distribution of playing talent among opposing teams; that a more or less equal distribution of talent is necessary if there is to be uncertainty of outcome; and that uncertainty of outcome is necessary if the consumer is to be willing to pay admission to the game. This defense is founded on the premise that there are rich baseball clubs and poor ones and that, if the players' market were free, the rich clubs would outbid the poor for talent, taking all competent players for themselves and leaving only the incompetent for other teams.

> (p. 246)

Rottenberg argued that (a) the Reserve Clause did nothing to prevent the migration of talent to the big city teams and so would not affect the distribution of talent and that (b) by establishing monopsony power over a player throughout his career the team owners were able to hold down wages and raise profitability. Point (a) has since been identified as an example of the Coase Theorem at work: the initial distribution of ownership rights should have no impact on the efficient (here profit maximising) distribution of resources. El-Hodiri and Quirk (1971) and Quirk and El-Hodiri (1974) took this analysis one stage further in a formal dynamic model showing that if teams have differing revenue-generating potential, (i) profit-maximising behaviour will not lead to an equal distribution of resources (playing talent) and (ii) revenue redistribution on the basis of gate sharing will have no impact on the distribution of playing talent. Both points, (a) and (ii), are examples of the well-known *invariance principle*.

There have been two significant changes in talent allocation rules in North American sports over recent years. First, in 1976 major league baseball (MLB) players won the right of free agency after completing six years of service, and this practice rapidly spread to the other sports. Second, the draft rules of the NFL, which allocated the right to hire new talent entering the league on the basis of the reverse order of finish of the previous season's competition, were adopted by the other sports [see Paul Staudohar (1996) for more details on both these innovations]. These changes can be studied to identify the impact of changes in talent allocation rules on competitive balance.

Free agency

The advent of free agency in MLB in 1976 for six-year veterans is a clear natural experiment.[2] The owners claimed that as a result of this limited free agency the best veterans would migrate to the big city teams and competitive balance would be undermined. A number of studies have attempted to use this rule change to test the invariance hypothesis, and the findings from these studies are reported in Table 10.1.

Table 10.1   The impact of free agency on competitive balance in MLB

Study	Measure of competitive balance	Impact on competitive balance in NL	Impact on competitive balance in AL
Daly and Moore (1981)	Movement of free agents to large market team	(−)	(−)
Scully (1989)	Standard deviation of win percent and Gini co-efficient of pennant wins	(+)	(0)
Balfour and Porter (1991)	Standard deviation of win percent, persistence of win percent	(+)	(+)
Fort and Quirk (1995)	Standard deviation of win percent and Gini coefficient of pennant wins	(0)	(0)
Vrooman (1995)	Standard deviation of win percent relative to idealised standard deviation	(+)	(+)
Vrooman (1996)	Persistence of win percent	(+)	(+)
Butler (1995)	Standard deviation of win percent and serial correlation of win percent	(0)	(0)
Horowitz (1997)	Entropy	(−)	(0)
Depken (1999)	Hirschman–Herfindahl index of wins relative to ideal	(0)	(−)
Eckard (2001)	Analysis of variance of win percent	(+)	(+)

Source: Szymanski (2003).

Most of the studies simply look at the standard deviation of win percentages before and after 1976 (Scully, 1989; Balfour and Porter, 1991; Quirk and Fort, 1992; Butler, 1995; Vrooman, 1995), while other measures include persistence in win percent (Balfour and Porter, 1991; Vrooman, 1996), entropy (Horowitz, 1997), the Hirschman–Herfindahl index (Depken, 1999) and analysis of variance (Eckard, 2001). Most of these studies find either no change (seven cases) or an improvement in competitive balance (nine cases), contrary to the claim of the owners that free agency would reduce competitive balance (four cases only). However, this meta-data is hardly a ringing endorsement for the invariance principle, as 'no effect' is reported in only seven out of 20 cases. Of course, it can be argued that many other factors have altered competitive balance (e.g. the increasing dispersion of local TV revenues), but in that case the data, without controlling for these factors, can hardly be said to represent a test at all.

Some other studies have approached the invariance principle as a direct test of the Coase Theorem and tried to establish whether the distribution of talent in the league has been affected by the introduction of free agency. George Daly (1992) observes that under the Reserve Clause top-line players were seldom traded, a situation that has been affected by free agency where the top stars have a choice after six years leading to increased mobility. Timothy Hylan *et al.* (1996) in a study of pitcher movements found that these players have become less mobile as free agency, a surprising result and one that they claim does not support the Coase Theorem. However, Cymrot *et al.* (2001) examine player mobility in 1980, controlling for possible selection bias and find that, for that season at least, there was no evidence that restricted players (with fewer than six years of service) enjoyed more or less mobility than unrestricted free agents after controlling for player characteristics.

Daniel Marburger (2002) considers a different implication of the invariance principle. If trade is possible between two independent leagues then it should be more profitable to hire a player from the same league than from the rival league. Intra-league trade raises the winning probability of the buying team more than an inter-league trade does, as in the former case not only does the buyer have a larger share of talent, but the seller now has a weaker team. Under the Reserve Clause this effect will be built into the seller's price, but under free agency it will not, as the free agent is indifferent to the adverse effect on the team he is leaving. Thus with free agency the relative price of intra-league trades should fall and their share of total trades increase. Marburger found a statistically significant increase in the share of intra-league trades, from 60% to 73%, in MLB between 1964 and 1992. This finding seems consistent with the invariance principle.

The rookie draft

The stated intention of the rookie draft system is to provide weaker teams with opportunities to acquire talented players by awarding them first pick. Of course, an additional consequence of this system is the creation of monopsony power. The draft system was instituted by the NFL in 1936 as a way of strengthening weak-performing teams to maintain competitive balance, and has been adopted by all the other major leagues (Fort and Quirk, 1995; Staudohar, 1996 provide details).

Daly and Moore (1981) first analysed whether the draft achieved its stated intention by examining competitive balance before and after the introduction of the MLB draft in 1965. They found a significant improvement in the balance of the National League and a smaller improvement in the balance of the American League. The Japanese Professional Baseball League adopted a draft system at exactly the same time as MLB, and a study by La Croix and Kawaura (1999) also found that competitive balance improved over time (measured by the Gini coefficient for pennants) in both the Central and Pacific Leagues.[3] As they point out, these results are 'virtually identical' to Fort and Quirk's (1995) results for MLB. Grier and Tollison (1994) examined the impact of the rookie draft in the NFL by running an autoregressive specification for win percentage together with the average draft order over the previous three to five seasons, and found that a low draft order significantly raises performance. These results seem to provide consistent evidence against the invariance principle and in support of the owners' stated position.

IV   Trading mechanisms and the allocation of talent

One difficulty with much of the preceding analysis is that the relationship between the trading mechanisms in sports leagues and the efficient distribution of talent is poorly defined. The approach followed here is to derive the distribution that teams will select when they maximise profits and to compare this with a plausible candidate for an efficient allocation of talent.

Szymanski (2004a) considered a simple model of competition in a league where demand depends on (a) the success of each team and (b) the degree of competitive balance.[4] In the model it is assumed that there is a supply of talent to the market (which may be fixed or elastic) and that team success (measured by the percentage of games won) depends on the share of total talent hired. Teams are assumed to maximise profit. In a league of two teams this boils down to a contest success function

$$w_1 = \frac{t_1}{t_1 + t_2}, \quad w_2 = 1 - w_1, \tag{1}$$

where w is win percentage and t is talent hired, which is assumed perfectly divisible. This amounts to the simple Tullock (1980) rent-seeking model. It is natural to assume a simple profit function, where there exists an asymmetry between the teams, in terms of their ability to generate revenue from a given level of success on the field:

$$\pi_1 = (\sigma - w_1)w_1 - ct_1, \quad \pi_2 = (1 - w_2)w_2 - ct_2, \quad \sigma > 1 \tag{2}$$

where c is the (constant) marginal cost of talent, and σ indicates that team 1 is capable of generating a larger revenue than team 2 from any given level of success. Note that the demand for competitive balance ensures that revenues are ultimately decreasing in success, but that given the adding up constraint in equation (1), there is no guarantee of an interior solution.

How do teams choose talent? We can imagine this as a quantity-setting (Cournot-type) or price-setting (Bertrand-type) game. As a quantity game, teams allocate a budget to hiring talent and the talent they can hire is proportional to their share of total budgets. The first order conditions for talent choice are therefore

$$\frac{\partial \pi_1}{\partial t_1} = (\sigma - 2w_1)\, w_2 - cT = 0, \quad \frac{\partial \pi_2}{\partial t_2} = (1 - 2w_2)\, w_1 - cT = 0, \tag{3}$$

where $T = t_1 + t_2$, so that at the Nash equilibrium

$$w_1^* = \sigma/(1 + \sigma) \tag{4}$$

Team 1 dominates ($w_1 > 1/2$) in equilibrium because it has the larger drawing power ($\sigma > 1$). However, at equilibrium the marginal revenue of a win for team 1 exceeds the marginal revenue of team 2

$$\frac{\partial R_1}{\partial w_1} = \sigma - 2w_1^* = \frac{\sigma\,(\sigma - 1)}{(\sigma + 1)} > \frac{\sigma - 1}{\sigma + 1} = 1 - 2w_2^* = \frac{\partial R_2}{\partial w_2} \tag{5}$$

This implies a distribution of talent in the league that is not jointly efficient. To see this, note that joint profits are

$$\pi_1 + \pi_2 = (1 + \sigma)\, w_1 - 2w_1^2 - cT \tag{6}$$

which is maximised when

$$w_1^M = \frac{1+\sigma}{4} > w_1^* \tag{7}$$

Hence the quantity-bidding mechanism entails 'too much' competitive balance at the Nash equilibrium. Intuitively, this result is a consequence of asymmetry. Competition always involves an externality – each team's actions under competition fail to account for the negative effect that those actions have on rivals' profits. The externality imposed by the team with the lower win percentage in equilibrium is bigger precisely because the big team loses more than the small team when its rival wins more.

Dakhlia and Pecorino (2004) consider a rent-seeking model where teams not only bid for a quantity of talent but also submit a bid for the wage rate per unit of talent. If each team offers the same wage rate then the Nash equilibrium distribution of talent will be the same as above. However, if one team bids higher than the other it can attract all the talent, generating a corner solution. In their model, where teams only have a demand for winning and there is no value in competitive balance, they show that the dominant team will be willing to preempt all of the talent by offering a bid at which its rival's demand for talent is zero, as long as the quantity of talent is not too great. However, if the supply of talent is large enough, pre-emption is not profitable, given that the team would have to hire all of the talent in order to pre-empt the market.[5]

The incentive to pre-empt can be identified by comparing the profit level at an interior equilibrium for a given marginal cost of talent with the profit made by one team raising price by ε above marginal cost, hiring all the talent and winning all the time. If this deviation can be shown to be profitable then a form of Bertrand's competition will ensue.

To derive the condition for a profitable deviation, first consider the demand for talent at the interior equilibrium. First note that $w_1/w_2 = t_1/t_2 = \sigma$. Writing equation (3) in terms of t_1 and t_2, substituting for t_2 we obtain

$$t_1^* = \frac{\sigma^2(\sigma - 1)}{(1+\sigma^3)c}, \quad t_2^* = \frac{\sigma(\sigma - 1)}{(1+\sigma)^3 c}. \tag{8}$$

This implies that team 1 makes profit equal to

$$\pi_1^* = \frac{\sigma^4 + \sigma^2}{(1+\sigma)^3}. \tag{9}$$

It can now be shown that team 1 would want to pre-empt by offering a wage rate '$c + \varepsilon$' if the total supply to the market $T^s = t_1^* + t_2^*$. For ε small enough, the profits from pre-emption are

$$\sigma - 1 - cT^s = \frac{\sigma^3 - 1}{(1 + \sigma)^2}. \tag{10}$$

Pre-emption can therefore be profitable if[6]

$$\sigma^3 > \sigma^2 + \sigma + 1 \Rightarrow \sigma > 1.84 \text{ approx.} \tag{11}$$

Thus pre-emption can be a profitable strategy if the dominant team is sufficiently large. As Dakhlia and Pecorino show, pre-emption additionally requires that the marginal profit of team 2 is negative when it hires zero units of talent, requiring that $bT^s > 1$, where b is the pre-emptive bid of team 1 and T^s is the total supply of talent. In addition, however, if $T^s > t_1^* + t_2^*$ then it becomes less and less likely that pre-emption is profitable.

Thus, when there is bidding for talent, there is a possibility that we shift from an inefficient interior solution to a pre-emptive corner solution, which is also inefficient. In both cases it is assumed that any market-clearing mechanism must involve identical treatment for each unit of talent. If talent were sold for different prices to different teams then there would be no equilibrium among the players, as low-paid players with identical skills would be willing to move to high-paying teams.

V Some empirical evidence

The theory described in the previous section implies a simple empirical experiment. Because data exist for attendance at league matches and the success rates of teams, it is feasible to identify a statistical relationship for each team in a league. From this relationship it is possible to estimate a distribution of wins that would maximise attendance at home matches, and to compare this distribution with the actual distribution, which may be imagined as an approximation of the competitive Nash equilibrium. Szymanski (2004b) estimates this relationship for Major League Baseball, while Leach and Szymanski (2005) do the same for the lower divisions of English soccer. The first of these papers shows quite clearly that the attendance-maximising distribution of wins will be much more unbalanced than what we observe in practice, and that the optimal distribution gives more weight to already dominant teams. The key to the analysis is to estimate separate slope parameters for a quadratic equation relating home attendance to wins. While this has seldom been done before (a notable exception is Dobson and Goddard, 2001), the regression fits the data well in the case of English football, although the analysis must be restricted to the lower three divisions because such a large fraction of Premier League matches are sold out, and therefore attendance in these cases is largely insensitive to success. But in general, attendance is strongly dependent on success in winning matches – this should not be surprising given that in any team sports league, the majority of those attending a game is fans of the home team.

Leach and Szymanski used attendance and wins data for all professional league clubs in England over the last 30 years and produced club-by-club estimates, a sample of which is shown in Table 10.2.

The size of these sensitivities varies considerably by club, and the restriction that coefficients are identical across clubs is easily rejected. The regressions seem well defined, with level and quadratic terms having the right signs in all cases, and about three-quarters of the estimates are significant at the conventional level. Using these estimates,

Table 10.2 Estimated sensitivity of attendance to wins for a sample of clubs

Club	Level term (WPct)		Squared term (WPct^2)	
	Coefficient	Standard error	Coefficient	Standard error
Aldershot Town	21,450	4627	−15,159	6752
Aston Villa	1,41,207	80,300	−1,03,652	1,15,000
Barnsley	40,018	22,100	−44,124	35,200
Birmingham City	73,007	18,000	−60,110	27,200
Blackburn Rovers	36,529	21,900	−24,005	34,200
Blackpool	25,535	6764	−17,645	8523
Bolton Wanderers	74,357	9735	−53,469	16,100
Bournemouth	21,700	3694	−11,255	6926
Bradford City	59,411	17,100	−51,505	23,700
Brentford	25,103	7938	−10,149	11,300
Brighton & Hove	92,932	9154	−84,248	12,000
Bristol City	72,672	33,500	−84,299	65,000
Bristol Rovers	29,861	1951	−22,318	3664
Burnley	21,804	11,800	−6079	21,400
Bury	21,555	1724	−13,862	2604

Source: Leach and Szymanski (2005).

we can proceed to estimate the attendance-maximising distribution of wins for any team in any particular season. By way of example, consider the estimates for two teams, Sheffield Wednesday and Watford. These were selected for simple arithmetical expedient that the quadratic terms for these two clubs are more or less identical. The two equations are

Sheffield Wednesday : attendance $= 75,000$ (%wins) $- 44,000$ (%wins)^2

Watford : attendance $= 59,000$ (%wins) $- 44,000$ (%wins)^2

From these estimates we can calculate the attendance-maximising percentage of wins for each team: 85% for Sheffield Wednesday and 67% for Watford. In each case, attendance does start to decline when the team wins too big a share of its matches. Imagine a league that contained only these two teams. Clearly, they cannot jointly reach their individual optimum, as the total number of wins must sum to 100%. A central planner would choose an allocation of wins between the two teams which equalised the marginal attendance from a win for each team – in other words where

$$75,000 - 88,000w_1 = 59,000 - 88,000w_2$$

which implies $w_1^M = 59\%$ is the optimal win percentage for Sheffield Wednesday. However, if we now consider the Nash equilibrium of a talent-hiring contest between the two teams, the marginal benefit of a unit of talent for each team is

$$(75,000 - 88,000w_1)\,w_2 = (59,000 - 88,000w_2)\,w_1$$

which implies that at the Nash equilibrium Sheffield Wednesday's win percentage would be $w_1^* = 56\%$, less than the attendance-maximising optimum, as illustrated in Fig. 10.1.

The calculations are somewhat more tedious, but it is straightforward to reproduce this result for any league division and any particular season, and the result always appears to be the same – the attendance-maximising distribution of wins is much more unequal than that which we observe in practice (which is presumed to be a Nash equilibrium). For example, Table 10.3 shows the actual standard deviation of wins for the second tier of English football over the last decade and the attendance maximising distribution.

Thus the empirical evidence on attendance seems to support the theory. Several objections have been raised to these results.[7] First, it might

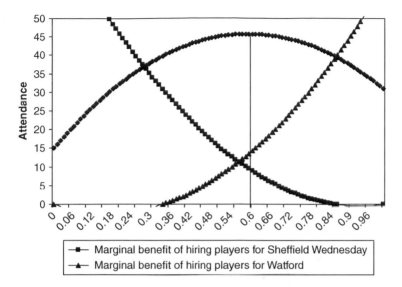

- ■ — Marginal benefit of hiring players for Sheffield Wednesday
- ▲ — Marginal benefit of hiring players for Watford

Figure 10.1 Total attendance at Sheffield Wednesday–Watford games

Table 10.3 Standard deviation of actual and optimal win percentages for the second tier of English football 1994–2003

Season	Second tier actual standard deviation of win percentage	Second tier constrained standard deviation of optimal win percentage
1994	0.086	0.241
1995	0.081	0.187
1996	0.072	0.232
1997	0.094	0.232
1998	0.115	0.235
1999	0.116	0.242
2000	0.111	0.237
2001	0.115	0.246
2002	0.112	0.227
2003	0.106	0.203

Source: Leach and Szymanski (2005).

be said that attendance is only one source of revenue, and that for many leagues TV income is as important. As a matter of fact, this may be true of the Premier League but is certainly not true for the lower divisions that attract only small TV revenues. If TV income did matter, and TV viewers wanted balanced contests (being less partisan than the typical supporter attending a match), then these results would be to a degree mitigated. However, even TV fans can be partisan, and even in the most TV-oriented leagues, clubs still obtain a large fraction of their income from gate money. Second, it might be said that a very unbalanced contest is all well and good in the short run, but that a league that was persistently unbalanced would be likely to lose its supporter base. This point is in fact addressed in the estimation technique, as the reported estimates are derived from a regression that includes lagged variables on the right-hand side, and these are used to estimate a long-run relationship. Critics might say that these estimates are unlikely to give a reliable indication about a much more unbalanced world as the optimal levels of balance estimated have never been observed in practice. However, it has been shown by Buzzacchi *et al.* (2003) that despite the fact that European football is much less balanced than the US major leagues (measured by the likelihood of teams entering the highest-ranked positions), it has not been the case that attendance at European football has been declining relative to attendance at the US major leagues. What the data certainly do not suggest, contrary to the claims of many federations and sports economists, is that increasing competitive balance will lead to an increase in attendance in the short to medium run.

VI   The future of the Champions League

In what sense does any of this contradict the Coase Theorem? What has been shown in the model is that different trading mechanisms generate different allocations, none of which is efficient. However, the model does not exhaust the potential range of mechanisms nor does it show that other forms of bargaining between teams would not achieve the productively efficient allocation. Indeed, owners of US major league teams might argue that they adopt the panoply of restrictive devices, for which they are famous precisely to combat these potential inefficiencies (roster limits, salary caps, etc.). However, perhaps the model does shed some light on what a Coasian mechanism must look like. The analysis suggests that simple rules often fail to reach optimality. It suggests that agents need to have some idea of what constitutes a globally efficient outcome, and that then they may need to adopt quite complex bilateral bargains to achieve the efficient outcome. Reliance on conventional market signals (e.g. prices, quantities) may not be enough. Significant planning and coordination among firms may be required to reach a Coasian bargain – often in ways that might, when viewed in a mundane fashion, violate antitrust laws. The most obvious mechanism for dealing with the inefficiency of specific trading mechanisms is to integrate the teams in the league into a single enterprise. In sport, it has been argued that a league should indeed be viewed as a single entity (see e.g. Roberts, 1984) since the 'product' is the league competition, rather than any particular games played in the league. This view is much debated in the sports literature, but the more general implication that the solution to the problem of Coasian bargaining is monopoly is surely not a very attractive one.

In the context of a sports league, such mechanisms are generally accepted on the grounds that teams must cooperate in order to produce 'the product' defined as the league competition, even if the single-entity defence is rejected. In this view, leagues are treated as a joint venture (Flynn and Gilbert, 2001). In the United States, redistributive mechanisms are supported in the name of competitive balance and are generally established in order to redistribute resources from strong teams to weaker teams. It could be argued that even if redistribution in this direction does not maximise attendance in the short run, it will serve to maximise interest in the long run, as excessively unbalanced competitions may cause loss of interest in the long run.[8] However, such effects are difficult to prove, and the evidence that many European soccer leagues have remained highly popular over many years, despite being consistently and significantly unbalanced, suggests that this link may be weak or even non-existent. Moreover, even in the united states, redistributive measures have not been deemed adequate to maintain balance within a league. Team relocation is a controversial issue, with many motivations being attached to desire of team owners to move from one city to another (e.g. expansion into larger markets, extracting stadium subsidies, pre-empting the entry of rival leagues) (see e.g. Zimbalist, 2003, pp. 29–33; Quirk and Fort, 1992, pp. 298–302). However, it is clear that if a team owner relocates from a weak-drawing city to a strong-drawing city, competitive balance is likely to improve. Carlton *et al.* (2004) go so far as to argue that league restrictions on the right of teams to relocate are an efficient mechanism for internalising the externality caused by the loss of rivalry when a franchise moves (initially, any traditional rivalry that many have existed between a team at its old location and nearby cities will be diluted or lost completely, imposing an economic cost on these other franchises). They supply some evidence from ice hockey (the NHL) to show that franchise movements have only been permitted where they have been expected to add to league-wide profits.[9]

In the context of European football, the system of promotion and relegation should automatically ensure that teams with roughly equal levels of support should reach similar competitive levels (i.e. divisions) without the need for team relocation. Tied to the very strong evidence that (a) team expenditure generates success on the pitch and (b) team success generates revenue (e.g. Szymanski and Smith, 1997; Szymanski and Kuypers, 1999; Forrest and Simmons, 2002), it is clear that both intra- and inter-divisional league rankings in European football should accurately reflect revenue-generating potential. The difficulty in Europe, however, is that this system still fails to produce competitive balance in domestic leagues, which tend to be dominated by a very small number of teams.

Szymanski and Zimbalist (2005) discuss the extent to which the national leagues of countries such as Portugal, Norway, Belgium, Greece and Turkey, among others, have historically been dominated by a small number of teams. Smaller European countries have tended to be unbalanced because teams from only one or two dominant cities, usually the capital, have resources that far exceed those of teams representing smaller towns. Even in larger countries where it might be expected that a larger national population will generate a more diverse set of teams (e.g. Italy, Germany, England), competitive balance, measured by the number of teams effectively contesting the championship, is much weaker than in the US major leagues.

One plausible reason for this historical lack of balance is the balkanised nature of European football. If almost the entire world supply of baseball talent is insufficient to maintain competitive balance among 30 teams, as Major League Baseball appears to believe (e.g. Levin *et al.*), then what chance is there that the world's supply of football talent, divided between 50 or so European domestic leagues, will stretch far enough to maintain competitive balance in each? Historically, the talent has been spread thinly across the nations, particularly as mobility was limited in the pre-*Bosman* era by various national restrictions. Post-*Bosnian* we have seen a dramatic increase in player mobility combined with even greater concern about competition. This concern has taken two forms:

- The fear that teams from larger nations dominate Europe at the expense of teams from smaller countries.
- The fear that strong clubs in larger countries increasingly dominate national competition.

The common factor linking these two fears is the Champions League. UEFA have expressed concern about the effect that the Champions

League is having on the distribution of resources in Europe and on the level of competitive balance:

> The Champions League has created, in almost every country in Europe, an elite of rich clubs whose increasing dominance is turning their domestic title races into predictable turn-offs for fans, UEFA are warning (Observer, November 7, 2004).

> UEFA created this fantastic competition in 1992, but that it has now become a monster that has produced this unequal struggle between haves and have-nots in countries across Europe (Lennart Johannsen, UEFA President).

> It's a serious concern for us that in many European countries only a small number of teams can win the domestic league title.... This competitive imbalance is not unique in England, but it is quite pronounced there (William Gaillard, UEFA Director of Communications).

It is not hard to see how the Champions League could have added to the level of competitive imbalance. Champions League revenues derive principally from gate receipts and from the distribution of TV revenues. Each team retains the gate revenues from its home matches, while in the 2003/2004 season around £280 million was distributed between the 32 teams that participated in the group stages. Exactly half of these teams came from the big five TV markets (England, France, Germany, Italy and Spain) and these teams received over 70% of the money distributed. Partly this reflected the greater success of clubs from these countries, as the payments are partly based on results, but in part it reflected pure pulling power. For example, the eventual winners, Porto, received a smaller distribution than Arsenal, Monaco, Manchester United or Chelsea.

The resources that are distributed to these teams are likely to be used to invest in talent in order to dominate the competition in the future. For example, a modest Champions League run to the quarter finals for Manchester United is likely to generate income in the region of around £30 million (about £20 million in broadcast fees and £10 million in ticket sales), while more than half of the Premier League has a total annual income of less than £50 million. It is hard to see how the smaller teams could generate the financial resources to compete effectively in the domestic league.

It would appear that the Champions League has created chronic imbalance both inside the competition itself and outside in the domestic league championships. UEFA's response has been to introduce restriction on the size of squads fielded by teams in the Champions League, and to oblige teams to field at least four players who were trained by the club, and an additional four players who were trained inside the national association. These rules were agreed at a UEFA Congress in April 2005 and their introduction was explained by UEFA thus: 'restoring football's competitive balance is one of the reasons why UEFA is proposing new rules on locally trained players'.[10] However, when introducing these proposals, UEFA Chief Executive Lars-Christer Olsson admitted that 'there had been negative responses to the proposals from some major leagues and their larger clubs'. In fact, these proposals seem quite mild compared with some of the restrictions to be found in North America, and yet even these seem to meet resistance from the dominant teams.

One explanation for this apparent difference in attitude is the following: All teams in the US major leagues are recognised to be the dominant teams and have little or no fear of being disenfranchised, thanks to the 'closed' league system. In Europe, however, presently dominant teams that make concessions to weaker teams have every reason to fear that in the future they will sink into obscurity – and one need only consider the present status of former European Champions such as Nottingham Forest (outside of the Premier League since 1999 and relegated to the third tier in 2005) to see how severe the penalty for poor performance can be. In the US, concessions by currently strong teams are expected to be repaid in future when the tables are turned. Hence, all can be persuaded to make agreements that are collectively optimal. Under the promotion and relegation system, however, concessions that might make sense collectively do not make much sense individually, and certainly make much less sense than they do in the context of a closed league (see e.g. Szymanski and Valletti, 2003). This is not to say that the promotion and relegation system is itself a bad thing – indeed Ross and Szymanski (2002) argue that many of the inefficiencies observed in the US closed league system would be remedied by the application of promotion and relegation. The point is that reaching agreement on decisions that are collectively efficient in sports leagues is extremely difficult and the actual decisions made often seem to fall well short of Coasian efficiency.[11]

Strong teams that compete inside the Champions League also perceive themselves to face an alternative to sharing income and resources with a large number of weaker teams. As in the early 1980s, there has been more or less persistent discussion about the creation of a European Superleague. Such a league could be formed by an elite group of European teams on a closed or near-closed basis. There are clearly many formats that such a league might take – Hoehn and Szymanski (1999) discussed one such format – but it is clear that such a league would be likely to be built more around TV income. For example, if the 16 large-market teams competing in the Champions League can generate an income of around £200 m from playing around 40 matches, a full-scale European Superleague of 20 teams might be capable of generating ten times this amount from a schedule of 380 games. Two thousand million pounds, however, is more than the combined total turnover of Europe's 20 richest teams, according to this year's Deloitte and Touche rich list.[12] A figure of £2000 million for European Superleague TV rights would be in line with the 6–8-year deals recently signed by the NFL in the United States for about $3000 million per year, and indeed such thoughts may well be tied up with the continuing interest of Malcolm Glazer, owner of the NFL's Tampa Bay Buccaneers, in acquiring Manchester United. Any such income, of course, would be before considering potential income from ticket sales, merchandising, sponsorship and so on.

The fact that a breakaway superleague has been considered many times before is no secret. Most recently, plans for a mid-week league developed by Media Partners, associated with Silvio Berlusconi, owner of AC Milan, were eventually shelved in 1998 following reform of the Champions League that favoured the largest teams in Europe. In recent years there have been continuous rumours that G-14, a lobby group of the top European clubs formed in 2000, is preparing its own plans for the formation of a superleague. Of course, critics would accuse any clubs that were part of such a plan of financial greed and a betrayal of the traditions of the sport. However, it should also be observed that a superleague of 30 clubs organised on lines similar to the US major leagues would likely be more balanced than the present Champions League or any domestic league, even absent redistributive measures. This is simply because the distribution of talent among the 20 or 30 largest European teams is already more balanced than it is in existing competition.[13] By eliminating competition from the weakest teams, the competitive externality identified in this chapter would be mitigated, if not eliminated. This would seem clearly to involve the kind of Coasian bargaining described in this chapter. Whether any such bargains come to pass remains to be seen.

Notes

1. In fact, the two systems were so similar that it is hard to believe that the Football League did not copy the National League. However, no evidence to this effect has ever been produced.
2. In this case the change was exogenous – i.e. not itself motivated by a desire to affect competitive balance (see Bruce Meyer, 1995, for a discussion of natural experiments).
3. Although the within-season measure (standard deviation of win percent) was significant only for the Pacific League.
4. A more general model that is used to analyse the impact of gate revenue sharing is to be found in Szymanski and Késenne, 2004).
5. Efficiency in their model of pure rent seeking (à la Tullock) is slightly peculiar in that the most efficient result is for team 1 to win all the time as it values the pay-off more. Moreover, even if team 1 pre-empts all the talent, it only needs to use ε of it to win with certainty, since team 2 hires zero in equilibrium. The point here is that the simple rent-seeking game requires more structure in order for an interior solution to be efficient. If, for example, there is a demand for competitive balance, then an interior solution can be efficient.
6. The exact value of σ^* is $\dfrac{1}{3}\left(1 + \sqrt[3]{19 \pm 9\sqrt{\dfrac{11}{3}}} + \dfrac{4}{\sqrt[3]{19 \pm 9\sqrt{\dfrac{11}{3}}}}\right)$.
7. I am grateful, *inter alia*, to Robert Sandy, Peter Sloane and Andy Zimbalist for their insights.
8. Humphreys (2002) shows that a combination of within- and between-season competitive balance affects attendance. The relative decline of interest in the English FA Cup as the financial gap between the different divisions of English football has grown might also be interpreted in this light (Szymanski, 2001).
9. This is not quite the same as a competitive-balance argument, but the general proposition is consistent with a competitive-balance justification for relocation if increasing competitive balance increases league-wide profits.
10. 'UEFA out to get the balance right', Thursday, 3 February 2005, Mark Chaplin. http://www.uefa.com/uefa/news/Kind=128/newsId=277348.html, accessed 5 August 2005.
11. Ross and Szymanski (2006) argue that part of the problem lies in the vertical integration of championship organising and club management functions that prevails in most team sports leagues. Efficient structures are more likely to emerge when organisers are distinct from competitors, as is the case with many individualistic sports contests such as marathon running or golf.
12. 'World's top 20 football clubs set to break €3 billion income mark in 2005' Deloitte & Touche, 17 February 2005. http://www.deloitte.com/dtt/press_release/0,1014,sid%253D1017%2526cid%253D74209,00.html, accessed 5 August 2005.
13. Note that the Champions League does not include all of the strongest teams since each country is limited by the number of teams that can compete, a restriction that works against some of the largest clubs.

References

Aivazian, V. & Callen, J. (2003) The core, transactions costs, and the Coase theorem, *Constitutional Political Economy*, **14**, pp. 287–299.

Balfour, A. & Porter, P. (1991) The reserve clause in professional sports: Legality and effect on competitive balance, *Labor Law Journal*, **42**, pp. 8–18.

Butler, M. (1995) Competitive balance in major league baseball, *The American Economist*, **39**, 2, pp. 46–52.

Buzzacchi, L., Szymanski, S. & Valletti, T. (2003) Static versus dynamic competitive balance: Do teams win more in Europe or in the US? *Journal of Industry, Competition and Trade*, **3**, 3, pp. 167–186.

Canterbery, E. & Marvasti, A. (1992) The Coase theorem as a negative externality, *Journal of Economic Issues*, **XXVI**, 4, pp. 1179–1189.

Carlton, D., Frankel, A. & Landes, E. (2004) The control of externalities in sports leagues: An analysis of restrictions in the national hockey league. *Journal of Political Economy*, **112**, S1, pp. S268–288.

Coase, R. (1960) The problem of social cost, *The Journal of Law and Economics*, **3**, pp. 1–44.

Coase, R. (1988) Notes on the problem of social cost, in R. Coase, *The Firm and the Market*, University of Chicago Press, Chicago, IL.

Cymrot, D., Dunlevy, J. & Even, W. (2001) 'Who's on first': An empirical test of the Coase Theorem in baseball, *Applied Economics*, **33**, pp. 593–603.

Dakhlia, S. & Pecorino, P. (2004) Rent-seeking with scarce talent: A model of preemptive hiring, Finance and Legal Studies, Working Paper No. 04-09-01, University of Alabama Economics.

Daly, G. (1992) The baseball players' market revisited, in P. Sommers (ed.), *Diamonds Are Forever: The Business of Baseball*, Brookings Institution Press, Washington, DC.

Daly, G. & Moore, W. (1981) Externalities, property rights, and the allocation of resources in major league baseball, *Economic Inquiry*, **29**, pp. 77–95.

Depken, C. (1999) Free-agency and the competitiveness of major league baseball, *Review of Industrial Organization*, **14**, pp. 205–217.

Dixit, A. & Olson, M. (2000) Does voluntary participation undermine the Coase Theorem? *Journal of Public Economics*, **76**, pp. 309–335.

Dobson, S. & Goddard, J. (2001) *The Economics of Football*, Cambridge University Press, Cambridge, UK.

Eckard, W. (2001) Free agency, competitive balance and diminishing returns to pennant contention, *Economic Inquiry*, **39**, 3, pp. 430–443.

El-Hodiri, M. & Quirk, J. (1971) An economic model of a professional sports league, *Journal of Political Economy*, **79**, pp. 1302–1319.

Ellickson, R. (1991) The case of Coase against Coaseanism, *Yale Law Journal*, **99**, pp. 611–633.

Flynn, M. & Gilbert, R. (2001) An analysis of professional sports leagues as joint ventures, *Economic Journal*, **111**, pp. F27–46.

Forrest, D. & Simmons, R. (2002) Team salaries and playing success in sports: A comparative perspective, *Zeitschrift für Betriebswirtschaft*, **72**, 4.

Fort, R. & Quirk, J. (1995) Cross subsidization, incentives and outcomes in professional team sports leagues, *Journal of Economic Literature*, **XXXIII**, 3, pp. 1265–1299.

Grier, K. & Tollison, R. (1994) The rookie draft and competitive balance: The case of professional football, *Journal of Economic Behavior and Organization*, **25**, pp. 293–298.

Hoehn, T. & Szymanski, S. (1999) The Americanization of European football, *Economic Policy*, **28**, pp. 205–240.

Horowitz, I. (1997) The increasing competitive balance in major league baseball, *Review of Industrial Organization*, **12**, pp. 373–387.

Humphreys, B. (2002) Alternative measures of competitive balance in sports leagues, *Journal of Sports Economics*, **3**, 2, pp. 133–148.

Hylan, T., Lage, M. & Treglia, M. (1996) The Coase Theorem, free agency, and major league baseball: A panel study of pitcher mobility from 1961 to 1992, *Southern Economic Journal*, **62**, pp. 1029–1042.

La Croix, S. & Kawaura, A. (1999) Rule changes and competitive balance in Japanese professional baseball, *Economic Inquiry*, **37**, 2, pp. 353–368.

Leach, S. & Szymanski, S. (2005) Tilting the playing field: Why a sports league planner would choose less, not more, competitive balance: The case of English football, Mimeo, Tanaka Business School, Imperial College, London.

Levin, R., Mitchell, G., Volcker, P. & Will, G. (2000) *The Report of the Independent Members of the Commissioner's Blue Ribbon Panel on Baseball Economics*, Major League Baseball, New York.

Marburger, D. (2002) Property rights and unilateral player transfers in a multi-conference sports league, *Journal of Sports Economics*, **3**, 2, pp. 122–132.

Meyer, B. D. (1995) Natural and quasi-experiments in economics, *Journal of Business and Economic Statistics*, **13**, 2, pp. 151–161.

Quirk, J. & El Hodiri, M. (1974) The economic theory of a professional sports league, in R. Noll (ed.), *Government and the Sports Business*. Brookings Institution, Washington, DC, pp. 33–80.

Quirk, J. & Fort, R. (1992) *Pay Dirt: The Business of Professional Team Sports*, Princeton University Press, Princeton, NJ.

Roberts, G. (1984) Sports leagues and the Sherman act: The use and abuse of section 1 to regulate restraints on intraleague rivalry, *UCLA Law Review*, **32**, 219, pp. 286–287.

Ross, S. F. & Szymanski, S. (2002) Open competition in league sports, *Wisconsin Law Review*, **3**, pp. 625–656.

Ross, S. F. & Szymanski, S. (2006) Antitrust and inefficient joint ventures: Why sports leagues should look more like McDonalds and less like the United Nations. Mimeo, College of Law, University of Illinois, Urbana-Champaign.

Rottenberg, S. (1956) The baseball player's labor market, *Journal of Political Economy*, **64**, pp. 242–258.

Samuelson, P. (1995) Some uneasiness with the Coase Theorem, *Japan and the World Economy*, **7**, pp. 1–7.

Scully, G. (1989) *The Business of Major League Baseball*, University of Chicago Press, Chicago.

Sloane, P. (1969) The labor market in professional football, *British Journal of Industrial Relations*, **7**, 2, pp. 181–199.

Staudohar, P. (1996) *Playing for Dollars: Labor Relations and the Sports Business*, ILR Press, Cornell, NY.

Szymanski, S. (2001) Income inequality, competitive balance and the attractiveness of team sports: Some evidence and a natural experiment from English soccer, *Economic Journal*, **111**, pp. F69–84.

Szymanski, S. (2003) The economic design of sporting contests, *Journal of Economic Literature*, **XLI**, pp. 1137–1187.

Szymanski, S. (2004a) Professional team sports are only a game: The Walrasian fixed supply conjecture model, Contest–Nash equilibrium and the invariance principle, *Journal of Sports Economics*, **5**, 2, pp. 111–126.

Szymanski, S. (2004b) Tilting the playing field: Why a sports league planner would choose less, not more, competitive balance: The case of baseball, Mimeo, Tanaka Business School, Imperial College, London.

Szymanski, S. & Késenne, S. (2004) Competitive balance and gate revenue sharing in team sports, *Journal of Industrial Economics*, **LII**, 1, pp. 165–177.

Szymanski, S. & Kuypers, T. (1999) *Winners and Losers: The Business Strategy of Football*, Viking Books, London.

Szymanski, S. & Smith, R. (1997) The English football industry, profit, performance and industrial structure, *International Review of Applied Economics*, **11**, 1, pp. 135–153.

Szymanski, S. & Valletti, T. (2003) Promotion and relegation in sporting contest, Mimeo, Tanaka Business School, Imperial College, London.

Szymanski, S. & Zimbalist, A. (2005) *National Pastime: How Americans Play Baseball and the Rest of the World Plays Soccer*, Brookings Institution Press, Washington, DC.

Tullock, G. (1980) Efficient rent seeking, in J. Buchanan, R. Tollison & G. Tullock (eds), *Toward a Theory of Rent Seeking Society*, Texas A&M University Press, College Station, TX, pp. 97–112.

Usher, D. (1998) The Coase theorem is tautological, incoherent or wrong, *Economics Letters*, **61**, pp. 3–11.

Vrooman, J. (1995) A general theory of professional sports leagues, *Southern Economic Journal*, **61**, 4, pp. 971–990.

Vrooman, J. (1996) The baseball players market reconsidered, *Southern Economic Journal*, **62**, 3, pp. 339–360.

Zimbalist, A. (2003) *May the Best Team Win: Baseball Economics and Public Policy*, Brookings Institute, Washington, DC.

11
The Economic Impact of the World Cup

Stefan Szymanski
Imperial College, London

Introduction

The 2002 World Cup will be the principal sporting event of the year. For the first time two nations, South Korea and Japan, will share the responsibilities of hosting the football tournament, and both plan to use the opportunity to offer foreigners a window into their world and stimulate the development of soccer domestically. The hosting of the World Cup, as with the Summer and Winter Olympics, represents a major investment in public relations both for the national associations involved and for central and local governments. It is these latter institutions that fund most of the investment associated with the event, and they look to reap substantial advantages.

Not least among these is the hope that the World Cup will produce a substantial economic boost to economies that have struggled over the past decade to maintain the astonishing rates of growth they achieved from the 1960s to the 1980s. Economic studies of the likely economic impact of the 2002 World Cup have been produced by respected economic forecasters in both countries. The Dentsu Institute in Japan has forecast that the Japanese share of World Cup will generate a combined total of ¥1,400 billion (around $11 billion) to produce a long-term boost to the economy of ¥3,300 billion ($26 billion). This is the amount by which they predict Japanese GDP will increase above the level expected without the World Cup. It is equivalent to an increase in GDP of six-tenths of one percent. Considering that Japanese economic growth has averaged only 1.1% per year over the last decade, this represents an enormous boost from the playing of 32 football matches.

The Korea Development Institute (KDI) has produced a forecast that is, if anything, even more optimistic. They estimate that investment of $1.54 billion has been made in stadia, with $2.6 billion invested in total. They forecast expenditure related to the event at $6.18 billion and a total economic impact of $11.47 trillion won, around $8.8 billion and equal to 2.2% of GDP. Even set against Korea's faster economic growth over the last decade (averaging 5.6% per year), this would still be a remarkable outcome for a single sporting event.

How are these forecasts developed? How reliable are they? What evidence is there that staging large sporting events can produce such significant impacts? These are the questions that will be addressed in the remainder of this chapter.

Modelling the impact of sporting events

(i) Multiplier effects

The basic idea behind the measurement of the impact of sporting events is that it injects a significant increase in the demand for goods and services into an economy. This effect is not simply the *direct effect* created by investments prior to the event (e.g. in new stadia) or consumer spending during the event (e.g. ticket purchases), but also the *indirect effects* caused by the stimulus to the economic activities of others induced by the direct effects. For example, if expenditure by spectators produces $100 of income for a hot-dog seller, then some fraction of this income (say 50%) will be spent on goods and services supplied elsewhere in the economy, and generate an economic gain of $50 for those suppliers. If those suppliers also spend 50% of what they receive, then another round of economic stimulus occurs ($25). This process will continue endlessly, but after a small number of rounds the size of the increment will be negligible. In this example, the sum of direct and indirect effects is $100 + 50 + 25 + 12.5 \ldots$ and so on, with the stimulus in each round equal to half the stimulus from the previous round. Another way of saying this is that the total impact is equal to the direct impact multiplied by a sum equal to $1 + 0.5 + (0.5 \times 0.5) + (0.5 \times 0.5 \times 0.5) \ldots ad$ *infinitum*. It turns out that the value of this sum is equal to $1/0.5$, which equals 2, so the total impact is the direct impact multiplied by 2, that is, $200. The sum of the fractions that determine the size of the stimulus is called the multiplier, as it is the total economic impact of an amount of spending injected, expressed as a multiple of that injection.

Anyone who has ever studied economics is familiar with the concept of the multiplier, since it was used by Keynes to explain how government spending might be used to inject demand into an economy and ultimately produce very large economic effects for a small initial outlay. Keynes even suggested that if public funds were used merely to dig holes in the ground and refill them, that activity would still produce an economic benefit since the money paid out would circulate and stimulate. The multiplier concept is extremely powerful and can be used to produce very large predicted effects from initial injections. But it is an easily abused concept. From the point of view of macroeconomic demand management, the notion that government spending can produce large multiplier effects has been widely discredited. The essential reason for this is that the idea of a multiplier relies on the notion of spare capacity in the economy – resources that are lying unused and waiting only for the necessary stimulus to be brought into action and supply the demand that has been created. When Keynes wrote in the middle of the Depression, this description of an economy had some resonance, but in general, resources tend not to lie idle, but to seek out their most profitable employment. Thus any demand created by government spending will tend to divert resources from alternative activities, and therefore whatever multiplier effects exist on the positive side must be counterbalanced against negative multiplier effects due to diverted expenditures no longer providing income to some individuals whose own spending is thus curtailed. Overall, the net multiplier effect of government spending might be closer to zero.

Moreover, once it is allowed that government spending may divert spending from other areas, one is led to consider whether government spending is as effective as the alternative, and what effect boosting demand has on the economy as a whole. On the whole, the issue of government spending is one of targeting – will the spending be directed at the most productive activities? If not, then it is plausible to suppose that it will undermine national productivity by reducing economic potential. How much of the extra income will those targeted spend? The larger the proportion they spend compared with those who would have received the displaced expenditures, the more likely it is that the net impact is positive. The likelihood that government bureaucracies, facing political pressures from elected representatives, can fine-tune spending packages to achieve a significant net benefit seems somewhat remote.

Furthermore, government spending packages can have nasty side effects. If demand is boosted but the capacity to increase supply is limited, then suppliers will simply raise prices, and the overall impact of the stimulus is likely to be inflationary. Increased investment by government is likely to raise interest rates, and therefore render unprofitable some investment projects that would otherwise have taken place. Crowding out private-sector investment in this way is likely to undermine long-term growth prospects. Taking into account these possibilities, the multiplier effect might actually be negative.

(ii) Multipliers and sporting events

Expenditures associated with investment in facilities for, and consumption of, goods and services at major sporting events unquestionably provide an economic stimulus, and so the multiplier analysis of Keynesian macroeconomics is applicable. From the point of view of a sporting event, the first problem is to determine the boundaries of the region to be affected. Macroeconomic demand management is usually concerned with the operation of the economy as a whole. Most sporting-impact studies are constructed at a more local level – either a region within a country or perhaps only a city – depending usually on who is funding the facility. If the municipal authorities fund the stadium, they are only interested in the economic impact within the boundaries of their jurisdiction.[1]

Where you draw the boundary it has important implications for the estimated economic impact. The smaller the region considered, the larger the stimulus to it is likely to be, since the greater the number of visitors entering from outside the region to attend the event, the greater is the amount of expenditure (demand) which will be created by these visitors. Visitors from inside a given region are unlikely to offer much of a stimulus, simply because their spending on the event will be to a large extent diverted from other activities that they would otherwise have undertaken in the region. To see this point, suppose we are interested in the multiplier effect of attending World Cup matches in Japan. Consider a Japanese who decides to buy a ticket to the World Cup Final, and suppose the ticket costs $500. To analyse the impact of this spending, we have to ask where the money spent on the ticket came from. If it was from income that would otherwise have been spent on going to baseball matches, then there is no injection and no multiplier – or rather the positive impact created by going to the football match is cancelled out by the negative effect of not going to the baseball matches.[2] The only circumstance in which there could be a positive injection due to consumption within the relevant region would be if that consumption was funded out of savings – money that was not intended for consumption expenditure (at least in the near future). Will the ultra-cautious Japanese buy World Cup tickets out of their long-term savings? It does not sound a very likely proposition.

Since we are interested here in considering the economic impact on Japan and Korea of staging the World Cup, we have to consider consumer demand effects derived from the impact of foreign visitors, setting aside the impact of domestic visitors who are largely substituting alternative domestic activities. While this is bad news if the aim is to estimate a large overall impact, the larger the size of the region the larger the multiplier itself is likely to be. For expenditures to produce multiplier effects, the goods and services purchased must have some local content. Otherwise, any expenditures simply create demand for products and services to be imported into the region and boost incomes of outsiders but not insiders. For this reason one should be sceptical about city-based studies that suggest large multiplier effects estimated for municipal investments, since most of the income produced will flow to people living outside the city. From the point of view of Japan and Korea, however, the leakages of demand to outsiders are likely to be quite small, since these economies will supply most of the goods and services domestically. While there may be some increase in imports, most of the benefit of demand from foreign visitors is likely to translate into income for Japanese and Korean citizens, to be spent inside those countries.

How large might the multiplier be? If a fraction c of each round of income is used for consumption (where c lies between 0 and 1), then the summation $1 + c + c^2 + \ldots$ is equal to $1/(1 - c)$. Thus if $c = 0.5$, the multiplier is 2; if $c = 0.9$ the multiplier is 10. The larger the fraction of income spent on consumption, the larger the multiplier. However, we must remember that the government takes a share in the form of income tax which cannot be assumed to circulate further. Given an income tax rate of around 25% for Japan and Korea, this means that c can be no larger than 0.75. However, various studies suggest that for Japan at least, only about 55% of available income translates into consumption, and of this consumption around 22% is spent on imported goods, and so further reduces the knock-on effect inside the country. This suggests that c has a value of around $0.32 (= 0.78 \times 0.55 \times 0.75)$, so that the multiplier would be around 1.47.

(iii) Estimating the economic impact

Investment in new facilities and consumption expenditures by visitors are the two sources of economic stimulus associated with staging a major event. Of these, the size of the investment in facilities is easiest to measure. What is striking about the 2002 World Cup is the scale of the investment in facilities.

(a) Investment expenditures

Each country is using 10 different venues to stage matches, and out of these 17 are purpose-built facilities. This has generated around $1.5bn of investment in Korea and $3bn of investment in Japan. This compares with the World Cup France 98, where only the Stade de France was built from scratch, and total investment in stadium construction was no more than $500m.[3] World Cup specific stadium investment for Germany 2006 is estimated to be no more than $350m.[4]

Total investment is somewhat higher than simply stadium investment, because of additional transport infrastructure that usually accompanies the construction of new sites, and also because of the other investment costs associated with preparing for the event. We may assume from the figures for stadium investment that total investment is somewhere around $2.5bn for Korea and $5bn for Japan.

(b) Consumption expenditures

If the injection of consumption expenditures is derived only from foreign visitors, the forecast numbers are critical. The forecast for France 98 was 500,000 foreign visitors; the forecast for Germany 2006 is 1,100,000, spending a total of $800m. The forecasts for Korea are 400,000, and Japan, 350,000. Assuming these visitors are all supporters from the countries participating in the matches, that makes for about 25,000 fans per country.[5] Given that stadium capacity is less than 50,000 for most of the facilities, total capacity is around 3.2m seats, suggesting that foreign visitors will account for just under a quarter of total capacity assuming they attend only one match each.

How much will they spend? Japan is notoriously expensive, and since a large fraction of visitors will be travelling a great distance to support the 15 European teams participating, the expected stay and expenditure is likely to be much higher than it would be in Germany. If the forecast for Germany is $700 per visitor, a forecast for 2002 might be two to three times this amount for Korea and four to five times this amount for Japan. There are also significant transport costs, a large fraction of which will be paid to Japanese and Korean airlines. A spend of $2000 per person in Korea and $3000 per person in Japan would yield a visitor spend of $800m for Korea and $1050m for Japan.

(c) Total effect

These back-of-the-envelope calculations suggest that the total injection of new spending to Korea equals around $3.3bn, and for Japan, $6.05bn. Adopting a multiplier of 1.47, this suggests a total impact of $4.85bn in Korea, equal to around 1.2% of GDP, and $8.89bn for Japan, equal to around 0.2% of GDP. These are considerably smaller estimates than the headline figures suggested in the introduction, but there are grounds for concern that even these estimates are significant overestimates.

The single biggest weakness with this analysis is the assumption that investment expenditures produce a multiplier effect with no offsetting effects elsewhere in the economy. It is as if we had assumed that the construction sector has been sitting idle waiting for work to come along and, in the absence of the World Cup stadium programme, would not have found anything else useful to do. Even in the case of the Japanese construction sector, which has suffered as the economy has stagnated, it is reasonable to suppose that firms have been diverted from other projects and have to some extent been able to raise their prices. This effect will not only reduce the net impact, but may also lead to crowding out of projects that would otherwise have been profitable. In Korea, where the economy has managed to sustain a much higher level of economic growth in recent years, the possibility of such displacement and crowding out is much greater.

There are also grounds for scepticism in relation to the estimated visitor numbers. While large numbers will visit Japan and Korea for the World Cup, there can be little doubt that many potential visitors may stay away, particularly from cities where teams noted for their hooligan following, such as England, are playing. This may not be too significant if these are potential visitors who simply postpone their visit rather than cancel altogether. On the other hand, it also seems quite likely that many people who planned to visit Japan anyway will choose to visit during the World Cup in order to see some matches. In that case, the additional number of visitors due to the World Cup might be considerably smaller. Figure 11.1 offers an interesting insight into the impact on foreign visitors to France due to the World Cup held there in 1998.

Taken over the whole year, the additional number of tourists attracted by the World Cup in 1998 did not show up as a significant deviation in the trend increase in visitors. Certainly the figures for 1998 were well up on 1997, but then they increased in every other year shown in Fig. 11.1, and often by larger percentage amounts. It would be hard to see in Fig. 11.1 any grounds for believing that the World Cup had any significant effect on French tourism.

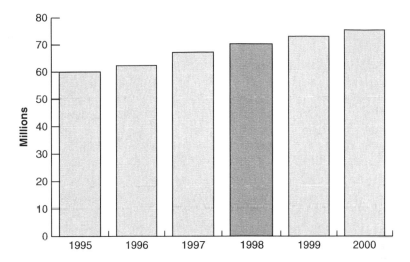

Figure 11.1 Foreign tourist visitors to France 1995–2000

A further point to note is that any effect of increased investment spending has in fact been spread over a number of years as construction progresses. Thus the annual economic impact over the three years leading up to the World Cup could be as little as one-fourth of 1% even if there is no crowding out.

Is the impact of a major sporting event statistically visible?

One problem frequently identified with economic-impact studies is that they tend to be upwardly biased since, in general, the studies are commissioned before the event by promoters anxious to claim that investments – usually from the public purse – have been well spent. There is little occasion to go back after the event and try to establish whether the claimed benefits actually materialised, and it is much harder to provide concrete evidence that a benefit materialised than to claim that the benefit *will* occur in the future.

One very crude method for assessing the effect is to look at the impact of hosting a major event such as the World Cup or Summer Olympics on economic growth, taking a range of countries over time. To do this, I collected data on the 20 largest economies measured by current GDP[6] over the last 30 years. Many of these countries have hosted at least one of the events over the 30 years, and several have hosted more than one. Table 11.1 shows the estimated impact of holding either the World Cup or Summer Olympics in the year before, during or after the event.

Table 11.1   The impact on economic growth of hosting a major event*

Effect	Impact on economic growth	*t*-statistic
Economic growth rate in previous year	0.249	6.271
Year before hosting World Cup	0.218	0.198
Year of hosting World Cup	−2.353	−2.160
Year after hosting World Cup	−0.099	−0.096
Year before hosting Summer Olympics	0.415	0.376
Year of hosting Summer Olympics	1.190	1.086
Year after hosting Summer Olympics	−0.640	−0.534

* Dependent variable is annual percentage change in GDP. Panel data estimates include both country-specific fixed effects and year effects.

The most important point to note from Table 11.1 is the last column that contains the *t*-statistics. These are measures of the statistical significance of any effects. To be considered statistically significant, it is conventionally required that the *t*-statistic be larger than 1.96 (in absolute value). For all the event effects bar one, the *t*-statistics are all substantially smaller than 1.96 in absolute terms. The only exception is the impact of holding the World Cup in the year the event takes place – and this effect is in fact negative, suggesting that economic growth declines rather than increases.

Is it very surprising that major events do not show up at the national level? Not really. For all that sport dominates the thoughts of many of us, it is still a relatively small economic enterprise. Compared to consumer spending on, say, food, sports expenditures are tiny. Moreover, the largest part of sports-related expenditures are on clothing and sports shoes. While major events may contribute to generating these expenditures, there is no direct link. Ultimately, for most economies of any size $1bn is a small amount, yet in the sporting world this is more money than that gets spent on almost any event.

Conclusions

There is a substantial literature in economics explaining why the economic impact of major events is likely to be quite small. There is also a substantial industry in generating large estimates of economic impact. Does it matter? In the long term, it probably does. Trying to persuade governments that major sports events will generate substantial economic benefits will not succeed forever. An increasing number of public authorities are asking for *ex post* evaluations of economic impact, and large *ex ante* forecasts are likely to be increasingly discredited. Once word gets around, what will promoters do to obtain government support? There are two possible lines of argument that promoters can develop. First, while the economic impact may be small, the publicity value may be high, as shown by the Sydney Olympics. Promoters must then persuade the government that there are greater promotional benefits in hosting a major sporting event than in any alternative. Second, rather than thinking of an event as an investment generating an economic return, it should be considered a form of public consumption – a reward for past efforts. Whether taxpayers want to devote their tax dollars to this kind of consumption is an open question, but one which might plausibly be answered in the affirmative. If not, event organisers will need to look increasingly to private sponsors rather than to governments to fund events.

Notes

1. There are a number of useful studies that explain both the methodology and problems associated with impact studies, e.g. Siegfried and Zimbalist (2000), Crompton (1995), Baade (1996), Coates and Humphreys (1999) and Porter (1999). These are reprinted in Zimbalist A. (ed.) (2001) *The Economics of Sport* Vol. II. Edward Elgar.
2. This assumes that the multiplier for spending on these two activities is the same. In practice they might be slightly different – in which case a small positive or negative effect will occur.
3. See Barget, E. "Coupe du Monde de Football pour une synthese des effets economiques". *Revue Juridique et Economique du Sport.*
4. See Ahlert, G. (2001) The Economic Effects of the Soccer World Cup 2006 in Germany with regard to different financing, *Economic Systems Research*, 13, 1, pp. 109–127.
5. Although this does ignore the possibility that lots of Koreans will go to watch the matches in Japan and *vice versa*.
6. These are Argentina, Australia, Belgium, Brazil, Canada, China, France, Germany, India, Italy, Japan, Korea, Mexico, Netherlands, Spain, Sweden, Switzerland, Taiwan, the UK and the US.

Index